RELIGION CAN CONQUER COMMUNISM

by

O. K. ARMSTRONG

and

MARJORIE M. ARMSTRONG

The Capitol Hill Press
Washington, D.C.

The Capitol Hill Press
A division of Prospect House, Inc.
1825 Connecticut Ave., N.W.
Washington, D.C. 20009

FOREWORD:
A CALL TO BATTLE

With all our hearts, we, the authors of this work, believe that RELIGION CAN CONQUER COMMUNISM.

We did not start out with this title; it grew upon us!

We began this study with the purpose in mind to alert our fellow believers in religion, living in all areas of the free world, to the plight of those who are deprived of their freedom of conscience and worship because they live under Marxist rule. We hoped to find and to suggest ways and means to alleviate the lot of those persecuted under communism and to encourage them to remain faithful to their spiritual ideals.

We found more than that! As our research progressed at home and abroad we discovered the hopeful, inspiring fact that *communism cannot conquer religion.*

From the day in 1917 when the cruel, crafty Nikolai Lenin forced Bolshevism upon the Russian people, communist dictators have toiled hard and long at the task of trying to eradicate religion. Atheism is a basic principle of communism. "There is no God. All things are material. Religion is the opium of the people!" declared Karl Marx. "Religion is obsolete; it is bourgeois superstition," said the heartless Joseph Stalin. All communist dictators have echoed these sentiments. Religion is the chief enemy of communism, for religion calls for man's highest loyalty to be pledged to his Creator, the Supreme Being, and to the tenets of the faith. Communism demands highest loyalty for itself alone. Therefore, unless communism can wipe out religion from the hearts and lives of the people, it can never fulfil its announced purpose of conquering the world.

Communist regimes have closed churches and turned the buildings into museums and dance halls; arrested, tortured, exiled, and executed ministers, priests, rabbis, and lay leaders; outlawed all the sacred ordinances of religious worship; forced children and young people to learn the foul dogmas of atheism.

Still, in all the vast Marxist empire of the Soviet Union and its captive colonies of eastern Europe, in Red China, in the Cuba that Fidel Castro betrayed, and in all other areas held in communism's iron grip, religion survives and grows. Despite all the persecutions, harassments, and restrictions, spiritual ideals still glow in the hearts of the faithful.

Furthermore, we discovered that the Marxist rulers face three insoluble problems in their campaign to eradicate religion: First, the rising demands by the people for freedoms enjoyed in noncommunist lands. Second, an actual spirit of religious revival among all faiths, Russian Orthodox, Roman Catholic, Protestant, Evangelical, and Jewish. Third, a revolt against denial of religious liberty on the part of young people—the very group the communists hoped to win in order to create a godless generation.

Like the steadily increasing light of morning the great truth dawned upon us: since communism has failed to conquer religion and is doomed to fail in the future, this tyrannical ideology has met its one unconquerable enemy. Religion is the irresistible force that can lead to the final triumph of human freedom over Marxist slavery.

Communism cannot conquer religion, but religion can conquer communism!

But another fact emerges as clearly: it will take all the dedicated efforts of believers in religion in the free world, encouraging and strengthening resistance to atheistic Marxism in the communist areas, to win the battle. In this book we suggest how peoples of all faiths may unite in this great crusade.

This generation may decide whether truth, honor, decency, and love inherent in religion will triumph over tyranny, materialism, degradation and hatred that are the ugly brood of Marxism. The crusade can and must be won by people of vision and determination. Let the trumpets sound the call to advance!

O. K. ARMSTRONG
MARJORIE MOORE ARMSTRONG

ACKNOWLEDGMENTS

We the authors express our sincere gratitude:

To Congressman Durward G. Hall of Missouri and his staff for obtaining authentic material relating to our study; and to the members of the staff of the Library of Congress for their thorough, up-to-date reports of religion's status and struggle in each area under Communist control.

To the New York and Washington offices of Religious News Service for making available their releases.

To each of the authors of works quoted in this book, listed in the References.

To the scores of churchmen, clergy and laity, of many faiths and fellowships, whose names do not appear but who have given most valuable assistance with their writings, interviews, and suggestions.

To Mr. Robert Lutnes of Thomas Nelson & Sons, and his staff, for helpful guidance in planning and organizing this work.

THE AUTHORS

CONTENTS

CHAPTER ONE

COMMUNISM ISSUES ITS CHALLENGE

"Help us! Protect us! Please let us stay here until we can go to America—or anywhere else, to get away from the persecutions of the Communist authorities!"

Such was the plea of thirty-two Siberian peasants who in early January 1963 sought refuge in the United States embassy in Moscow, capital of the Soviet Union.

The refugees declared they were Evangelical Christians, living in the community of Chernogorsk, a manufacturing city in Krasnoyarsk Territory, and that they were being persecuted because of their religious beliefs. The six men, twelve women, and fourteen children had journeyed more than 2,400 miles to Moscow hoping they could be granted asylum by U.S. authorities.

Some of the families of their sect had been deprived of their children, said the refugees, because the Soviet commissars objected to the parents and their church leaders teaching them about God and religious faith.

These devout people carried with them only a few personal belongings, but they were ready and anxious to leave the Soviet Union forever to find a place where they could worship in freedom.

They brought with them also a dangerous package: a roll of names, many pages of them, of their relatives, neighbors, and friends, petitioning the U.S. embassy officials to intervene in their behalf to prevent the loss of their children, to ask the Soviet government to allow them to worship as they chose, and to beg the

U.S. government to admit any who wanted to emigrate and find a new life in a free land. They were aware that if this list fell into the hands of Soviet officials they could be charged with treason, punishable by long imprisonment or death.

Officials at the American embassy were embarrassed. They expressed their sympathy for the plight of the Siberians, but declared they could not grant asylum to the group. "It would produce complications with your government," U.S. spokesmen said, in effect.

So after four hours the Siberians were handed over to the Soviet authorities, who loaded them into trucks and headed for the railway station, presumably to send them back to their home community.

Time after time as the police were herding the evangelicals away, members of the group tearfully begged to be allowed to stay in the embassy as political refugees.

"We shall be persecuted more than ever now!" they wailed.

An American employee of the embassy reported that the last words he heard members shout were these: "Now our children will all be taken from us! All our brothers and sisters who believe in God—Please help us!"

Although the American embassy did not permit newsmen to interview the Siberians, news of the incident leaked out and within a few days the matter became known all over the free world. Devout people, of all faiths and creeds, were shocked and dismayed.

"Why? Why!" was asked everywhere by people concerned for human liberties and justice. "Why did the Americans refuse to grant asylum? Why, at least, did not the U.S. authorities have some understanding with the Soviet government that if the would-be refugees were handed over to them they would be humanely treated?"

The Siberian sect is listed officially by the Council for Cults, which controls all religious affairs in the USSR, as "Evangelical-Christians-Baptists," a designation for most Protestant groups as distinguished from the dominant Russian Orthodox Catholic Church. While the sect is a Pentecostal type, with no relationship to any denomination in the United States, church leaders of many faiths, expressing the concern of religious believers in countries all over the world, took up the matter with both the government of the Soviet Union and the U.S. State Department.

MANY PERSONS WERE CONCERNED

Officials of the Baptist World Alliance, representing 24 million Baptists in 104 countries, from their headquarters in Washington made a direct approach to the Soviet ambassador, Anatoly Dobrynin. Through Dr. Josef Nordenhaug, exective secretary of the organization, the officials declared:

"Regardless of the precise religious convictions of these Siberians, the Baptist World Alliance desires to express its deep sympathy with them in their feelings of religious oppression and to express the concern that religious liberties should be accorded to all peoples of various religious convictions in every nation."

Pointing out that the USSR constitution guarantees all citizens the right to religious worship, the statement asked for "more information regarding the beliefs and practices of these Evangelical Christians who came to the U.S. Embassy in Moscow and regarding the pressures of policies which brought them the long trip from their homes."

The statement continued: "We would be interested to know from the Secretariate for Religious Affairs in Moscow whether some local authority may have violated this guarantee in the case of these Evangelical Christians. Accordingly, it is our wish that a group of known and responsible leaders from international organizations of government and of churches might be given access to the facts."

The National Association of Evangelicals took up the matter directly with Nikita S. Khrushchev, chairman of the Soviet Council of Ministers. In a cablegram to the Kremlin, Robert A. Cook, president of this religious organization representing 42 denominations in the United States, declared that if the Soviet Union would let the Siberian Evangelicals leave the country to settle in America they would be given every possible help by the association's world relief committee; and, the message added, "by all who love freedom in this nation."

A Russian Refugee Committee, formed by Anthony Palma, a Roman Catholic layman, for the express purpose of helping the Siberians, sponsored a letter-writing campaign to the State Department to urge further inquiries by the U.S. government as to the safety and welfare of the would-be refugees.

"Through an alerted Christianity and world opinion by the press and radio, it is conceivable that the Soviet government may back off from effecting any further reprisals against these devout people for their attempted escape," Mr. Palma said.

Spokesmen for numerous other religious denominations in the United States appealed to the State Department for information as to why the embassy in Moscow could not or at least did not in some manner help the devout Siberian refugees who sought asylum to escape religious persecution.

Now it was the turn for both the United States government and the Soviet dictatorship to be embarrassed. The State Department issued a statement to the effect that its embassy officials had no legal right to grant asylum to those citizens of the Soviet group. The petition has never been made public. The embarrassment of the Soviet Union rose from the fact that its propaganda agents have carefully cultivated the myth that there is freedom of religion in its monolithic empire, and at the same time, the Marxist program of complete eradication of religion moves forward in every area of Communist control, throughout the Soviet Union and its captive countries.

It is understandable, therefore, that a spokesman for the Soviet Union announced to an American news service that there was indeed religious liberty in his country. The Siberian Evangelicals, he maintained, were not under any harassment because of their beliefs, but that they were being dealt with because of "criminal" activities. Specifically, said the spokesman (with the built-in duplicity of all Communist propaganda), the members of the sect were "cruel" to their children, and so the children had to be taken from them. He did not mention, of course, that the "cruelty" consisted of teaching the children religious beliefs.

Although not a word of the affair appeared in the press of the Soviet Union, foreign correspondents were told in a statement issued through a Communist press agency *Novosti* that the members of the sect had practiced "savage rites." The release continued:

"Their fanatic parents kept them away from school and children's games, forbade them to read books, and dragged them along to their tiring meetings."

A TIME TO WAKE UP

The affair of the Siberian peasants, although involving only a few families in a far-off corner of the Soviet Union, prompted millions of people all over the free world to ask:

Just what is the present status of religion in the USSR and in other countries with Communist governments?

The incident brought a sharp reminder that, beneath the smiling countenance of the Soviet dictators, as they talk amiably of "coexistence" with the nations they contemptuously call "imperialist warmongers" is the grim determination to bury all governments that do not embrace Marxism and all religious "superstitions" along with them.

It is time for thoughtful people who believe in freedom of conscience and worship and in all other cherished human liberties that flow from that fundamental freedom to realize that religion, in all its varied expressions of faith and practice, stands today at its most important crossroads in recorded history.

As these words are written, it is quite clear that religion as the great spiritual force among peoples of all races, colors, creeds, and conditions is being challenged to fight for its very life.

The challenge comes from the advocates of this atheistic, materialistic ideology, communism, which now holds in its iron grip of political, economic, and social control more than 1,073 million peoples of the world.

"There is no God!" declare the Communist rulers. They echo the theme of communism's chief founder, Karl Marx, that embittered, dogmatic thinker, agitator, and writer of the mid-nineteenth century. He taught that all things are material. In Karl Marx's revolutionary creed there was no such thing as a Creator. All things came about by chance. The universe was set in its course by material forces alone, and all creation that followed the beginning is governed solely by matter and energy.

For people of all religious faiths, man is the highest and most noble of the Infinite Creator's handiwork. In Communist thinking, man is merely a bit of organic matter, more intelligent than other forms of animal life, but no better nor worse; he possesses no soul, no spirit, no reason except that which springs from instinct and desire.

"Religion is the opium of the people!" declared Karl Marx.

All the Communist conspirators, working underground to overthrow established governments in the years before World War I, identified their campaigns with Marxist atheistic materialism. With the seizure of the government of Russia at the downfall of the Tzarist dynasty in 1917 by that cruel, crafty foremost disciple of Marx, Nikolai Lenin, religion became a chief enemy of the new Communist "dictatorship of the proletariat" in that vast nation, second only to the hated property owners and other "capitalists."

"Religion is bourgeois superstition! The philosophical basis of Marxism is dialectical materialism . . . materialism that is absolutely atheistic, and resolutely opposed to all religion," declared Lenin, as he went about the task of establishing firmly the monolithic tyranny that since late 1917 has ruled the Russian peoples.

"We are proceeding steadily with the elimination of the illusions of religion," said Joseph Vissarionovich Djugashvili, known by his own designation as "Stalin" (man of steel), who by intrigues and rewards, betrayals and murders rose to the top of the heap of Lenin's followers and remained dictator of the Soviet Union until his death in 1953. During his bloody rule this cruel maniac realized even better than his predecessors in the monolithic government of the 219 million Russian peoples that communism can never completely triumph in Russia or elsewhere unless and until religion is stamped out from the beliefs and actions of the people.

"Let it be understood that the superstitions of religion are no longer needed in the Socialist (Communist) State," the former chief dictator of the Soviet Union, Nikita Khrushchev, declared. The present foremost enemies of mankind's liberties have found it necessary to accommodate themselves to the pressure of circumstances in dealing with religion in numerous areas of their homeland and their colonial empire in Eastern Europe. Still they hold firmly, steadily to the aim that guides all Communist thinking, planning, and movements: religion *must* be conquered, by whatever means necessary, so that triumph of worldwide Communist control can some day be realized. By stark, direct persecution, by prohibitions and restrictions, by crippling decrees, by constant and countless harassment the Communist rulers proceed relentlessly to liquidate the religious practices of the "believers"—as those rulers themselves correctly call those of all faiths who profess spiritual ideals.

In China, that unhappy subcontinent of nearly 700 million people where Communist rule seized complete power in 1949, the combinations of persecutions, restrictions, and harassments have been openly bloody and cruel, with little of the devious refinements utilized by the tyrants in the Soviet Union and their puppet satraps in governments of the present captive countries.

In Cuba under Fidel Castro, at present the beachhead of Communist control in the Western Hemisphere, center of Communist subversion, infiltration, and revolution for all Latin America, the methods of persecution of religion and its progressive elimination from the lives of the Cuban people vary little from those employed by Castro's sponsors in the Kremlin in Moscow.

How Goes This Battle?

For all the Communist leaders and regimes in every area of the world where their iron grip has fastened upon the people, the situation is the same: religion is the enemy of dictatorial control, identified with freedom of conscience, with liberty to think, to plan, to debate, to decide, to act freely in conformity to law established by government with the consent of the governed. Those freedoms simply cannot exist under Marxist communism. Therefore the Marxists insist that religion must be eliminated, root and branch, as quickly as possible, from the hearts and lives of the people.

In early 1959 directives were issued to Communist authorities in communities all over the Soviet Union with instructions that the drive to eliminate religion must be stepped up. The directives carried a master "seven-year plan," indicating that with vigorous activity on the part of atheist teachers and leaders, with the constant backing of official personnel, religious sentiments could be eliminated. By 1966, the plan declared, religion will have died out except among a few elderly survivors who will be the last of the foolish dupes who believe in the worship of a nonexistent God.

Dutifully, the quisling Communist leaders in the captive Communist nations of eastern Europe adopted the plan and meshed the gears of their antireligion apparatus with those of the USSR. In China there was no acknowledgment that the program to eradicate religion had not succeeded. Actually, there has been no let-up in the steady, cruel, massive battle against all religious faiths in the China mainland.

Even before the seven years of the plan were completed, a tacit admission that the program had not gone well was given in the announcement of a new and still more vigorous program to combat religion. On March 2, 1964, the Central Committee of the Communist party of the USSR announced in its official paper *Pravda* (which means, ironically, "Truth"), that the new program would begin at once. The announcement reported that the plan was perfected and presented by the Party's Ideological Commission, headed by Leonid F. Ilyichev.

The program will have as its primary object the thorough indoctrination in atheism of three groups: members of the Party themselves, members of the Komsomol (Communist Union of Youth), and officials of the trade unions. These, in turn, are to carry on the fight against religion in communities all over the country. The announcement called for the reviving or establishing of atheist "action committees" in all cities and towns that have religious groups. It mentioned that an Institute for Scientific Atheism would be established as a part of the Communist Party's Academy of Social Sciences. The Institute will coordinate all research, train propaganda experts, arrange lectures, sponsor discussion groups, hold conventions, and initiate public demonstrations.

Beginning with the fall term of 1964, the announcement of the plan disclosed, a complete course in atheism will be given in all schools where party officials and young Communists are trained. Writers, speakers, actors, and artists are to be recruited to help with the drive. Popular journals will present antireligious features and materials. Nonreligious ceremonies for births, coming of age, marriages, and deaths will be substituted for those with religious significance.

The *Pravda* article made this significant admission: "It must be remembered that remnants of religious illusions cannot be overcome with one sweep or with administrative measures alone."

This is the new challenge thrown down to the world of religion, clear and plain for all to know and understand. Will the Communist program succeed? In this study we shall attempt to answer that question. To do so, we shall notice in some detail how the constant, relentless campaign against religion has been carried out and how far it has progressed. We shall cast the searchlight of truth on this assault against the people's faith in God and their devotion to the sacred teachings of Holy Writ. We shall observe the open and the subtle attacks upon spiritual ideals and programs, the varied campaigns designed to crush all those who refuse to embrace materialism and who cling to the ideal that "man does not live by bread alone."

We shall attempt an answer to these three questions that now trouble millions of devout people of all faiths, of all ages, and in every area of the globe:

How are churches, and religious organizations and programs generally, faring in the countries and areas under Communist government?

To what extent has the determined drive to eliminate religion in Communist nations succeeded in the past?

Can the intensified antireligion crusade be halted and religion emerge triumphant over this challenge to its future existence? If so, how?

CHAPTER TWO

ATHEISM SWINGS ITS CLUB

"We must step up the drive against religion," Leonid F. Ilyichev, chairman of the Soviet Ideological Commission, is quoted as telling the Central Committee of the Communist party in full session in June 1963. Significantly, the session's chief topic for consideration and discussion was "what to do about religious matters." Commissar Ilyichev continued:

"Religion is the chief enemy of the scientific outlook within the Soviet Union. Also, religious superstitions are most difficult to get rid of in quite a few segments of the population."

There can be no doubt that Ilyichev spoke with the full approval of Nikita S. Khrushchev, chairman of the Council of Ministers in the dictatorship of the misnamed "Union of Soviet Socialist Republics." In fact, in that same speech before the Central Committee, Ilyichev extolled the official policy of peaceful coexistence" with the imperialist countries, which he said must now be practiced by the Soviet Union, and he added:

"However, this does not mean *ideological* coexistence with the West. There must be unceasing ideological struggle against Western ideas and influences—including that greatest ideological enemy of all—religion."

Ilyichev called for a more vigorous campaign to teach atheism, and severely criticized "those who think religion will die out of its own accord without any effort to eradicate it."

It is well for anyone who holds religious faith to understand how serious is the problem of this intensified attack upon religious beliefs and practice in every area under the Red flags of Marxism, in the Communist homeland of Soviet Russia, in the great subcontinent of China, in the captive Communist colonies of Asia, eastern Europe, and Cuba.

Whatever variations in methods and intensity the persecution of believers may take, whatever the means employed, such as the snatching away of children from their devout parents, closing of churches, prohibiting the propagation of the faith, and sending ministers, priests, and rabbis to prison and death, the end will be the same:

The steadfast purpose of worldwide communism is to eradicate religion from the lives of present and future generations.

The recently announced campaigns against religion not only indicate the grave concern of Communist rulers because of the survival of religion among their subjects and captive peoples, but also betray their fear that religion may be gaining in the struggle despite all their efforts at extermination.

One thing is certain: the Communist leaders consider the suppression of religion a deadly serious matter. They are determined to move forward in their double-pronged campaign, one branch to make religion harder and still harder to profess and practice, the other branch to step up the positive program of the teaching of atheism as a substitute for religious faith.

Reviewing past campaigns to exterminate religion in Marxist countries for indications of future action, we discover five categories of action:

First, *forthright persecution* of leaders and members of religious groups, including arrests, imprisonments, false accusations, rigged trials, forced confessions, long prison terms or death for the accused.

Second, *severe harassments,* such as the closing of churches, expropriation of religious properties, levying of exorbitant taxes upon church organizations, constant surveillance of priests, ministers, and rabbis in order to trap them into counterrevolutionary statements or activities, heavy penalties upon youth who attend religious services.

Third, *hampering restrictions* upon all religious activities: strict control by a government agency, licensing of ministers and church leaders, confinement of all religious activities to the buildings used for worship, secularization of the schools, social and enonomic pressure to prevent parents teaching religion to their children, refusal to permit propagation of the faith beyond the immediate congregation, censorship of all speeches and publications.

Fourth, *temporary toleration:* For the sake of expediency, permission may be given to religious leaders and groups to function with some degree of freedom, but always with the uncertainty of future policies and the fear of sudden changes that can terminate all concessions.

Fifth, *tenuous "coexistence"* between the Communist regime and religious leaders based upon understandings that in return for the measure of temporary freedom religious organizations will cooperate with the government, silence their opposition, and become the tool of the regime for propaganda purposes.

Now let us examine some illustrations of the many and devious methods of Communist persecution.

THE CROSS CAME DOWN

May we go first to Latvia, that small nation of brave people that lived under the rule of the Russian Tzars from 1795 until the end of the imperial regime in 1917. Latvia was granted independence after World War I, in keeping with the ideal of that far-sighted exponent of "self-determination of peoples," President Woodrow Wilson.

For twenty-two years, from 1918 until 1940, Latvia was free, its people prosperous and happy. Naturally a hearty, friendly folk, for the most part devoutly religious, the Latvians built up their churches, cathedrals, and synagogues, under complete freedom of worship.

One such church was the Agenskalna Baptist Church, in Latvia's capital city of Riga. The church building was begun in 1914, and despite the hardships of World War I the congregation completed the edifice in 1918. The auditorium held about 700 people. Grandly the church stood in the heart of the city. Crowning glory of this house of God was its steeple, a lofty spire about one hundred feet high, topped by a cross of wood covered with gilded metal. For the peoples of all faiths in Riga, the Agenskalna church stood as a symbol of righteousness, its very presence seeming to echo the words of the Psalmist,

> Enter into his presence with singing,
> And into his courts with praise.

In 1940, in stark violation of a specific treaty of friendship between the Soviet Union and Latvia which pledged "mutual friendship and protection," the Soviet government sent its Red army crashing into the small republic. Many Latvian people, including its most outstanding religious leaders, were arrested and imprisoned. In the summer of the following year most of these "criminals" were herded into boxcars like cattle and deported to Siberian labor camps.

Under Soviet control of Latvia the Agenskalna church was allowed to function, but severe restrictions prevented any of its activities outside the church building itself. In the course of the war the Nazi armies came and replaced the Russians. With the victorious allies pressing upon Berlin in April 1945, Hitler's troops withdrew and again the Red army occupied Latvia.

Again the Agenskalna church of Riga and all other religious bodies in the Baltic countries were encircled with the heavy chains of Communist restrictions. Still, many of them were permitted to hold services, but only after being "licensed" by the authorities. Their priests, ministers, and rabbis had to be registered with the authorities and had to subscribe to required regulations. Reverend Augusts Korps, Agenskalna's pastor, continued to preach on Sundays. His congregation numbered about 500 believers. Earnestly they prayed for strength and guidance under their difficulties, and fervently they sang.

> Faith of our fathers, living still,
> In spite of dungeon, fire and sword.
> Oh how our hearts beat high with joy,
> Whene'er we hear that glorious word!

In the summer of 1961 a Russian "inspector," an agent of the secret police, visiting Riga in line of his duties, sat in the office of a local Communist official. Pointing toward the lofty steeple topped with the cross on Agenskalna church, he rasped:

"How does it happen, Comrade, that you permit that symbol of superstition to stand in this city?"

The Latvian lackey of the Soviet regime explained that Agenskalna was a congregation of influential persons, and that it had been thought wise to permit the church to continue as closing it might bring unfavorable reactions from the public.

"But that cross!" continued the commissar. "It must come down. You set a very bad example, Comrade, to the youth of Riga, who must be taught that religion is superstition and reactionary. And besides, your city needs another cultural center. Perhaps that church auditorium would do for a television and drama house."

The discussion resulted in a decision to send a delegation of Communist officials to inspect Agenskalna church, who dutifully reported to their chief that the auditorium would indeed be suited for cultural purposes. The pastor, Rev. Augusts Korps, was so informed. The anguished minister announced the shocking news to his congregation.

Agenskalna's members protested vigorously to the local officials against the appropriation of their church. They even sent the Pastor with a committee to Moscow to plead that the church be spared. But it was to no avail. Khrushchev's minister of cults told the delegation that he could do nothing. "It is a matter of local administration," he declared.

The Agenskalna congregation held their last meeting in their beloved church on the first Sunday of September 1961. Tearfully they sang for the last time in their sanctuary,

> Blest be the tie that binds
> Our hearts in Christian love.

The Soviet inspector left behind his final orders: "Tear off the steeple, so the building will never again look like a church. But first—*cut down that cross!*"

So one morning a squad of workmen under a Communist foreman appeared in front of Agenskalna church with ladders and tools to cut down that gilded cross. Several of the church members, and many other citizens of Riga, gathered in angry silence to witness this desecration of the house of God. From some eye-witnesses we have the story of what happened:

None of the workmen would volunteer to climb up the steeple and cut down the cross. Whatever their religious faith, they did not want to be a party to such a deed.

"We are not steeple-jacks, and we cannot risk our lives to do this job," a spokesman for the workers said.

The foreman scolded and cursed the men, but still no one volunteered to climb the steeple. Finally a young man, later identified as a leader of Komsomol, the young Communist league, stepped from the crowd and declared he would climb up and cut off the cross. While the workmen gingerly held the ladders for him the youth scaled the steeple, adjusted his safety belt, and began cutting through the metal covering of the cross.

Like the workmen, the young man was no steeple-jack. In his cramped position he worked with great difficulty. The metal was hard to cut. After an hour or so the youth climbed down to the roof to rest, complaining that his legs were numb. Securing a rope he scaled the steeple again. The workmen below held the rope end to yank the cross down when its base was sufficiently cut. Tensely the crowd below watched and waited for the cross to fall. Finally the young Communist volunteer screamed, "Pull now!"

The rope tightened and the gilded cross came clattering down upon the pavement. In the next instant, as the eyes of the spectators again turned upward, the youth's safety belt broke loose, and he came falling spread-eagle fashion from the steeple. With a sickening thud he fell by the cross, and lay quivering in a widening pool of blood.

Gazing at the lifeless form, the workmen removed their caps. Those of the Catholic faith crossed themselves. Ashen and shaken, the foreman dismissed the men. In half an hour or so an ambulance came and carted away the remains of the young Komsomol. He wanted to be a hero, but now he was only a cadaver to be sent to some medical school.

Next day a squad of Russian army engineers came with a huge battering ball and demolished the steeple. Today the edifice, shorn of its once stately steeple and cross, is a television and dance center. Many people of Riga cross the street rather than step over the spot where the cross fell.

The Baptist World, official organ of the Baptist World Alliance, in its issue of September 1962 presents two pictures, "before and after" the decapitation of Agenskalna's steeple. And the devout people of Riga tell us:

"Yes, the cross came down, but the Communist came down with it."

The Very, Very Bad People

Let us now talk with Pastor Heinrich Steinbis, one of the Protestant leaders of West Berlin. Dr. Steinbis is a forthright, vigorous minister, who fell into disfavor with Adolf Hitler when the Fuehrer was at the height of his power, for declaring from the pulpit that no government should restrict freedom of worship, and specifically for remarks made in a sermon on the text: "Render unto Caesar the things that are Caesar's, and unto God the things that are God's."

Brought before a Nazi trial court, Pastor Steinbis was asked to explain: "Did you mean to imply that our Fuehrer is a Caesar?"

"Oh no," answered the pastor. "I was merely quoting scripture, and advocating that our people give all due support to the government, while at the same time giving spiritual allegiance to a power greater than Hitler, and that is God himself."

Dr. Steinbis was released, but during all the remainder of the Nazi regime, including the years of terror while American and British bombers, then Russian cannon, pounded Berlin to rubble, he continued to minister to his congregation and to the people of his war-marked city, under strict surveillance.

"All dictatorships are alike in their determination to prevent freedom of worship," Dr. Steinbis told us. "Freedom of religion is the mother of all other freedoms, such as freedom of speech, the press, and assembly, and no dictatorship can coexist with these human liberties.

"Today our brethren in East Berlin—beyond the cruel wall that divides our city, and those in the entire sector ruled by the

Soviet Union through the German Communist puppets, are experiencing persecutions far worse than Hitler imposed."

One example Dr. Steinbis gives us from his own immediate family. His son Peter, also a minister, began serving a substantial Protestant church in East Berlin some years ago to fill the need for a congregation whose pastor "disappeared" one night—for whatever reason might be known to the East German Communist authorities headed by that thoroughly despised puppet of the Soviet Kremlin, Walter Ulbricht.

The young pastor moved his wife and small children to East Berlin to be near his parish people. He was duly registered by the commissar of cults and he submitted to all the restrictions imposed upon religious leaders and their spiritual programs under the Soviet-German regime.

On the early morning of Sunday, August 13, 1961, Pastor Peter Steinbis came to West Berlin on an unusual mission. He was to substitute for a pastor who was speaking to a youth-camp group sponsored by his denomination, and perform an evening wedding ceremony.

On that black morning of Communist infamy, rolls of barbed wire were strung along the entire distance of the border dividing West from East Berlin. Here was violation of postwar agreements among the allied conquerors of Germany so crass and inexcusable that the very heavens cried out for a correction. Pastor Steinbis approached the entrance from East Berlin which he had used in early morning and found it closed by the rolls of barbed wire and guarded by the guns of the "Vopo"—*Volks Polizei*.

Obviously under orders of the Kremlin masters, Ulbricht waited anxiously for a day to see the reaction of the Western powers to this flagrant infringement of the rights of these same Western powers, to say nothing of the rights of the people of all Berlin. When American and other authorities in West Berlin offered no resistance to the diabolical act, and sure then that nothing *would* happen except for mild and meaningless protests, Ulbricht proceeded with the building of solid masonry, concrete, and steel.

Pastor Steinbis was never able to return to his home and his parish, despite earnest, almost frantic, efforts by himself, by his father, and by West Berlin officials, until the brief visit permitted him at Christmas time of 1963. He was under closest watch during the short hours he spent at home. He was not permitted to hold a religious service in his still pastorless church, nor even to meet with his parish leaders. He was forced to return to West Berlin through that small opening so "charitably"—as Puppet Ulbricht called it—made in the wall to allow short visits of West Berliners to relatives in East Berlin, because, in the words of the East German authorities, he had "deserted his place of work in the *Deutsche Demokratische Republik.*" But Peter Steinbis gave to his father and mother this story:

My wife told me that our daughter Hilda, now eight years old, came home from school one day in tears. "I did not know that my grandparents are such wicked people," she said. Her mother, shocked, replied: "What can you mean by that? You hardly know your grandmother and grandfather. They are kind, loving people, and they hope they can visit us sometime."

"Oh no," said Hilda. "Grandmother is a very bad woman."

"Who told you that?" my wife asked the girl.

"My teacher," Hilda answered. "She tells us all about bad people and she said they live in the bad part of Germany. My teacher said that all the people in West Berlin want war and do not want peace, just like the Americans do. I told her that my grandfather is a preacher, like my father was before he went away. She said that since my father and grandfather are preachers, they are very, very bad, because they tell people lies!"

How to Treat Religious Spies

Father James Huysmans, of Dutch descent, spent 37 years as a Catholic missionary in China. His service included parishes and administrative duties in Shanghai and many other parts of China. He learned to speak Chinese fluently and was greatly beloved by the people he served.

At the close of World War II, Father Huysmans, like all Christian missionaries in China, saw with growing concern the efforts of the United States government to "settle" China's political problems by insisting upon a coalition government made up of the Nationalist regime headed by Generalissimo Chiang Kai-shek and the Communist leaders that had gained a strong foothold in northern China under Mao Tse-tung. Like his associates generally in the great task of spreading the gospel among the peoples of the vast Chinese continent, whatever their denomination, this priest understood that Communist "coalition" for China meant what it always has in Marxist-Leninist terminology: a period of "coexistence" during which non-Communist leaders will be ruthlessly overpowered and replaced by the followers of Marxist-Leninist tyranny.

In 1949 the Communists took over, as expected, and Chiang Kai-shek was forced to move the Nationalist government to the island of Taiwan. Father Huysmans remained at his post until mid-summer of 1951. He endured as best he could the restrictions placed by the Communist authorities upon all priests and ministers. He saw with horror the persecutions of many of his fellow priests on trumped-up charges of being counterrevolutionary or, more frequently, of serving as "spies of the United States" whatever their original nationality might have been. Father Huysmans saw these men of God imprisoned in small, filthy cells, their hands manacled behind their backs. They were pushed into the degradation of solitary confinement without toilets or the comforts of cleanliness, fed once a day like wild beasts with a bowl of slop shoved through a hole in their cell doors. The prisoners were brought out only for questioning as to *why* they had committed their "crimes," why they were spies or "running dogs for the imperialists." The priest saw his fellows tortured beyond human endurance if their tormentors imagined they knew some choice bit of accusation against other priests or their parishioners, or if perchance they knew where some former landlord's money was hidden.

With his parish abolished, his people scattered, the church property confiscated, and the place of worship turned into a Communist school, Father Huysmans felt he must leave to continue his ministry elsewhere. He applied for an exit visa, and it was granted. The Communist authorities set the date for the priest's departure at July 27, 1951. Then like cats waiting to pounce upon a wounded mouse, they watched him until July 25. On that night the police came to his quarters, insisting that Father Huysmans must write a full "confession of his crimes" before he could go. He was informed that the confession would have to include an account of his spying. Since the revered leader, who had spent most of the years of his life ministering to the spiritual, social, and even material needs of his people, had committed no crime, he refused to write a confession. He was immediately arrested, handcuffed, and forced to stand facing a wall for hours at a time. For six weeks this ordeal went on while he was detained as a prisoner in his parish house.

Still refusing to "confess" to crimes never committed, Father Huysmans was carted off to prison. The *Sunday Examiner,* a Catholic paper published in Hong Kong, gives this further graphic account:

> As he still refused "to confess," his arms were screwed tighter and tighter behind his back. "Two helpmates" in his cell constantly discussed his "criminal record" with him; he was not released from the shackles for food, washing, or any other necessity of daily life. His refusal to "confess" and silence angered his tormentors and from cursing and swearing at him they descended to blows, that is to slapping his face, spitting on him, battering his chest until he would topple over, and then they would kick him until he collapsed. The 66-year-old priest faintly remembers one night having fallen about fifteen to twenty times, for he awakened each time under a douse of cold water.*

This sort of treatment went on until May 1954. Finding Father Huysmans ready to endure the death they had barely denied him during the nearly three years of torture rather than yield to their demands, the authorities released him and he was led by friends secretly to the freedom of Hong Kong.

Meantime, thousands of other spiritual leaders died of such treatment, or were mercifully executed for their faith.

SYNAGOGUES: NO LONGER NEEDED

The years since 1959 have been especially dark for Jewish people in the Soviet Union and the captive countries of Eastern Europe. Devout Jews have been persecuted in almost every aspect of their religious faith and practice.

Vigorous denials are issued by Soviet Union authorities as to persecutions of the Jews, for the matter is embarrassing. It rings a gong that sounds like an echo from the Tzarist days. It arouses world opinion against its perpetrators. That is why strenuous efforts are made by authorities in charge of restrictions upon religion to prevent publicity about their atrocities toward those of Jewish faith. Despite denials, reports from all areas of Communist control tell the tragic and irrefutable story.

As though slowly tightening the noose about the neck of Jewish worship to bring about ultimate strangulation, Communist officials have closed numerous synagogues on trumped-up and completely false charges running all the way from "profiteering" in the sale of *matzoth,* or unleavened bread, to "consorting with foreign agents." The synagogues thus closed were usually declared to be "no longer needed" in the Communist society.

According to information supplied to the United Nations on July 11, 1956, "worshipers of the Jewish faith have at their disposal about 450 synagogues." Yet in 1959, barely three years later, the Soviet government informed the United Nations Commission on Human Rights that the number of synagogues in active use had "fallen" to 150.

In the April 1963 issue of the English-language monthly magazine *USSR,* Moscow's Rabbi Levin is quoted as confirming that there were only 96 synagogues in active service. Thus in the course of four years no less than 300, or about two thirds of the Jewish places of worship in Communist Russia, were shut down. And apparently the process of gradual elimination is going on at an increased tempo, in the light of reports of new restrictions and harassments begun in 1964.

A typical example of the treatment of Jewish places of worship and of their rabbis and congregations is that of the synagogue in the Georgian town of Tskhakaya, where orthodox Jews form a substantial percentage of the population. According to the publication *Jews in Eastern Europe:*

During the summer of 1962, at the height of the series of economic trials in which Jewish defendants were most prominently featured, enraged anti-Semites burned down the synagogue, wrecked its furniture, and desecrated religious objects. The 2,000 Jews of the town, mainly artisans and agricultural workers, collected money to buy building materials for the restoration of the synagogue. The task took all autumn and winter, but by March of this year a new wooden roof had been built, new framing constructed, windows replaced, furniture acquired and the premises had been repainted. Having made full preparations, the congregation decided to re-dedicate the building on the first day of Passover, April 8.

Six days before Passover, on April 2, 1963, police officers called on the leaders of the congregation and brusquely informed them that the municipal authorities had decreed that the building could no longer be used as a synagogue but would be confiscated for municipal purposes. The authorities sealed the doors and impounded the furniture.

The Jews of Tskhakaya protested to the municipality without success, then sent a delegation to the provincial authorities in Tbilisi, a hundred miles away. They promised the delegation that instructions would be sent to the municipality ordering the return of the synagogue. But the promise was either not kept, or the municipality had little regard for the central Georgian authorities. The synagogue remained padlocked.*

What is this monstrous power that inflicts its harsh and cruel decrees upon the faithful in every area of its control? Is it invincible, or can the faithful topple it? Like a giant it stands defiantly, arrogantly, challenging religion as did a giant of old, described in the Holy Word:

And there came out from the camp of the Philistines a champion named Goliath, of Gath, whose height was six cubits and a span. He had a helmet of bronze on his head, and he was armed with a coat of mail . . . and he had greaves of bronze on his legs, and a javelin of bronze slung between his shoulders. And the shaft of his spear was like a weaver's beam, and his spear's head weighed 600 shekels of iron.

Truly a formidable character! Was he invincible?

CHAPTER THREE

COMMUNIST GOLIATH DEFIES RELIGION

Anyone familiar with the story of that great duel between David and Goliath, recorded in the Hebrew Scriptures, may well reflect upon the massive size and power of the giant Philistine, and ponder how he resembles the size and power of the Marxist movement today:

Now the Philistines gathered together their armies to battle . . . and Saul and the men of Israel were gathered together . . . and set the battle in array against the Philistines. And the Philistines stood on a mountain on the one side, and Israel stood on a mountain on the other side, and there was a valley between them. . . .

And there went out a champion . . . and he stood and cried unto the armies of Israel and said unto them, "Why are ye come out to set your battle in array? . . . Choose ye a man for you, and let him some down to me!" . . . And the Philistine said "I defy the armies of Israel this day!"

Like the Philistine challenger, the forces of communism confront the defenders of religious faiths, and especially those of our Judeo-Christian civilization.

On one side of the valley, filled now by an Iron Curtain, are the exponents of the monolithic state, the champions of the dictatorship of a few over the masses of the people, the supporters of the cult of materialism, the enemies of all that humanity cherishes by way of freedom of worship and the many other liberties that flow from that God-given fountain. On the other side are those who know that their liberties have been bought with the price of the blood of the martyrs, who value those liberties more than life itself and who understand that eternal vigilance is still the price for human freedom.

Beastly, arrogant, drunk with the power that comes with the control of nearly one third of the population of the globe, communism stands and defies those who believe that "In the beginning God created the heavens and the earth."

Who is this Goliath? What is the nature of this challenger? Who brought him into the world and who nurtured him to his present fearful strength? Why his burning desire to annihilate those who cling to spiritual ideals? Why does he consider religion his greatest enemy?

The giant of communism was sired by Karl Marx, who was born in Rhenish Prussia in 1818, son of a Jewish lawyer. He grew up to become a radical philosopher, renouncing the faith of his fathers for materialist atheism. From his youth he consorted with a mistaken, misshapen, truly reactionary concept that only material matter has reality and meaning in life.

From this unholy union was born the ideology that there are only two classes of society, constantly in conflict one with the other: the owners of property, known as capitalists, and the workers, known collectively as the proletariat.

Assisting at the birth of the concept of communism was a male midwife, Friedrich Engels, a German Socialist, son of a family of wealth and influence. Like Karl Marx, Engels early turned to radical philosophy. He teamed up with Marx, while both were living in England, to advocate the "working class struggle" and world revolution. Assisted by Engels, Marx explained the aims and methods of the new movement in the now historic *Communist Manifesto.*

To understand why communism must crush religion if it is to survive and triumph, let us examine the words of this historic *Manifesto.* Let us scan the principles embodied in the teachings of this product of two radical zealots.

"The history of all hitherto existing society is the history of the class struggle."

So begins the *Manifesto.* The entire document echoes the theme of struggle, conflict, violence, hatred between the classes, and predicts the final liquidation of one with triumph of the other. Like a minor-key symphony, returning again and again with even louder clashing of cymbals and a crescendo of discordant notes, the *Communist Manifesto* repeats the theme of class against class in a fight to the death.

MARX USES THE BLACK BRUSH

And who were the classes? Marx and Engels identified them simply as the capitalists and the workers. The class struggle was an irreconcilable fight between those who owned property and could employ others at wages, and those who had little and therefore must work for hire. The employers were the capitalists, and they were all villains, oppressors and exploiters of their workers. All the workers were exploited by the capitalist class, and were therefore good people, worthy to take from the capitalists all political power and to set up a government in which they would have complete control: "the dictatorship of the proletariat."

"The history of all past society has consisted of the development of class antagonisms,—antagonisms that assumed different forms at different epochs. But whatever form they have taken, one fact is common to all past ages—the exploitation of one part of society by another."

Numerous statements in the *Manifesto* emphasize that theme: "Our epoch, the epoch of the Bourgeoisie, possesses however this distinctive feature: it has simplified the class antagonisms. Society as a whole is more and more splitting up into two great hostile camps, into two great classes directly facing each other— Bourgeoisie and Proletariat."

Marx and Engels were adamant in their belief that the rich capitalists would get richer and richer, as greed for profit pushed them to still greater exploitation of the working people. They believed that conversely the workers would get poorer and poorer, since the capitalists were backed by their governments, which in the Europe of that day meant generally by crowned heads of the royal families.

In 1848 the industrial revolution, spurred by the widening application of the steam engine, was creating new inventions of machinery for manufacturing, transportation, and distribution. Still the *Manifesto* authors believed that this meant only more profits for the owners and greater injustices by employers toward their workers.

Marx recognized that the discovery of America opened up a great region for the expansion of commerce from the Old World, but he could see in this only an opportunity for the capitalist traders to get richer with no comparable benefits for the exploited workers. His *Manifesto* tarred all employers with the black brush of selfish greed and attributed to them no sentiments of charity, fair dealing, and cooperation for mutual benefits.

It was also Marx's theory that the owners of large factories would compete one with another on an unlimited dog-eat-dog basis, resulting in some capitalists being driven out of business while the survivors of this jungle war created monopolies, only to enrich themselves still further. Throughout the *Manifesto* the idea is persistently developed that all but wage-earners are villains of the worst kind. Ministers, lawyers, teachers, office workers, even farmers (whom Marx persisted in calling "peasants") are lumped together for his burning contempt—if they happened to own property. They were the mean and cruel "Bourgeoisie."

In justice it must be remembered that pay and working conditions in all the European countries at the time of the writing of the *Communist Manifesto,* and especially in Russia with its heritage of serfdom, were extremely backward. Wage-earners customarily worked an average of twelve hours a day, with pay a bare subsistence for the breadwinner and his family. Little or no thought was given by employers to the health or comfort of employees. The workers were supposed to turn out a given amount of production, and they were often penalized for not meeting heartless norms. If the toiler suffered an accident, it was his own bad luck; he could expect no compensation for lost time nor for disabilities incurred on the job, even if such were due to the negligence of the employer and even if they resulted in permanent loss of ability to work.

In the light of these conditions, as history neared the middle of the nineteenth century, it must be admitted that Marx's theory that working people were exploited in all industrial countries contained some truth. Marx pointed up his economic doctrines with the explanation that workmen, the wage-earners, never received their just pay because the capitalists reaped the "surplus value," or profits left over after the costs of production. And that was partially true at the beginning of the industrial revolution, for few owners of the means of production had developed any social consciousness that would prompt them to share more of their profits with their workmen. Very few felt obliged to grant any rights to an employee except the right to work at his job as decided by the employer alone. Few had any knowledge of the needs of the workers' families or any concern with their financial plight. Furthermore, the public generally shared this indifference to the welfare of the workers.

"Hire them as cheaply as possible, and get all the work out of them that you can!" was the idea generally accepted by the owner, the boss, the investor in the new machines for manufacturing and trade.

THINGS MARX NEVER KNEW

Never in his wildest dreams could Karl Marx have imagined that greater and more efficient machines, by increasing the goods needed by society, would thereby increase the wealth of workers and employers alike. Never could he have foreseen that instead of the rich getting richer and the poor becoming steadily poorer, the trend would be the other way, with the gap between rich and poor gradually narrowing as the great middle classes in the industrial nations became a majority in the population. He could not have understood that as the industrial revolution progressed there would grow along with its benefits an understanding on the part of the rich as to how their riches might be used to benefit a wide range of human interests.

An Andrew Carnegie, using his wealth to establish libraries for the common people of numerous communities, would have been impossible for Karl Marx to contemplate. Samuel Gompers, dedicated to establishing collective bargaining among employees, would have been unbelievable to Marx. As for Henry Ford, deciding to double his employees' wages to a maximum of $5.00 a day with the remark that this greater pay would make it possible for his workmen to buy the small automobiles they made—Ford would have been a fantasy to this original Communist zealot.

Marx and his radical associates could never have foreseen that "capitalism" as they knew it in the 1840s would no longer exist one century later in any industrial nation on earth. They had in mind the only capitalism they knew; one in which the owner of the source of production, such as the primitive factory of that day, or a large landed estate, hired workers as cheaply as he could, worked them 60 or more hours a week and pocketed all the profits. They could not have known such a capitalism as that would disappear with high wages, governmental control of hours and wages, and the high taxes that reduced the profits of most industries to narrow margins.

The original Communists could never have believed that there would be an awakening social consciousness on the part of peoples of all economic levels, prompting them to demand and secure laws that would curb the monopolies Marx predicted, establish better working conditions, compensation for injuries, pensions for the retired, and hundreds of other corrections for the economic injustices of their day. In their hatred for spiritual things, they would never have believed that this social consciousness would result for the most part from religious ideals. They would have been contemptuous of the principle of the stewardship of all material possessions for the good of others, accountability for the common welfare, and concern for fellow men as expressed by believers of all faiths:

"I am my brother's keeper; I will do unto others as I would have them do unto me!"

And what was to be the final outcome of this increasing class struggle?

The revolution of the proletariat. The uprising of the oppressed workers, when they reached the breaking point under the injustices they endured. Such was the inevitable course of history.

"Workers of the world, unite! You have nothing to lose but your chains!" trumpeted Karl Marx.

As the workers rebelled and united, they would destroy the hated capitalists, take over the means of production, of transportation, and distribution; create a government ruled only by the party of the workers, the Communist Party; and thus they would establish a true dictatorship of the proletariat.

THE END JUSTIFIES THE MEANS

By the use of intrigue, terror, bloodshed—whatever the means, since the means were justified by the end in view—the capitalist class would be smashed and the workers would create a regime in which all power woud be in their hands. As the *Manifesto* explains:

"The immediate aim of the communists is the same as that of all of the other proletarian parties: formation of the proletariat into a class, overthrow of the bourgeois supremacy, conquest of political power by the proletariat. . . . The abolition of bourgeois individuality, bourgeois independence."

Marx counseled that when the revolution had placed the workers in control, the workers would operate the factories for the common good, rather than for profit of the capitalists; that the workers, through a government set up by the Communist Party, would take over all land, implements, machines, and all other means of farm production.

Marx believed that private property was the basis of the exploitation of workers, and that therefore private ownership of property must be abolished in favor of ownership by the State. He declared:

"They [the proletariat] have nothing of their own to secure and to fortify; their mission is to destroy all previous securities for, and insurances of, individual property."

How the destruction of individual property could benefit the working class, since the cherished hope of most of its members was to be able some day to own property themselves, remains a question that Marx did not care to answer in his thorough hatred of all who owned any means of production.

Under communism, each citizen would contribute his productive labor according to his ability and each would be rewarded according to his needs.

Unquestioning obedience to the dictatorship of the workers

would be demanded and achieved through "liquidation" of all opposition to the revolution. The rule of the Communist Party would spread from its first beachheads of control—supposedly from Germany and England—to other industrial countries as its loyal comrades successfully infiltered, undermined, and brought down one government after another.

And what of religion in this new world of rule by one class of people through an all-powerful political party?

Materialism would be the guiding star of the new order, with science as its god, replacing the moral and spiritual values found in "obsolete" religion.

Which came first in the thinking of early Communists: atheism or materialism? This is like asking which came first, the hen or the egg. Atheism and materialism came together. They are the two faces of the same coin. They can be used interchangeably. That is why believers in Marxist materialism *must* be atheists, and why atheists have nowhere else to go but into materialism, whether Marxist or some other brand.

Time and again in his writings Marx tied religion to the despised capitalist oppressors. He argued that religion was a convenient device to cloak the exploitation of the proletariat. He wrote:

The bourgeoisie, wherever it has got the upper hand, . . . has drowned the most heavenly ecstasies of religious fervor, of chivalrous enthusiasm, of Philistine sentimentalism, in the icy water of egotistical calculation. . . . In one word, for exploitation, veiled by religious and political illusions, it has substituted naked, shameless, direct brutal exploitation.

Believers in religion must recognize that Communists, from their first founders and leaders to the present, are consistent. They were consistent when Marxism was but the dream of radical agitators, and they are consistent in this day when that dream has become a terrifying reality. They start with the theory that there is no God. Things were not created by a supernatural Power, but just happened. The elements came together and formed the solar and other systems. The laws of nature worked out the production of the earth, sun, moon, and stars, and set them in their courses.

No guiding hand controlled this. Only chance, and the rule of material forces.

Now for the consistency: If there is no God, no Father of all mankind, then there can be no such thing as a spiritual nature in any creature, including man, who admittedly even by the Communists is the highest form of animal life. If there is no spirit in man, then he is just another walking animal, smarter than the other animals about him, perhaps, but of no greater importance except as he can be used by the revolutionary State—such as a scientist, bureaucrat, or astronaut.

A Good Question

The Communist may be asked: "If there is no God as Creator, then who created things?" The good Marxist has a ready answer: "Why, of course, *labor creates everything.*"

Just how a cosmic proletariat existed to bring in the universe is never explained. One pat answer is always enough for a Communist to give to an inquiring mind.

Thus, if there is no such thing as a spiritual nature except in the deluded ideas of those not yet versed in materialism, then all the virtues that we associate with the things of the spirit do not exist either. Love? Mercy? Human understanding and helpfulness? Bourgeois rubbish! Truth? Justice? Honor? More rubbish! Words to lull the workingman into a supine acceptance of his fate!

To Marx and his associates in shaping the ideology of communism, all sentiment, including the deepest and most abiding principles of religious faith and conduct, were superstitious nonsense, to be eradicated as quickly as possible. They must have known—and feared—that religion had been the major influence in creating love to replace hatred, mercy to blot out tyranny, cooperation for conflict, charity for greed. Still they clung to the false theory that religion was mere superstition, and that it was doomed by the advance of scientific knowledge. In the enlightened society of communism, they taught that religion would be discarded by intelligent people and wither away.

That the disciples of the original Communists, in every area of the world under their control today, still hold to Marx's false ideology of the necessity of conflict between two classes, both of which have practically vanished in our complex modern society, seems fantastic in the extreme. That the Communist rulers in all their far-flung colonial empire still hold that religion is not needed in the world of today and tomorrow, and that material substances shorn of all sentiments and virtues must be sufficient to bring about a happy society, proves the stubborn tenacity with which they cling to a monstrous lie and continue to put their trust in the Goliath of atheistic materialism.

"Thou shalt love the Lord thy God with all thy heart, with all thy soul, and with all thy mind, . . . and thy neighbor as thyself," said a devout people chosen of Jehovah.

"Blessed are the poor in spirit, they that mourn, the meek, the merciful, the pure in heart, the peacemakers, . . . for theirs is the kingdom of heaven," spoke the Nazarene Teacher.

Through the centuries of Judeo-Christian progress the history of mankind has been one of developing understanding of the problems and needs of one's neighbor, a growing spirit of oneness with all humanity, a way of life based upon an ever-increasing cooperation rather than conflict.

But without conflict, without the class struggle and the upraised fist of hatred and vengeance, communism could not exist. That is why all Communists of the past, and all today, know that religion is their greatest enemy, a force totally irreconcilable with their program of world control. In their world, love, liberty, justice, and brotherhood can have no place.

It is clear then that believers in religion, throughout the entire world, face a struggle for the survival of their priceless heritage of faith: those in the free world to rally in a tremendous crusade of encouragement of these millions who must suffer the loss of religious liberty, and to marshal worldwide public sentiment in their behalf.

Dedicated Communists expect that the David called religion will not come forth to battle, but will hide in the caves of fear, indifference, weakness, and collaboration. Are these true Marxists correct in their conjecture?

CHAPTER FOUR

LENIN STRIKES WITH CRUEL FIST

Karl Marx passed away in 1883, leaving behind his legacy of the class struggle, and tangible evidence of it in an organization, *the First Internationale,* made up of radical agitators working underground in many countries of Europe.

Soon a vigorous young Communist, Vladimir Ilich Ulyanov, who later changed his name to Nikolai Lenin, was leading the Social Democratic Party, the group in Russia most nearly fitting the pattern of radical Communist action. Thoroughly indoctrinated in Marxist philosophy and dogma, Lenin was eager to devote his life to the coming revolution of the masses.

"Out with the Romanovs! Long live the workers! Down with the capitalists! Death to the exploiters!" were some of the mottoes he repeated whenever and wherever he could assemble secretly with fellow revolutionaries.

Lenin was a born leader, with never a doubt as to his mission on earth and never any hesitation to assert himself and his opinions. In 1903, at the second Congress of Communist Parties held in Brussels and London, Lenin led a majority of his fellow radicals, the Bolsheviks, to endorse the overthrow of the government of Romanov Tzar Nicholas II. They vowed to aim steadily at the breaking up of landed estates, liquidation of capitalists, and expropriation of private property. In a word, Lenin's mission was to establish the Marxist revolutionary rule of the workers.

Only persons of Lenin's eager, dedicated, ruthless nature could consider such a program attainable. To most statesmen and citizens of that era the idea of the rule of the proletariat seemed like the fantasy of tortured minds.

But Lenin was no ordinary person. He saw his brother hanged for plotting to assassinate Tzar Alexander III. He took part in the Social Democratic uprisings of 1905, and was imprisoned. Released and exiled to Switzerland, Lenin kept up his radical campaign by a voluminous correspondence and a steady stream of publications.

Meantime, during the latter four decades of the nineteenth century and the first decade of the twentieth, Russia progressed appreciably in education, literature, music, the arts, sciences, and even in some aspects of local representative government. As a result of sweeping reforms of the courts in 1864, the judicial system of Russia was just and humane.

None of this progress swerved Lenin from his determined campaign to overthrow the imperial government and set up the Communist dictatorship.

The assassination of Archduke Francis Ferdinand of Austria and his wife at Sarajevo, Bosnia, on June 28, 1914, set the match to the powder keg of European rivalries that exploded into war in August. In less than three years Russia was bled white by the armies of Kaiser Wilhelm II of Germany. Wracked by conflict, with much of the country overrun by German troops, with the majority of the people in cities, villages, and countryside hungry and rebellious because of their hardships, Mother Russia sank to her knees.

By February 1917 the Tzar's soldiers were deserting in droves, wandering over the land, looting and robbing. In early March the radical Socialists forced the collapse of the imperial regime. Tzar Nicholas II and his family were imprisoned. On July 16 they were taken into a room, seated as though to have a photo made, and machine-gunned to death in cold blood.

The news of the historic downfall of the Romanov dynasty reached Lenin, who was in exile in Zurich, Switzerland. Sensing that the day for revolutionary action had come and burning with eagerness to take charge of the campaign for communism, Lenin approached the German authorities with a plan. If they would make it possible for him to return to Petrograd, said Lenin, he would make sure that a radical regime took over. The regime would officially withdraw Russia from the war and promptly make peace with the Imperial German Government.

Snatching at this bait, the German authorities in Zurich put the Russian revolutionary and a companion in a sealed train and sped them to Petrograd. That one train ride likely provided the most far-reaching and tragic consequences of all rides in all history! The incident brought together that rare combination of the time, the place, and the man that shapes history for better or worse. Lenin was the man, and perhaps the only man alive, with the daring, the cunning, the cold-blooded contempt for truth, honor, and decency, along with the knowledge of how the government of the prostrate country could be seized and how to crush all opposition at the moment it was weakest and his own influence the greatest.

How to Rape a Whole Nation

Coolly, calmly, Lenin brought the Bolsheviks together. Leon Trotsky, another leading disciple of Marx, came out of exile from London. Through the months of the summer of 1917, while the people of America were arousing themselves to get into the European War "to make the world safe for democracy," the Communist leaders plotted and planned the steps for what they called "armed insurrection" (rather than the Marxist "revolution") to seize the government.

A new parliament, called the Constituent Assembly, had been elected as the basis for a Democratic-Socialist government. It was widely representative of the Russian people, and held their hopes for a fresh start as an infant republic. The Constituent Assembly had the task of drafting and promulgating a new constitution.

Lenin realized that he and his Bolshevik associates would have to move fast to get ahead of the Constituent Assembly. With shrewd, cold calculation of the odds against him, Lenin quickly organized a "Soviet Council" made up of soldiers, workers, and peasants. He specifically denied, with that cunning duplicity for which he later became infamous, that his group intended to introduce communism as the government of Russia. With hearty contempt for the dupes willing to believe his lies the chief Bolshevik promised that all the rights of the people mentioned in the Constituent Assembly would be respected by his Soviet group. A newspaper which Lenin had founded as his mouthpiece repeated the slogan, day by day: "Long live the Constituent Assembly, the master of the Russian Land!"

In a voting by the Russian people from November 25 to December 9, Lenin's Bolshevik Party received only 35 per cent of the ballots. Millions of Russians then supposed that their new democracy was safe. But when the Assembly came to Petrograd for its first post-election meeting, Lenin took the action that was to become the standard, familiar Communist method of seizing the full power of government. He posted his soldiers, for the most part Lettish infantrymen, about the Tauride Palace where the Assembly was to meet. How Lenin and his troops thwarted the will of the Russian people, blocked the formation of a truly democratic government, and set up the iron gates of Bolshevik tyranny is vividly told by Eugene Lyons, former United Press correspondent in Moscow:

On the morning of January 18 massive columns of unarmed workers and students marched from different parts of the city toward the center to greet their new parliament, under banners proclaiming faith in democracy. As they proceeded, thousands more joined in the procession, making it as genuine a demonstration of popular feelings as that city had ever witnessed. But as the procession approached the Tauride Palace, their path was blocked by the Lettish sharpshooters, who opened fire without warning. About a hundred of the demonstrators were killed, hundreds were wounded, the rest dispersed in panic.

With this bloody overture, the Constituent Assembly, embodiment of vision that had been Russia's for a century, gathered in the afternoon for its first—and last—session. The elected deputies found the corridors patrolled by Letts, Red Guards, and sailors in a derisive and insulting temper. They found the galleries packed by noisy, drunken, jeering Communists; admission tickets had been managed solely by Lenin's police.

The Social Revolutionary leader, Victor Chernov, was elected president but could barely make himself heard above the hurricane of catcalls and whistling. Toward evening Lenin arrived to survey his handiwork. He sprawled himself contemptuously on the stairs leading to the rostrum and winked wickedly as his handpicked soldiers and sailors guffawed and banged the floor with their rifle butts. At one point he stretched out on a bench and pretended to go to sleep to underline his disdain for the proceedings, to the utter delight of his rowdy henchmen.

The Bolshevik faction presented a "program" which in effect was an ultimatum calling for the Assembly to turn over its power to the Soviets and commit suicide. It was of course voted down, whereupon Lenin's deputies left the hall in a body. Amidst the organized pandemonium Chernov managed to present and obtain passage of a basic land reform bill, providing for the orderly distribution of land to all peasants. Gruff sailors repeatedly intruded on the platform, pulled at Chernov's coattails, and threatened to turn out the lights if he did not wind up the meeting.

When the session was adjourned toward dawn everyone knew that it would never reopen. The first and only genuine expression of the people's will after the revolution was wiped out in cynicism and violence. The more optimistic deputies, who returned to the Tauride Palace next day, found its doors locked and sealed and guarded against the people, with artillery and machine guns.

The doom of the revolution too was sealed. A sinister tyranny, despising the people in whose name it had taken control, was in the saddle.*

Few persons living in the world at that time could possibly have understood the ominous, sinister meaning of what had happened that January day in Petrograd, Russia, by the iron will of one utterly unprincipled, ruthless character, Nikolai Lenin. But on the following day the liberal journalist Maxim Gorki wrote:

Yesterday the streets of Petrograd and Moscow resounded with shouts of "Long live the Constituent Assembly!" For giving vent to these sentiments the peaceful paraders were shot down by the People's Government.

On January 19 the Constituent Assembly expired—until the advent of happier days—its death foreboding new suffering for the martyred country and for the masses of people. . . . It can be resurrected only through a new alignment of forces, only if the masses of the people will come to their senses and soberly realize the impasse to which their own ignorance, cleverly used by a handful of madmen, has brought them.*

NOT A QUESTION OF RUSSIA

Even some of Lenin's associates in the coup, fearful of possible counteraction on the part of friends of the Assembly, complained about his reckless behavior in seizing the government in defiance of the wishes of the Russian people. Lenin gave them this answer:

"It is not a question of Russia at all, gentlemen. I spit on Russia. . . . This is merely one phase through which we must pass on the way to a world revolution."

Truly, this man was Karl Marx's complete and thorough disciple. You need not look for any accounts of the diabolical events of January 18 and 19, 1918, in official Soviet Union histories. All references to this rape of democracy and triumph of Communist imperialism under Lenin have been entirely expunged from the record. In the "unthink" of the Communist conspiracy for world revolution they just did not happen. Rather the myth has been carefully cultivated among intellectuals of free nations that Lenin was merely the benevolent tool of the popular uprising against an old, despotic regime, a regime that had expired with the overthrow of the Romanov dynasty ten months before.

In the orgies of arrests, imprisonments, tortures, degradations and executions that followed the establishment of the Soviet government in Russia, the Russian Orthodox Church, because of its close ties with the old Tzarist regime, came under immediate and harsh attack. Bishops and priests were rounded up, imprisoned, and shot by the hundreds. Numerous Orthodox places of worship were closed. The church as an organization was largely paralyzed.

Roman Catholic, Protestant, and Jewish groups fared somewhat better, for a time. Lenin's major task was to strengthen the sandy base of the new monolithic government by liquidating any and all "reactionary enemies" and building about it a rim of iron control against which opposition would decisively crumble. Trotsky summarized the murderous process, in 1920, in these words:

"As for us, we were never concerned with the Kantian priestly and vegetarian Quaker prattle about the 'sacredness of human life.' "

The Bolshevik rulers were not concerned about the sacredness of human life because they never believed in it. They never believed in it because it was, is now, and evermore shall be a spiritual concept, a part of the religious beliefs of all the devout of humankind. Since religion is merely an expression of obsolete superstition for the Communist, there can be nothing sacred about its teachings or its evaluation of what God hath made in His likeness.

The Russian Orthodox Patriarch, Bishop Tikhon, excommunicated all Communists soon after the persecutions of his church began. Lenin's answer to this man who dared to defy him was to clap him in jail. From his prison cell Patriarch Tikhon wrote these burning words:

It is not enough that you have stained the hands of the Russian people with the blood of their brethren. You have instigated the people to open, shameless robbery. You have befogged their conscience and stilled their concept of sin. But, under whatever name you may disguise an evil deed, murder, violence, and plunder will always remain crimes and deeds of evil clamoring to Heaven for vengeance. Yes, we are living through a dreadful time under your domination, and it will be long before it fades from the hearts of the people, where it has dimmed the image of God, and impressed that of the Beast.

Lenin's opposition to religion in all its forms and faiths was constant and intense. Some of his bitterest polemics were directed at what he called the "bourgeoisie scalawags" who taught the "superstitions of religion." Lenin saw in religion the greatest possible enemy of his dictatorship, a wall standing in the way of the complete control of the people which the worldwide sweep of communism would have to accomplish.

The Russian murderer of the newly born democracy in Russia knew that religious convictions presupposed liberty of conscience, freedom to think, to discuss, to debate, and to decide what is true and what is false. This he could not allow. Religion would have no place in his scheme, except to be abolished as promptly as possible.

Soon after Lenin announced his official policy of atheism for all Party officials and members, and set in motion his persecutions of religious leaders and beliefs, a cartoon appeared in the *Christian*

Science Monitor that would have angered him further had he seen it. The cartoon showed Lenin dressed like a Bolshevik soldier, standing by the side of a tremendous rock rising from the landscape. The rock was labeled "Religious Faith," and was crowned by the rays of light from the heavens. Lenin had one hand upon the rock and was saying:

"I think I'll just push this out of my way!"

George Vernadsky, in *Lenin, Red Dictator,* says of Lenin's attitude toward religion:

Lenin divined that religion is the fundamental basis of human individualism; it creates a place, if only a small place, in the individual's soul, as an unapproachable refuge, a shelter from the supervision and control of a political party. Fighting against individualism, wishing to turn all persons into useful implements for the Party, Lenin naturally had to direct his blows against religion as the last sanctuary of the individual.

He fought not only against the established church, it must be kept in mind, but against religion in general, against any reverence for the Supreme Being even though preserved only in the human heart. It was exactly such inward religion of the spirit that seemed to Lenin an evil much more dangerous than a church, since he could battle more easily against a visible church.

The turning of the spirit toward God meant the impossibility of its absolute and unreserved submission to the Communist ideal and the Communist party. And Lenin demanded from all his followers just such unreserved submission. . . . All other political parties Lenin gradually debarred. But since the Communist party was not only a political organism, but above all a church of its own kind, or rather an antichurch, it had to attempt to destroy all churches and religions throughout the earth. This aim Lenin set for himself, but he considered it only necessary to move very gradually toward its achievement.

A MILITANT ATHEIST'S HATRED

In a discussion of the "problem" of religion, in 1913 Lenin had written to Maxim Gorki these blasphemous words:

Every sort of religious idea, every concept of any kind of a little godhead, every coquetting even with a little god, is an inexpressible baseness, . . . the most horrible sort of infection. Millions of sins, vilenesses, violences, and physical diseases can be far more clearly revealed to the masses, and are therefore much less dangerous than this delicate, spiritual idea of a nice little godlet, dressed up in most decorative "idealistic" robes.

In numerous such statements this militant atheist showed his hatred and contempt for all things religious. Actually, his political ideology took the place of religion, and still does for millions of Party members throughout the world. It was Lenin's decree that all Party functionaries, and indeed all members, should embrace atheism unreservedly, and this is still the rule for dedicated Communists.

Lenin was especially enraged by the fact that in the villages and small town communities religion was almost the sole cultural outlet for the people. While the intellectuals of the Russian cities under the Tzars as a class gave lip service to the established church, considering it a necessary adjunct to the imperial government, there was little depth of feeling among them and there were few expressions of religious fervor in the perfunctory worship. It was the peasant class, therefore, that valued religious activities most highly. It was the substandard class, the workers on the land and in the small factories, that took most comfort from their religion. And this was the class which Lenin and his Bolshevik associates were determined to weld into the ruling class, together with soldiers and some intellectuals. These were to make up the proletariat. So by every means at Lenin's disposal, including political and social pressures, exhortations, rewards, and punishments, he began the process of winning the masses away from the faith of their fathers.

Lenin was shrewd enough, however, to realize that he could not abolish religion from the minds and hearts of the Russian people, or any other people who joined the uprising of the proletariat, with a few strokes of his pen. He understood how deeply most of the people of his sprawling new dictatorship revered the Orthodox Church, and how many others held tenaciously to the faith of their Roman Catholic, Protestant, or Jewish forebears. He told his Supreme Soviet on one occasion:

"To combat religious prejudices, it is necessary to be extraordinarily cautious."

Cautious or not, Lenin made a vigorous start in his crusade to stamp out "prejudices" born of religion by placing his Number One Comrade, Leon Trotsky, a zealot who had abandoned his Jewish faith for atheism, in charge of a thriving bureaucracy devoted to antireligious propaganda.

Nothing could illustrate more clearly how irreconcilable are religion and Marxism than the capture of the Russian people for communism. Marxism came to power by deceit, terror, and force. It established itself by torture and murder. It survived by the elimination of all human freedoms. We shall see how by these same tactics the Communist revolution spread to other countries now in the captivity of Marxist dictatorships.

We shall see also how the rock of religious faith still stands.

CHAPTER FIVE

RELIGION IS THE OPIUM
OF THE PEOPLE

Lenin wasted no time in laying down his basic, fundamental policy with respect to religion in the USSR under his dictatorship. The first meeting of the National Assembly of Commissars, a group of Lenin's hand-picked stooges in the Bolshevik movement, was held on January 23, 1918. In that Assembly a decree was issued, called "On Freedom of Conscience and Religious Societies." The exact wording of one article follows:

"The church is separated from the State, and the school from the church." Another article asserted: "Every citizen has the right to engage in religious and antireligious propaganda."

Shortly afterward these ideas were spelled out in Article 124 of the Soviet Constitution:

"In order to insure to citizens freedom of conscience, the church in the USSR is separated from the State and the school from the church. Freedom of religious worship and freedom of antireligious propaganda is recognized for all citizens."

Every possible effort was made to prove that these measures provided freedom of religion, so far as the public was concerned at home and abroad. "Separating" the church from the State was generally accepted to mean not only that the church—meaning all religious "societies"—could no longer depend upon the government for any support, but also that churches and religious organizations would be free from government interference. Especially did this seem to be the meaning of the words purporting to grant every citizen the right to engage in "religious propaganda."

Numerous religious leaders in the United States and other Western nations with well-defined policies that guaranteed religious liberty hailed this statement of policy as an advancement in the cause of freedom of religion in the great Russian nation so recently liberated from despotic control.

Actually, the statements, in their true meaning and application, constituted one of the most colossal frauds in history. Although carefully cultivated for a while, the intended impressions proved to be monstrous lies.

Separating the church from the State meant that the church could expect no more support from the government, to be sure. But it also meant that religious societies were placed on the same footing with all other organizations in the Communist State: they lost all privileges they might have claimed as religious groups. It meant that the property of all church bodies, whatever the name or faith, was confiscated; that far from being free to worship and to practice their spiritual activities, religious leaders and members would have to look to the government for permission to exist at all.

As for the right to engage in "religious and antireligious" propaganda, the bitter truth was not long in emerging. Religious propaganda was allowed as long as it was confined within the walls of the place of worship, was not critical of the government, nor in any manner "reactionary," which could mean anything the authorities decided it meant.

On the other hand, the right of "antireligious propaganda" gave to the Communist rulers, from the top commissars down to the local satraps, the power to persecute, restrict, harass, and impede the practice of religion.

Actually, Lenin's cleverly worded decree and the Soviet Constitution, disguised to indicate freedom of religion, were meant to pave the way for its progressive strangulation.

ENGEL'S THEME IS EXPANDED

Hatred and contempt for religion color the writings and sayings of Lenin like a black pigment. He was obsessed with the idea that religion was linked with the capitalist class. He wrote:

"The saying of Marx: 'Religion is the opium of the people,'

is the cornerstone of the Marxist point of view on the matter of religion. All contemporary religion and churches, all and every kind of religious organization Marxism has always viewed as organs of bourgeois reaction, serving as a defense of exploitation and the drugging of the working class."

Lenin was fond of quoting Engels, the associate of Marx in drawing the blueprint for an atheist society:

"Now all religion is nothing else than the fantastic reflection, in the minds of men, of those external forces which dominate their everyday existence, a reflection in which the earthly forces assume the form of supernatural forces."

The top man in the new proletariat dictatorship in Russia expanded Engels' theme in these words:

God (as he appeared in history and life) is before all a complex of ideas produced by the stupefying oppression of man both by the outer nature and class exploitations,—a complex of ideas which pacifies the class struggle. Economic slavery is the true source of the religious humbugging of man . . . the oppression of religion over humanity is but the product and reflex of economic oppression within society.

As though to clinch the matter that even ethics should be considered only as "reflexes" springing from social conditions, Lenin declared:

Our ethics is completely subordinate to the interests of the class struggle of the proletariat. Our ethics is deduced from the interests of the class struggle. . . . Ethics is something that serves for the destruction of the old exploiting society and unites all the toilers around the proletariat which creates a new communist society.

Lenin and his Bolshevik associates were shrewd enough to realize that an immediate and final prohibition of religious worship and the propagation of spiritual teachings would be too much.

The commissars knew that by sheer terror and force they could liquidate the capitalists, who were a minority of the population and the target of all the hatred of the oppressed proletariat. But to meet the forces of religion head on by a sweeping decree to abolish the whole "reactionary superstition" would be too risky to attempt. They knew that many believers among all the faiths were fully willing to die for their convictions, and that antagonizing too many of them would endanger the whole structure of their Communist revolution.

The original Communist plan, therefore, was to accomplish the defeat of this troublesome enemy by successive stages. Lenin made it crystal clear, however, that religion was an irreconcilable foe of the new regime. It is not known whether he set a blueprint with time schedules for the complete eradication of religion from the Soviet Union, but it is hardly believable that this detail escaped his thinking. Certainly he warned his henchmen that "caution" would be needed in the attack upon religious bodies. And certainly he moved directly to the attack where he could and detoured discreetly around opposition where he found it too formidable to smash promptly: the typical method of Communist offensives, whether for political, military, economic, or social aims, in every movement since the seizure of the Russian government, on through the Communist captivity of other vast areas of the world, and down to the present time.

Bukharin-Prebrajensky, a close friend, collaborator, and adviser of Lenin, whom Lenin called "the greatest theoretician of the Party and the most worthy to be listened to," in early 1919 pointed out:

The separation of church and State, and of school and church, has been relatively easy, almost an effortless task for the proletarian power. But it is incomparably more difficult to fight against religious prejudices which have already taken deep root in the conscience of the masses and which are extremely long-lived! The struggle will be long; patience must be accompanied by measures of extreme firmness.

War on the Believers

Behind the gloved hand of "patience" in the treatment of the churches was the iron fist of "extreme firmness," the Marxist intolerance of all things spiritual. Lenin launched a barrage of Party propaganda as an opening gun to remold all the thinking of "believers" (a term supposed to be in derision) and to win their acceptance of the idea that religion was obsolete superstition.

Then followed the direct attacks upon the churches. Since the

Russian Orthodox Church was the dominant religious group in Russia, persecutions and restrictions fell heaviest upon priests and believers of that faith. But soon Roman Catholics and Protestants were included in the campaign of antireligious propaganda.

An immediate aim of Lenin and his top commissars was to break up the unity of religious bodies and make each congregation strictly local in character. This struck directly at the hierarchy of the Orthodox and Roman Catholic churches. To accomplish this dismemberment of the churches, "religious associations" of more than one congregation were prohibited. The decree of the politburo was plain: "A citizen may be a member of one religious association only, and persons who are members of several religious associations may be prosecuted. . . . A religious association can use only one church building, or other premises, for prayers."

Since January, 1918, all church buildings and real estate had become the property of the State. Next step in the strangulation process was to declare church after church as "surplus" and proceed to close them down. In that process, all Christian faiths and Jewish congregations were treated with equal severity. Priests and pastors who resisted were arrested, imprisoned, and often given harsh prison sentences.

Indirect blows at religious worship quickly followed. Each congregation, whatever the faith, had to secure a house from the local Communist authorities. Soviet law declared that when permission was obtained for a place of worship, "use of church buildings is granted free of charge." However, in actual practice this was interpreted by the usual twist of Communist duplicity to mean only the building itself. Of course a "rental" had to be paid on the land occupied, along with obligatory insurance by the State. Fees and dues were assessed against the members who signed the contract for the use of the building. All this added up to a financial burden so heavy as to discourage all but the most dedicated believers.

In addition, members of the congregations were held individually responsible for any loss of property from the church building, even for thefts by nonmembers. If one member was convicted of an offense, all members were held equally to blame and the place of worship could be closed immediately. These diabolical devices allowed unscrupulous bureaucrats to keep the church members in constant fear.

All religious activities were confined to the place of worship itself. Religious ceremonies such as baptisms and marriages, spiritual teachings in schools or homes, missionary enterprises, and distribution of money for causes outside the congregation were strictly forbidden under heavy penalties.

All religious schools were closed, and either absorbed as "people's" schools or liquidated. All religious instruction was forbidden for youths under eighteen years of age. "Cultural" activities were offered as substitutes for religion, and many church edifices were turned into theaters. Movies and ballets, shaped to carry Communist propaganda, thrived under government sponsorship.

People in all walks of life were called into frequent party discussions, at which the virtues of the revolution were endlessly and boringly explained. Antireligious publications sprang up on every hand.

Conferences were held in communities in all the cities and towns of Russia, at which party workers gave instructions for organizing the people to combat religion in all its forms: the despised and dangerous "opium of the people."

In 1919 a "Museum of the Godless" was set up at 14 Petrovka Street in Moscow. It displayed numerous caricatures of religious beliefs and poked ribald fun at the most sacred tenets of the faithful. In addition the museum contained relics of saints and other consecrated articles, snatched from churches and monasteries closed by Soviet decree. To the astonishment of the authorities, devout visitors to the museum stood, bowed, or knelt in veneration of the sacred items. The guards were forced to prohibit such displays of worship in this and other museums of the godless set up in many cities and towns of the Soviet Union.

Disappointed at the slow pace of the antireligious program and impatient to get on faster with the task, Lenin in mid-1920 decreed the "liquidation of the holy relics." This was a cruel and shocking stroke. Relics of the saints, greatly venerated by Russian Orthodox believers, were seized by authorities. Exposed to public view, they were denounced as frauds and derided as not being "incorruptible" as the faithful had been taught.

The same barbaric Bukharin-Prebrajensky, now high in the council of the commissars, advised that the time had come to be much more severe on the "cults." He wrote:

A war of maximum intensity against religious prejudices must be waged at the present time when the Church, revealing itself as a counterrevolutionary organization, is using all its religious influence to launch the masses into a political struggle against the dictatorship of the proletariat. The Orthodox Faith supported by the popes tends to ally itself with the monarchy. Consequently the Soviet power should from the present moment engage in a most intense campaign of anti-religious propaganda. This can be done by special conferences, public discussions, publication of a whole new literature specially adapted for the purpose, or by the widespread diffusion of scientific knowledge which will insensibly, gently, and inevitably, undermine the influence of religion. An excellent weapon in the struggle against the Church has been employed recently in many parts of the Republic, namely, the opening of "incorruptible" relics. This has revealed to huge throngs of fervent believers the gross charlatanism which is at the base of all religion and of Russian Orthodoxy in particular.*

How to Use a Famine

In 1921 a famine of tremendous proportions struck great areas of southern Russia. It was the first tragic harvest of the systematic liquidation of the kulaks, the land-owning farmers, under Lenin's program of ruthless ending of private ownership of property. Seizure and expropriation of the farms was met with bitter resistance, not only by the gentry but also by small peasant landowners as well. Wholesale arrests, imprisonments, deportations, and executions framed the somber picture in deepest black. "Collective" farms were established, under rules laid down ostensibly by the farm workers themselves, but actually under the compulsion of local authorities answerable to the dictatorship.

The result was the same as has followed the collectivization of agriculture in every area in the Marxist empire: production fell alarmingly, despite the beratings and threats of the Bolshevik overseers. Private planning, sowing, reaping, all the elements of successful farming were replaced by bureaucratic incompetence. Passive resistance and covert sabotage by the victims of the system brought still lower farm production, with less and less food for humans and feed for livestock. The usual reserves of farm produce were exhausted.

In addition, the summer and autumn of 1920 saw the most severe droughts that had ever been experienced in that area of Europe.

As news of the great national tragedy filtered out of Russia countless church groups in many countries of the world made plans to send relief to the famine area. The United States established the American Relief Administration, under direction of Herbert Hoover. The Soviet government permitted Mr. Hoover to send in thousands of tons of food and clothing, and this helped stem the tide of hunger and privation.

Pope Benedict XV, deeply affected by the disaster in Russia, sent generous funds to be distributed through Catholic organizations throughout western Europe. He also won Lenin's agreement to admit a Pontifical Relief Mission into the area most affected.

Pope Pius XI continued the benign work of his predecessor, sending in the mission in July 1922. Lenin's Soviet ministers informed His Holiness that members of the relief group could in no wise engage in any type of religious activity while administering the famine relief, nor propagate their faith in any manner.

Furthermore, the Politburo insisted that the Catholic mission grant full diplomatic status to its members. This was a devious way of trying to force the Vatican to grant official recognition to the Communist regime, a step the Holy See had steadfastly refused to take. When Pope Pius refused this demand, Communist authorities laid down so many restrictions on the Pontifical Relief Mission that it carried on with greatest difficulty for only about a year.

Protestant relief efforts fared some better, largely because most non-Catholic groups coordinated their work with that of Mr. Hoover, until late 1923 when conditions in the famine region became appreciably better.

In late 1921 Lenin announced his "New Economic Policy,"

which permitted more private enterprise in farming and small businesses. Without relaxing control over big industries, the plan gave more liberal treatment of small producers. This brought a measure of recovery for the national economy. But the breathing spell allowed small capitalists was only a strategic retreat in the battle for the enslavement of the Russian people. And there was no change in the steady strangulation of religious bodies.

The famine took a toll of 3 million lives. Even this disaster was utilized by the Communist high command to persecute religion. On December 27, 1921, the All-Russian Central Executive Committee passed a resolution requiring all church priests, pastors, rabbis, and their congregations to list every valuable article used in their worship. Here was clear indication that the authorities planned to confiscate such articles.

The official atheist news magazine *Bezboznik* began beating the drums in behalf of confiscation of such articles of value, declaring that they were the symbols of opposition to "scientific materialism" and therefore enemies of the State.

On February 23, 1922, the blow fell. Giving the famine as the reason for the need for funds which would come from the sale of such church articles, the commissars decreed:

> The local Soviets are hereby instructed to remove within one month's time . . . from Church property, given for use to various groups of believers of all religions, according to inventories and contracts, all precious articles of gold, silver, and precious stones, the removal of which does not essentially infringe upon the interests of the cult, and surrender these to agents of the Commissariat of Finance, specially designating them for the fund of the central committee for famine aid.

The decree specified that there must be surrendered to the authorities "all the valuables of decorative nature as well as vessels and utensils . . . golden or silver chalices, reliquaries, metal adornments of icons, vestments, chandeliers, and precious stones."

The Robbery Is Challenged

The Patriarch Tikhon, highest prelate of the Russian Orthodox Church, who had been released from prison some months before, dared to challenge the move for what it was: A device to rob churches and their ministers of the very visible symbols necessary to their worship. Especially was this true of the Orthodox churches, with their traditional veneration of the cross, and their use of icons, candles, chalices, altar pieces, and works of art. Religious articles also played a most significant and necessary part in Roman Catholic worship, and even the services of Lutheran, Baptist, Jewish, and other faiths were enriched by the venerated symbols of their creeds and methods of devotion.

Many congregations hastened to raise the money to cover the value of the articles to be expropriated. With vast cruelty, Lenin instructed the local Soviet authorities to accept the funds, then to inform the church leaders that the valuables would be confiscated anyway, because the articles were still the property of the State.

In righteous anger, bishops, priests, pastors, rabbis, and their faithful believers resisted the move. Wholesale arrests followed. In several communities armed secret police enforced the order. *Pravda* ("Truth") reported in December 1922 that there had been 1,440 "bloody excesses," meaning the slaughter by gunfire of resisting clergy and parishioners in that many areas of the country. The report further stated that there had been 45 executions and 250 long-term imprisonments.

Ignoring for the most part these ghastly statistics, the Soviet press boastfully listed the totals of the value of the church objects "voluntarily" given over to the authorities from the various areas.

Typical of the treatment accorded church leaders who resisted this wholesale robbery of sacred objects was that of about a dozen leading Roman Catholics in the dioceses of Petrograd and Moscow. Lenin personally selected these priests for arrests, vowing to make examples of them in order to terrorize all other churchmen who dared oppose his orders. Typical also was the wording of the charge against the Catholic priests:

The accused have . . . set up a counterrevolutionary organization in Petrograd, to oppose the laws and decrees of the Soviet Government with regard to the relations between Church and State, and more particularly in opposition to the decree of the National Assembly of Commissars of January 23, 1918, relating to the separation of Church and State. By their action they tried to shake the loyalty of the people by exciting them at Petrograd in 1922 to oppose unanimously the nationalization of Church property, the closing of churches and the requisition of articles of value. They also gave evidence of being categorically opposed to the legitimate demands of the Government. . . . This opposition comes under Articles 63 and 119 of the Penal Code.*

Among the accused was Monsignor John Cieplak, Archbishop of Mohliev. The specific accusation related that the archbishop had sent a telegram to a priest urging him not to send an inventory of church articles to the local commissar. For this crime, the prelate was condemned to death, and all his personal effects and the property of the church to which he ministered were confiscated. Later, his sentence was commuted to banishment from Russia.

Monsignor Constantine Butkiewicz of Petrograd was similarly charged. The wording of his accusation was practically the same as that preferred against his colleague. He was condemned to death and was executed, with pointed significance as to the date, on Good Friday, March 30, 1923.

The charge against another of the arrested leaders, Bishop Hodniewicz, reads as follows:

Accused of resisting the expropriation of the valuables of the Church of St. Catherine at Petrograd on 24 June. When the Commissars Kolesnikov and Ivanov wished to examine a small altar furnishing in the tabernacle he declared that they would do it only over his dead body. Then he said to the faithful who were in the church: "Let us pray and let us keep them from touching the tabernacle except over our dead bodies." For this reason the tabernacle could not be examined. This crime is punishable according to Article 119 of the Penal Code.

Bishop Hodniewicz was given a long-term prison sentence, to which the authorities added: "With the approval of the People."

The closing of churches and persecution of the clergy continued unabated. Within five years of Lenin's coming to power only about one fourth of the places of worship of all denominations were open for services, and less than one fourth of the priests, ministers, and rabbis were permitted to perform their spiritual duties.

"Can we save Russia from becoming a spiritual desert?" was the question asked by many religious leaders. As we shall see, they fought a valiant fight to do so.

CHAPTER SIX

ATHEIST SCREWS ARE TIGHTENED

Never, during those dark days of Lenin's despotic rule, was there a direct accusation that the restrictions upon religion and its believers were due to the practice of their spiritual faith. Such a charge was carefully avoided, to keep up the fiction of "freedom of conscience."

Always the "crime" charged to leaders of the churches of all faiths consisted of some form of opposition to the State, such as counterrevolutionary activities.

The excuse most frequently given for closing the churches was the need for buildings for cultural centers, art galleries, and places of entertainment. Many churches in the rural areas were requisitioned for barns to store grain and other farm products.

The case of the pastor of an Evangelical church near the edge of Petrograd, Dr. L. Serpicov, was typical. In July 1923 this minister was informed that his church was "surplus." He was ordered to vacate the building within a week. Strongly supported by his members, Dr. Serpicov refused to give up his place of worship, pleading that he would have to have time to find another building.

Summoned again to local Communist headquarters, the pastor was scolded severely for his lack of "patriotic support" of the people's revolution, and warned that he would have to comply with the order or suffer consequences. The minister begged to be allowed one more service in his church, and this was granted.

In his sermon at this last Sunday morning's service, Pastor

Serpicov denounced the action of the authorities, declaring with considerable vehemence that believers in religion owed their highest allegiance to God rather than to men. Dr. Serpicov had failed to remember that there would be spies for the local Party in his audience taking note of all that he said.

Early that Sunday afternoon the minister was arrested and imprisoned. He was held for several weeks without a public hearing or trial. All efforts of members of his congregation to visit him were repulsed. Finally the local commissar announced that Pastor Serpicov had pleaded guilty to the charge of "reactionary and treasonable utterances," and was therefore serving a sentence of ten years in an unnamed prison.

Some three years later a political prisoner in a Siberian concentration camp was released. Returning to Petrograd (renamed Leningrad in 1924), he passed the word secretly to close friends of the former pastor that Dr. Serpicov was in that same concentration camp. The ex-prisoner told how in the three years' time the once robust and hardy man had been physically and mentally broken. He described him: "Gaunt, almost like a skeleton, hardly able to walk, but forced to rise at 4:30 in the morning with all the rest of the prisoners, and stand at his place of work all day even though he could hardly lift a shovelful of dirt."

Despite efforts of his bureaucrats to suppress it, late in 1923 news leaked out that Lenin was fatally ill. It is certain that millions of believers in Russia fervently prayed that when the curse of this atheist tyrant had been removed, someone would succeed him who was humane enough to permit the unalienable right of the profession and practice of religion.

While the dictator was still in his last illness a savage struggle for leadership of the monolithic regime began among his top henchmen in the Politburo. Many religious people of the Soviet Union hoped that the whole Bolshevist government would collapse during the intra-party fight. But no such good fortune came their way. The people learned to their sorrow that a Marxist dictatorship is a self-perpetuating parasite, fastening itself upon the living body of a people and sucking the blood of liberty from the veins of community and national life.

JOSEPH STALIN COMES TO THE TOP

Chief contenders for leadership were Leon Trotsky, who had been the man Lenin most depended upon to liquidate religion; Joseph Stalin, the stolid, earnest Marxist who had faithfully performed all the duties Lenin had assigned to him, including the murder of countless thousands of "enemies of the revolution"; and Bukharin-Prebrajensky, the great Communist founder's closest adviser on matters of inner policy.

From the bloody struggle, Stalin emerged on top. He banished Trotsky, put Bukharin-Prebrajensky to death, and gathered into his cruel fists the chief powers of the dictatorship.

How Stalin operated to smash all remaining vestiges of human freedom in the Soviet Union is graphically condensed in these words written by Eugene Lyons:

I must try to recapitulate it in terms of its essence, which was *a war of internal conquest,* a Homeric struggle between an all-powerful dictatorship and a desperately hostile population.

Stalin's offensive opened with swift and fatal blows at the counterfeit capitalism of the National Economic Policy, and by 1934, when I departed from Russia, nothing was left of the high mood of dedication, traces of which I had still found among Communists when I arrived. The very vocabulary of idealism had been outlawed. "Equality" and "compassion" had become dirty words, lampooned as bourgeois romanticism. Excessive concern for the people, their needs, or sensibilities, was punished as "rotten liberalism." It was a time when the verbal camouflage was peeled from arbitrary power. Terror was no longer explained away as a sad necessity. It was used starkly, arrogantly, and glorified as "human engineering." Among those who wielded power there developed grotesque pride in the "Bolshevik firmness" and "Leninist courage" that could torture and kill millions without sentimental self-reproach, so that officials sometimes even exaggerated the number of victims. If starving a million took Bolshevik daring, did not starving five million prove that daring fivefold?

The offensive was directed, at various times or at the same time, against the "technical intelligentsia": engineers, technicians, scientists, the educated generally; against the industrial proletariat; against the Communist Party itself. Its operations were reported to the outside world through "demonstration trials," industrial charts and statistics, figures on "socialized" acreage, edicts in effect chaining the worker to his machine and the farmer to the soil.

Its most ghastly piece of strategy was the man-made famine of 1932-1933. Its most sinister and enduring by-product was the institution of slave labor in conditions that made ordinary chattel slavery, ancient or modern, seem benign by comparison. An intensive attack on "superstition," meaning religion, was an inevitable part of the undertaking: The harried individual must be denied a spiritual sanctuary beyond the reach of the state. And everything that was creatively unconventional in the arts, the cultural sanctuary of the more sensitive citizen, was driven underground for the same reason.*

The "man-made famine" Mr. Lyons mentions was the starving to death of approximately 4 million men, women, and children in the USSR, in the process of forcing them into collective farming. In the Ukraine, the great "breadbasket of eastern Europe," the foremost wheat-producing area of the Old World, resistance was most intense. Here Joseph Stalin, "man of steel," pitted his most monstrous cruelties against the rights of the people. In all areas of the Soviet Union where rebellion reduced production far below the needs of the local population, Stalin allowed death by starvation to beat the people into submission.

In the Ukraine at that time there was a minor official, one of Stalin's bright young disciples of Ukrainian descent, Nikita S. Khrushchev. He was eagerly learning all he might need to know to follow in his master's bloody tracks. In that same region in the mid-thirties Khrushchev was to win the title of "the butcher of the Ukraine" by directing Stalin's murderous purges in that area.

Along with the man-made famine in the Ukraine came the famine of spiritual life, the almost complete eradication of church activities in that unhappy land. As in Russia proper the Orthodox Church was the dominant religious group in the Ukraine. By the early 1930s this church was reduced to a shell of its former vigorous life. Roman Catholic, Protestant, and Jewish believers were also persecuted almost to extinction.

During the first ten years of his iron rule Dictator Stalin clubbed the religious life of the people of his Communist empire in every conceivable manner. He closed churches, confiscated their properties, forbade religious activities outside the places of worship, restricted the number of students allowed to attend seminaries, harassed believers with devilish cruelty, and callously murdered those who opposed his program to abolish religion.

LIQUIDATION MOVES FORWARD

In true Marxist-Leninist fashion, Stalin and his henchmen would tighten the screws and racks of persecution of believers for a time, then relax them for a season, knowing that with every relaxation the persecuted ones would be so relieved they would figuratively kiss the hands of their tormentors in gratitude for their consideration and liberality.

In 1926 Stalin prompted the organization of the Society of Militant Atheists, an activist group aimed especially at youth. The young atheists were given instructions on how to combat religious superstitions, both among their elders and their fellow young people. They formed the true shock troops of the atheist movement, using speeches, conferences, parades, propaganda, and any other means at hand to downgrade religion in public thinking.

In early 1929 Stalin decided it was time to tighten the enormous screw of restrictions upon religious activities to a considerable degree. On April 8 he had his Soviet Assembly rubber-stamp his "Law on Religious Associations." This act codified many of the loose decrees respecting religious bodies and brought the churches under still stricter control of the government.

Principal item in the new law was the requirement for the registration of all religious associations. Actually, the act forbade any further activities by religious groups until they had been properly registered with the authorities. Any such group that did not register by May 1, 1930, was to be considered as dissolved.

Among other hampering restrictions upon the practice of religion were these:

1. All believers in each congregation had to sign a "consent" to their membership, thus automatically placing them on the Soviet books as enemies of the State.

2. The association had to agree to exercise its activities solely

within the walls of its licensed building (a provision that had been in effect since the beginning of Communist rule): cutting off outside teaching, missionary work, and propagation of the faith.

3. Each priest or pastor, and each "executive" of the religious association (no more than three of whom were allowed), had to be listed by name, occupation, former places of work, etc., with the proviso that the authorities could exclude any executive as "not acceptable": meaning that the authorities could name one of their own atheist spies to the governing body of the religious group.

4. No welfare or charitable work of any kind could be carried on by the churches: thus stifling all activities helpful to families of believers and the community in general.

5. Changes in membership, the clergy, and the executives were required to be reported to the authorities within seven days: so not to break the continuous control of the association by the local commissars.

6. Local authorities were given the right to examine all the records of a religious association at any time: a most convenient device to secure what the Communist leaders called "self-condemnation" for infractions of the law.

Even after all these and numerous other items of the 1929 act were fulfilled, local Communist bureaucrats could refuse to issue a permit for the functioning of the religious association.

Thus did Stalin compress religion in the USSR into such narrow confines of restrictive control as to make its practice almost impossible.

The new law started an extensive campaign to close places of worship throughout the Soviet Union. According to the most reliable statistics available, about 1,500 churches and monasteries had been closed prior to 1927. During that year 134 were closed, and in 1928 an additional 550. But in 1929 the number of churches and monasteries of all faiths liquidated rose to 1,440: their property confiscated with no compensation, and their leaders disgraced in countless ways.

All during 1930 the Soviet press reported the continued "demand of the people" in communities all over Russia for the closing of churches and the systematic destruction of icons, Bibles, paintings, and other articles used in worship.

In addition, bishops, priests, and pastors of all denominations were disfranchised. This punishment was not on charges of being active churchmen, but because they were branded officially as "nonworkers." Within three years of the 1929 law, it is estimated, more than half a million religious leaders were disfranchised. The effect of this wholesale degradation is tersely portrayed by Vladimir Gsovski, an authority on Soviet law:

> The disfranchise did not affect merely the right of vote. The disfranchised persons (*lishentsy*) constituted a special class of the Soviet citizens, a kind of outcast, whose right to work, earn, and even to get food was considerably restricted. Thus they could not be members of the trade unions and could not therefore be lawfully employed, especially in the governmental enterprises.
>
> Special regulations prohibited the clergy from holding any position in the institutions under the control of the Commissariats of Justice, Education, Agriculture, Food, and the Interior. They had to pay an increased rent for their apartments—from five to ten times higher than the "toilers." They could not rent rooms or apartments in municipalized or nationalized buildings, that is, in the prevailing number of buildings in the cities. Persons living in such buildings could not accept ministers of religion as lodgers.
>
> When for quite a long time food and other commodities were distributed by rations on cards, the disfranchised persons were deprived of such cards. The right to work and employment affected not only the disfranchised persons but also the members of their families. Their children were practically barred from education, especially in the higher institutions. Finally, the disfranchised persons paid a special, high income tax and an agricultural tax; and those 21 to 40 years old were forced to pay a military tax in peacetime and to enroll in the labor militia in war time.*

Since the seizure of the government in Russia by Lenin and his Bolsheviks and their destruction of the infant democracy in January 1918, the United States of America had never recognized the Soviet dictatorship as a government truly representative of the people of Russia and worthy to be honored by exchange of ambassadors. In 1933 President Franklin D. Roosevelt, on assurances of Stalin's agents that a greater measure of religious freedom would be granted to the Russian people and also that there would be no subversion of the American public and institutions by Communist authorities, granted the recognition Stalin so anxiously desired.

While subversion by agents of the international Communist conspiracy remained at a minimum for some years following U.S. recognition, there was no appreciable liberalizing of the treatment of religious bodies. Stalin simply ignored this promise, as he did any promise which he considered better broken than kept. A new Soviet constitution was issued in 1936, making few changes in the 1929 law, and the systematic strangulation of the churches proceeded with its characteristic tightening and loosening of the screws and racks as suited dictatorial whims.

Following 1936 Stalin became engrossed with the progress of another ruthless dictator to the west, Adolf Hitler, who had come to power in Germany on the ruins of the German economy and his promises to rebuild a strong and prosperous Fatherland. It is certain, from his subsequent actions, that Joseph Stalin saw in Adolf Hitler a means to accomplish a most cherished ambition: the extension of the Communist revolution to neighbor lands, by peaceful means if possible, by war if necessary.

SPEAK UP, COMRADES!

Meantime, never were Stalin and his Politburo able to announce that they had eradicated religion from the hearts of the people. Always there were those who remembered the old days and worshiped quietly in their homes, where two or three or more were gathered together. Always there were those who walked many miles to attend the one church of their faith still allowed for propaganda purposes to function. Like trying to hold down the steam in a heated kettle, in one place or another the lid of restrictions would be lifted by the pressure of those who would not be denied their spiritual beliefs and practices.

M. Yaroslavsky, Stalin's most able hatchet-man in the program to eradicate religion, took note that acceptance of atheism by the people was not progressing as he had hoped. This infamous leader of the Union of the Godless was quoted by *Pravda* on May 7, 1937, as saying in a discussion of a report by his atheist organization:

> In the towns more than half of the workers, about two thirds of the adult population above sixteen class themselves with atheists. *In the villages,* on the other hand, probably more than half or about two thirds believe in God, and that means not only old men and women, as some think, but among the *young* in the villages the percentage is very high. . . . Another mischievous theory is that only old men and women are believers. This is not true.

Continuing his discussion, Yaroslavsky urged the people to be diligent and vigilant to make their antireligious work more effective.

One constant method of persuasion of the people to abandon religion was to send trained speakers into all communities to instruct the masses in atheism. Attendance at these meetings was compulsory, unless a "worker" could show it was necessary for him to be on duty.

Big attendance did not insure a warm reception for the atheist lecturer. Generally the crowd sat in stony silence, showing no emotion but seething inwardly at the blasphemous tirades forced upon them, while instructors mentioned that the constitution of the great Union of Soviet Socialist Republics, the People's Revolutionary Government, enjoined the duty of "antireligious propaganda."

Numerous such discussion meetings were timed for the days sacred for religious observances, such as Christmas and Easter. On those occasions the attack upon religious superstition was specific and direct.

A man respected in the ministry of his Protestant denomination in the United States, born in the Soviet Union and fortunate enough to escape as a young man, recalls for us what happened at one of the community gatherings for atheist instruction. Knowing the spiritual significance of Easter to the Christian people of the village where our friend lived as a youth, the local commissars scheduled the meeting for Good Friday night. Our friend recalls that the eager young lecturer faced the townsfolk with arrogant confidence in his ability to "re-educate" their thinking.

The speaker began quietly, persuasively, pointing out that the Marxist revolution had freed the people from the old, unscientific illusions, such as they had erroneously learned from that bundle of myths, the Scriptures. The people were now at liberty to follow the only true and scientific teachings, those announced by Marx and Lenin, and now so well explained by the man who was like a father to them all, Comrade Stalin.

Warming to his subject, the speaker declared that Jesus Christ may have lived, and perhaps was a truly good man, but if so, he assuredly was a good Communist.

"As for his death and resurrection, these are lies!" shouted the young man. "All lies! You must not believe such nonsense. You must turn your backs on this Easter superstition. Be at your work, all of you, on this Sunday, and you can have Monday off. Now— what do you think now of this impostor, Jesus Christ?"

There was complete silence for a moment.

"Speak up, Comrades!" urged the atheist instructor. "What do you think of Jesus Christ now?"

The silence was broken by a tall, raw-boned worker who rose from his seat in the back of the hall, shuffled into the aisle, and glaring at the young man on the platform declared in a clear voice:

"I think Christ is risen from the dead!"

Spontaneously from the audience as in one voice came the response, in the words of their beloved liturgy,

"He is risen indeed!"

CHAPTER SEVEN

COMMUNISM TEACHES HARD LESSONS

Why have we pursued this brief review of the history of the Communist seizure of a great country, the Russian nation and people, and the treatment of religious believers by the godless regime?

Why "look back to the past" to recall the origins of the Marxist-Leninist principles and their application under the iron rule of Dictator Stalin?

Why take from the voluminous files of Communist duplicity and cruelty these few examples of persecutions of religious leaders, the strangling restrictions upon their spiritual ministrations, the heartless harassments of the believers—these examples we have noted from the time of Lenin to that most tragic war of 1939?

The answer may be found in words inscribed on a building in Washington. Near the portal of the stately structure that houses the most cherished documents relating to the founding of the United States of America and its government, the Archives Building, are these words: THE PAST IS PROLOGUE. Truly, communism's past is prologue to its present and its future.

All that happened before 1939 in the efforts of Communist leaders to exterminate religion in the Soviet Union drew the blueprint for similar—often identical—treatment accorded those who have clung to their spiritual beliefs although condemned to live in the Communist colonial empire of post-World War II.

All that was planned by the disciples of Karl Marx between the issuing of the *Communist Manifesto* of 1848 and the year 1917, and carried out between 1917 and 1939 in the USSR, tested and proved the methods that guided the antireligious campaigns after World War II to the present, in the nations of eastern Europe, of China, of North Korea and North Viet Nam, of Tibet, of Cuba, and of all other areas now under the heel of Communist control.

If we of the free world do not heed the lessons taught by the Marxist leaders during those tragic years, our world will find its most cherished liberty, freedom of conscience and worship, increasingly beset by this irreconcilable enemy of all spiritual things.

By heeding those lessons, people who are still free can use their moral and spiritual strength to challenge, to combat, to beat down, and finally to conquer this monstrous force whose continued existence will prevent the creation of a just and lasting peace in the world.

Furthermore, the developments that precipitated that greatest holocaust of history, World War II, costing the lives of millions of men, women, and children all around the globe and the destruction of immeasurable resources, teach a most unforgettable lesson. The lesson is found in the clever manner the Soviet rulers switched tactics to fit the war situation, the duplicity with which they won from democratic nations the material support needed to preserve their dictatorial power during and after the great conflict, the lowering of the Iron Curtain after the attainment of their purposes: all these explain the true situation confronting believers in religion in atheist Marxist empires today.

The past explains clearly what the free world must expect in its dealings with communism in the future. There can be no doubt that the people of the free nations stand at the most critical "forks of the road" in modern times. They must quickly decide whether to drift along in the supposed security of a "coexistence" with the Communist rulers or to stand and fight with all the mighty weapons of their economic, political, social, moral, and spiritual power until victory. The free peoples must understand that coexistence implies that Communist regimes will not disturb the "capitalist" nations if in turn these "imperialists" do not disturb the Communist regimes while the Marxist tyranny digests the peoples it has swallowed. Will peoples who still have freedom and who still cherish their liberties agree to this?

On this decision will depend not only whether governments of, by, and for the people will long endure, but also whether religious faith and practice are to be preserved for mankind.

PEACE IN OUR TIME!

Let us review briefly the events that brought about the enslavement of about one fourth of the people of the world and see their effect upon that most priceless right of humankind, freedom of conscience and religious worship.

Partly with the idealism of Woodrow Wilson's motto for Europe, "the self-determination of peoples," ringing in their ears, and partly because of the pressure of revived nationalism within ethnic groups that made up the old empires, new nations emerged from the collapse of Tzarist Russia and Kaiser Wilhelm's Germany, the dismemberment of Austria-Hungary, and other "adjustments" made in middle and eastern Europe. The three Baltic areas, Estonia, Latvia, and Lithuania, ruled by Imperial Russia since 1795, were given their independence and with great rejoicing unfurled their national flags. Poland, partitioned between the German states and Russia since 1795, was again made an independent nation. Principally from the fragments of Austria-Hungary and Serbia emerged the countries of Czechoslovakia, Austria, Hungary, and Yugoslavia.

Despite these gains in self-government for several nations, World War I did not make the world safe for democracy. Contrary to the hopes and prayers of millions of people all over the globe, the war proved only that the destruction of material and human resources leaves economic distress, social problems, and the certainty of political upheavals.

A League of Nations was established, but it had no power to prevent the rise of aggressive dictatorships. A disarmament conference set quotas of naval strength for the United States, Great Britain, and Japan, in the fond illusion that disarmament can bring peace. The world learned—or should have learned—that only world order under law can bring peace and only with a secure peace can there be hope for effective disarmament.

All the major nations signed the Kellogg-Briand Pact of 1928 renouncing war as an instrument of national policy: some of the nations in earnest, more of them in cynical compliance with what seemed to be expected of them.

Economic distress with its unemployment and poverty, especially in Italy and Germany, brought political earthquakes of historic dimensions. In Italy a veteran of the war, Benito Mussolini, marched with his Black Shirts upon Rome, seized the government, and established a Fascist corporate state. In Germany another veteran of the war, Adolf Hitler, scrambled to power and set up a National Socialist (Nazi) party built around his own dictatorship.

Hoping to extend the glory of Italy by creating a modern Roman Empire, in 1935 Mussolini sent his armies to conquer Ethiopia, while the League of Nations covered its eyes or wrung its hands impotently. Hitler, rebuilding the national economy of Germany while robbing the people of all semblance of freedom, in 1938 began a series of aggressive moves that by military force brought Austria under his control and annexed the Sudetenland of Czechoslovakia to his *Reich*. In September of that year Prime Minister Neville Chamberlain of Great Britain met the Fuehrer at Munich and granted concessions to the Nazi leader that included recognition of the seizure of the Sudetenland, in return for promises by Hitler that he had no more "territorial ambitions."

"Peace in our time!" hopefully announced Mr. Chamberlain. This appeasement won for the free world the only harvest the sowing of appeasement can ever win from a dictatorship: still more aggression and still more demands, which must be met either with more appeasement or with firm resistance.

In March 1939 the new aggression began, once more against Czechoslovakia, resulting in the annexation by the Nazi regime of the western provinces of Bohemia and Moravia.

It is certain that Joseph Stalin, top man in the dictatorship of the Soviet Union, watched these developments with keen interest. Fascism and nazism were popularly supposed to be poles apart from Marxism. The dictatorships of Mussolini and Hitler were thought of as "right" and communism as "left." Actually, all three systems were firmly based upon monolithic control; all permitted no freely elected parliaments; all considered the courts not as guardians of impartial justice but as agencies for support of the dictatorship; all considered citizens as servants of the State, rather than the State as the servant of the people.

All three dictatorships considered religion as unnecessary and an enemy of the regime.

While using a basis different from atheistic materialism for their control of religion, both Mussolini and Hitler enforced the policy that religious belief and practice must be subordinate to the demands of the State.

Like all dedicated Communists, Stalin was saturated with the Marxist urge to advance the cause of world revolution. His constant dream was to extend his Communist rule into the neighbor countries to the west of the USSR. The Tzars had ruled the Baltic nations and eastern Poland. Why should not these territories be "recovered"—with the help of Nazi Germany?

WHEN ROBBERS BECOME FRIENDS

On August 23, 1939, the statesmen of the entire world were startled by the news of the signing of a treaty between Hitler and Stalin, using their foreign ministers for the agreement, Ribbentrop for Nazi Germany and Molotov for the USSR. So much of the treaty as was made public pledged nonaggression and peaceful adjustment of any disputes between the countries.

Both Hitler and Stalin understood very well what the treaty meant: war against the nation lying between them. Caught like a nut in the jaws of a cracker, Poland was plainly the object of the agreement. By the treaty, the *Reichsfuehrer* would not have to worry about an attack from the Soviet Union in case Britain and France went to war to defend Poland. The Soviet Union would get its share of Poland, all the Baltic states, and other loot after the dust of Poland had settled.

It is known now that all but a few details of this infamous treaty were decided upon far in advance of its signing—perhaps in early spring. Mobilization of troops in both countries went quietly forward. On September 1, 1939, Hitler sent his military legions moving like an irresistible juggernaut into Poland. Stalin cleverly waited five days, so that it could be firmly fixed in world opinion that only the Nazis were responsible for starting the war. Then he loosed his powerful infantry and artillery divisions against Poland from the east. Within a few weeks, that hapless victim nation was bombed into submission, lying at the mercy of the two big aggressor regimes.

To prepare the Baltic countries of Estonia, Latvia, and Lithuania for their executions, the Soviet Union forced their leaders to sign "nonaggression" pacts, permitting the Stalinist government to establish military bases upon their territories. The same arrangement was offered another intended victim, Finland. The Finns refused, and in late November 1939 the Soviet forces invaded Finland. Repulsed at first by the tenacious Finns, the Red invaders used their overwhelming military power to force their small neighbor to surrender.

Sensing that dictators could extend their aggressions with impunity, Mussolini attacked and absorbed Albania, then threw in his lot with Hitler against the Western nations of Europe.

In the spring of 1940, while Hitler's air force, the *Luftwaffe,* was pounding away at Britain, the Soviet Union ousted the democratic governments of the Baltic countries. In cynical disregard of the nonaggression pacts, the Stalin regime took over the sovereignty of these little nations. Thousands of patriotic people, including most of their religious leaders, were arrested and executed or deported to Siberian work camps.

The American people were shocked by all these examples of stark aggression and genocide by the dictator powers against their neighbor countries. With respect to the seizure of the Baltic countries by the USSR, Sumner Welles, deputy secretary of state, declared:

"The United States will never recognize the taking over of Estonia, Latvia, and Lithuania by use of force."

Meanwhile, Communist leaders in the United States joined peace organizations and loudly beat the drums for Americans to stay out of the European war. THE YANKS ARE NOT COMING! declared signs carried by pickets in front of the White House. Stalin encouraged a wave of vicious propaganda calling the United States an imperialist, war-mongering nation and its people slaves to the "capitalist clique" that did not support the joint efforts of Germany and the Soviet Union to bring "peace" to Europe.

Then on June 21, 1941, *Reichsfuehrer* Hitler, understanding that Stalin's word was no better than his, executed one of the most historic double-crosses of history. He turned on his ally in crime and began his invasion of the Soviet Union.

Confused and embarrassed, Stalin sat in silence behind the Kremlin walls for some days, fearful that his oppressed people would now brand him for the lying tyrant that he was and rise up to get rid of him. However, during that anxious interval the governments of both Great Britain and the United States assured Stalin that he would have their full support in the war against Nazi Germany. Stalin then went on the air to inform his people that Hitler was a Fascist beast and that the people of Britain and the United States were pretty good after all.

After the Japanese attack on Pearl Harbor officially bombed the United States into the war, this nation began to pour out its manpower and resources for victory. Stalin was now in position where he could virtually blackmail the nations allied against Germany, Japan, and Italy into granting his political and territorial demands as reward for his remaining an enemy of the Axis powers. And that is precisely what this expert in Marxism accomplished.

THE ATHEIST FINDS RELIGION HELPFUL

As the war spread its searing flames across the face of Europe, churches suffered heavy losses of their leaders, members, and places of worship. Poland was completely occupied by the Nazi forces after Hitler's double-cross of his former Communist partner. Since Poland was and is now predominantly a Roman Catholic country, let us note how this church suffered under the Nazi occupation. According to Alberto Giovannetti (pseudonym, Albert Galter):

"From 1939 to 1945 about 3,000,000 Poles were deported. Of 21 ordinaries of the Latin Rite in 1939 only six remained in their Sees in 1945. Priests were reduced in the same period from 12,200 to 8,605. Those killed numbered 584, and 1,263 had died in concentration camps. Polish priests made up 80 per cent of the Catholic clergy in the Dachau camp."

Hard pressed by the invading Nazi forces, Stalin shrewdly decided to seek the help of that archenemy of communism, religion. With typical Marxist cunning, the atheist dictator called for all believers to rally in the great patriotic campaign to defend the Russian homeland. Stalin decreed freedom to worship for members of any religious association, provided they offered prayers for the success of the Red forces. He reduced the taxes of church properties, although keeping the properties in State ownership. He allowed Christian churches to celebrate feast days such as Easter and Christmas, and Jewish congregations to observe their days of special spiritual significance.

This loosening of the persecution screw to gain the support of religious leaders had its effect. In November 1942, on the twenty-fifth anniversary of the Bolshevik seizure of power, acting Patriarch Sergius sent congratulations to Stalin, whom he addressed as "God-given leader of the military and cultural forces of the nation." The church offered prayers for victory and blessings to the soldiers at the front.

On September 5, 1943, *Izvestia* announced that "Stalin received the acting Patriarch Sergius, Metropolitan Alexius of Leningrad, and Metropolitan Nicholas of Kiev." As a result of this meeting, Sergius was installed as Patriarch of Moscow and All Russia on September 12, 1943. The first issue of the political publication of the newly restored patriarch, the *Journal of the Moscow Patriarchate,* also appeared on this date.

In October 1943 the Kremlin authorities set up a "Council for the Russian Orthodox Church," to work directly under the Council of People's Commissars. Heading this "religious" organization was a notorious secret police official, G. E. Karpov. In early 1944 the publication *Izvestia* went so far as to issue an appeal by the patriarch urging the faithful to attend confession and communion.

In August 1944 the Council for the Russian Orthodox Church announced that "priests may go to their parishioners or engage in proselytizing work either in church or outside." In September it decreed that "Parents may religiously educate their children themselves . . . or send them to the homes of priests for such education. Children of different families may also gather in groups to receive religious instruction." The government was thus able to take the wind out of the sails of the Germans, who had decreed full religious freedom in the occupied areas.

In the Ukraine, Mgr. Joseph Slipyj was enthroned as Metropolitan of the Ruthenian Church. Given to understand that he was expected to arouse the faithful to support the war effort, the prelate made a gift of 100,000 rubles from Ukrainian parishoners for the relief of the Red Army wounded.

In the areas occupied by the Red Army troops, both during the war and as the defeated forces of the Nazi regime retreated, officers and men were commanded to be lenient with believers.

Crucifixes and other religious objects were brought back into the churches. Soldiers in uniform often assisted in religious worship. In Galicia, where the Polish population had been treated with severe cruelty by the German occupiers, antireligious propaganda was quashed on specific orders of the Soviet military authorities.

Blackmail on a Big Scale

With Stalin's home front buttressed by the patriotic efforts of religious believers whom he utterly despised, with his agents sitting in on all the Allied committees in Washington to plan the conduct of the war and the postwar agreements, with the bulk of his war matériel pouring in from the United States, the Soviet dictator was free to push with all his might to obtain from the war what he and Adolf Hitler had agreed upon when they started the great conflict—and even more.

The first meeting of the so-called "Big Three" statesmen, British Prime Minister Winston Churchill, President Franklin D. Roosevelt, and Party Chairman Stalin himself, was held at Teheran, Iran, in the fall of 1943. Stalin, the atheist Marxist, confidently confronted these two gentlemen of high position, these believers in religion, morality, and the impact of spiritual values on mankind. The two great spokesmen for democracy were facing a man thoroughly steeped in Communist ideology, chicanery, and duplicity; a man who never wavered in his belief that the end justifies the means, nor questioned that the end was the inevitable triumph of the Communist revolution throughout the world.

With what must have been amazement at the pliability of his adversaries temporarily turned into allies, Stalin calmly demanded an agreement that after the war had been won certain areas, specifically the "corridor" of countries in eastern Europe, would be marked as within the "sphere of influence" of the USSR. Stalin called for confirmation of annexation of Estonia, Latvia, and Lithuania. He demanded that Germany be completely dismembered after the war, with such destruction of German industries as would leave that country impotent ever to make war again. Then came his clinching argument:

"You would not want me to pull out of the war and make a separate peace with Hitler, would you?" Stalin is quoted as saying, in substance, by officials who were there, to his opposite numbers of the Big Three.

Here was international blackmail of colossal proportions. It is quite certain that Stalin had no intention to pull the USSR out of the war. But his threat had its effect. At that conference, or at later meetings of the Big Three, annexation of the Baltic states by the Soviet Union was confirmed, although for political reasons the United States government insisted it would have to deny recognition of this *fait accompli*. Confirmation was also given for the annexation to the Soviet Union of a slice of eastern Poland, and an addition to Poland of a slice of eastern Germany—"east of the Oder and Neisse rivers"—all without any idealistic prattle about "self-determination of peoples" involved in these transfers of sovereignty.

Thus were principles sacrificed to satisfy the demands of a man who even then was plotting to gain enormous prestige and power from the shambles caused by the war, and to emerge from the conflict the greatest victor of them all.

CHAPTER EIGHT

IRON CURTAINS ARE ERECTED

In his memoirs former Prime Minister Winston Churchill relates his efforts to convince the two other members of the "Big Three," President Roosevelt and Chairman Stalin, that the war could best be won by an allied attack from Italy northward through the countries of eastern Europe.

That was the area that the British statesman called "the soft underbelly of Europe." He meant that the Nazi occupiers in the countries east of Germany and Austria could not possibly put up the strong military resistance they could mount against an invasion of Germany.

Mr. Churchill recalls the immediate, firm, and unbendable opposition of Stalin to such a plan. The Soviet dictator was not open to any arguments about it. He insisted that the invasion had to be made through occupied France and across Germany. While that was being done, Stalin asserted, his own Red armies would take care of the "soft underbelly."

It is clear now, as it was clear then to statesmen and ordinary students of Communist strategy, that in Stalin's grand design for the expansion of Marxism he had marked those countries for speedy and permanent subjugation, and that occupation by forces of the free nations would upset the plan.

The Red dictator's spokesmen in Washington, armed with specific instructions from Moscow, had the major voice in dividing Germany into zones of occupation. Berlin, they insisted, must be far inside the Soviet zone. If troops of the invading Americans and

British got beyond the line of Soviet occupation, they must retire to their own zones on the surrender of Hitler's forces.

One Soviet official presented a map showing the Stalin-approved division of Berlin into the proposed Soviet, British, and American zones, with Berlin's Templehof airdrome under Soviet control. An alert U.S. military officer, familiar with Berlin, caught the significance of that and refused to approve. The Soviet official reluctantly left Templehof in the American zone, a fact which saved Berlin from Communist takeover at a time of the Soviet blockade of the city in 1948.

By his actions in clamping down that cruel blockade over Berlin, as well as sealing off the Russian zone of Germany in violation of his agreements on the administration of the defeated country during the allied occupation, the Soviet dictator made clear his original design to take over all of Germany and transform it into a Communist satellite. Meanwhile, his advance agents and political shock troops would be moving westward into France and southward into Italy.

Urged by the Western Allies to bring the USSR into the war against Japan, Stalin flatly refused to do so until three months after the surrender of the Nazi forces. In return for this promise the Soviet leader won concessions of tremendous importance for his design to extend communism into the Far East: He would have the privilege of taking the surrender of the Japanese forces in Manchuria and retain a sphere of influence there. He would have control of North Korea southward to the 38th parallel, and a free hand to assist "democratic" forces in northern China that would result in a coalition government for that war-weary land.

And what concessions did the Communist dictator make in return for those given by the spokesmen for the great democracies, whose manpower and resources were making possible Allied victory?

First, there was his promise not to pull out of the war, which must have given him vast amusement, for pulling out would have meant throwing away his chance to spread the Communist revolution over many areas of the world.

Second, Stalin promised that although the Soviet Union must have the countries of eastern Europe in its sphere of influence, his government would permit free elections to determine the new regime—"in due time."

Third, there was agreement that the Big Three powers (later raised to the Big Four by inclusion of France) would administer Germany and Berlin as a unit, with freedom of communications, trade, and transportation from one zone to another.

THE ADVISERS WERE WINDOW DRESSING

President Roosevelt, with wise foresight, during 1944 was making plans for a United Nations, to keep the peace of the world in the future. In Stalin's last personal conference with the President and Mr. Churchill, at Yalta in the Crimea in February 1945, the Red leader agreed to bring the USSR into the new international organization.

But there were important strings attached to that promise. Stalin insisted that the Soviet Union must have three votes in the General Assembly of the United Nations, by giving a vote each to the Ukraine and Byelorussia, rather than the one vote given to each of the other member countries; and the USSR must be a permanent member of the Security Council, with a veto, along with the other permanent members, over matters pertaining to enforcing the peace and over the admission of new members.

James F. Byrnes, who attended the Yalta conference as U.S. director of war mobilization, later secretary of state under President Harry S. Truman, has recorded:

"No enthusiasm was shown by Stalin for the project [the United Nations], though he expressed no opposition. Dedicated as he was to controlling the world, he simply was not interested in a peace organization."

To win support for the formation of the new United Nations, the State Department invited all major religious denominations in the United States to send committees to the organization meeting at San Francisco to begin April 25, 1945. The spokesmen for the religious groups, clergy and laymen, acted as "advisers" to the official delegates of the United States government.

This writer * had the honor to be a member and secretary of

* O.K.A.

one of those committees. Since President Roosevelt had passed away just a few days before the session began, the new chief executive, Mr. Truman, greeted us. Calling the first meeting to order was the secretary-general, Alger Hiss, an important official in the State Department. *Our church committees were instructed to clear all matters through Mr. Hiss.*

Catholic, Protestant, Jewish believers: all were there. All listened with intense interest to the reports and discussions. For some of the advisers, the glaring weaknesses of the proposed charter were apparent: It was a document produced in the heat of the greatest war in history. Its original 46 members were only those nations who had declared war on Nazi Germany. Consequently it placed the responsibility for enforcing international peace upon the powers emerging as victors, rather than to bring victors, vanquished, and neutrals together in a common effort for all mankind.

Furthermore, the charter presumed to present a plan to prevent aggression, but completely detoured around any definition of aggression or who might be an aggressor. This was understandable, since every big colonial nation represented had committed aggression in the past. The charter held out the high ideals of equality of peoples but placed the permanent members of the Security Council in a class by themselves. They were to be responsible for keeping the peace, but privileged to veto the efforts of all the other nations of the organization to keep the peace.

Finally, it was clear to many of the advisers that the charter failed to come to grips with the basic fact that just as peace has been established in communities and in nations, it must finally be established on the international plane, by world order that denies the right of any man to trample upon the liberties of his people or the sovereignty of his neighbors; a world order under law, able to hold any national leader accountable for his breach of international peace.

Whatever their misgivings, the religious advisers at San Francisco took up the task of offering suggestions to the delegates representing the United States, earnestly hoping that they might strengthen the organization dedicated to preventing future wars. From those representing the Protestant, Catholic, and Jewish committees came two important suggestions. It might be well for people of good will, who believe that "righteousness exalteth a nation" and who hope to preserve and strengthen the United Nations, to reflect upon them:

First, that there be included in the charter a recognition of God as the Father of all mankind.

Second, that the charter include a Bill of Rights, so that people of all nations in the future would enjoy freedom of conscience and worship and the other basic human liberties which Thomas Jefferson called "unalienable."

The answer? Gently but firmly the answer given to our committees came down in substance to this:

We appreciate the efforts of the religious people of the United States to advise us, but it would be very difficult at this point to make any changes in the basic draft of the charter. As to the specific suggestions, we must inform you that the success of the new United Nations depends upon cooperation of the Soviet Union. Its representatives will not agree to any statement with religious implications. And as to a Bill of Rights, we must use only general terms, for the Soviet Union does not interpret the rights of its citizens in the same way we do.

So again, at a most important moment in the history of man's struggle for world peace, principle was sacrificed for expediency, hard knowledge was laid aside for wishful thinking, and the birthright of future generations to begin the erection of a structure of a just and lasting peace was traded for a mess of doubtful political pottage.

COMMUNIST PROMISES ARE BROKEN

At a conference of the Big Three at Potsdam, Germany, in July 1945, attended by Stalin, President Truman, and British Prime Minister Clement Attlee, agreements made at previous meetings of the Big Three were affirmed, with certain modifications, and with additional concessions to the Soviet dictator.

Perhaps the most tragic decision made by those three men, in point of the vast human suffering which resulted, was agreement to uproot and expel from their homelands the "ethnic Germans" living in eastern European countries. More than 12 million people of German ancestry were forced to gather up a few belongings and leave behind forever their homes, their property, their cherished communities and places of worship. Many expellees were descendants of people who had lived in the eastern countries for hundreds of years. They were in no way responsible for the crimes of the Nazis. Hundreds of men, women, and children lost their lives from hunger, privation, grief, and cruel treatment by their captors. It was perhaps the second most glaring example of genocide in human history—second only to the extermination of about 6 million Jews by Hitler's Nazi regime before and during World War II.

Compounding this tragedy is the fact that the expellees were forced upon families and communities in all the zones of Germany, with no consideration whatever of religious affiliations. As through design, whole communities of Catholic people were transplanted into predominantly Protestant areas of East Germany, while Protestant groups were forced into traditionally Catholic regions of Bavaria.

As bombs and cannon pounded German cities into rubble and the Nazi regime collapsed, Western allied military forces dutifully stopped at the borders or pulled back to position as promised the Soviet authorities. As he had agreed, Stalin entered the war against Japan on August 8, 1945, exactly three months after the war ended in Europe. Just two days before, the world had been blasted into the Atomic Age by the first atomic bomb to fall upon human beings, at Hiroshima, Japan.

So the great war ended, and its tragic aftermath began. All that had gone before was prologue to the postwar developments that have robbed 800 million people of the world of their cherished liberties, including that priceless heritage of religious freedom. Even before the fighting stopped, the Iron Curtain of Communist control began to descend from the Baltic Sea to the Black Sea.

Every promise made by the Red dictator, in return for those costly concessions made by the Western Allies, was soon broken, cast aside, or simply ignored, except Stalin's agreement to enter the war against Japan and to bring the USSR into the United Nations.

No free elections to set up new governments in the eastern European nations were permitted by the Soviet occupiers.

Almost as soon as the Soviet forces entered eastern Germany they sealed off their zone, refusing to permit a free exchange of communications, trade, and transportation across their areas of control. Soviet military authorities quickly abandoned any semblance of cooperation for joint allied administration of Berlin.

Every area taken over by Communist dictatorships in those tragic postwar years was conquered by subversion, betrayal, and terror, plus the combined force of the dread secret police and Red army troops.

Call the roll of the immeasurable tragedies that sprang full-grown from the dark womb of the worldwide Communist conspiracy as a result of concessions given this cruel Marxist leader and his associates!

COMMUNIST IRON CURTAINS GO UP

Close on the heels of the retreating Germans the Red armies came back into the Baltic countries, there to re-establish the iron rule that insured their absorption into the USSR.

A Polish government that had been in exile in Paris and London during the war returned to Warsaw to find itself replaced by a "provisional" Government of National Unity formed by a Communist agent in Lublin. By the time the first postwar elections were held in Poland the Communist-sponsored regime, backed by Red army troops, was able to suppress all freedom of speech, press, and assembly, and to refuse the right to vote to citizens known to be in opposition to Marxist control. The result was inevitable: A Communist government, with Boleslaw Bierut as president.

The Communist drive on Czechoslovakia began in the summer of 1944 when Soviet agents were parachuted into Slovakia. In May 1945 President Eduard Beneš returned from exile. At the polls one year later the Czechoslovakian people overwhelmingly voted against Communist rule. But again Marxist tactics of terror succeeded. A small Communist minority in the government, backed by Soviet troops, executed a *coup d'état* on February 25, 1948, installing the Communist Klement Gottwald as president.

During World War II a Croat Communist named Josip Broz, who used the name "Tito," seized control of all Yugoslav military forces. Belgrade, capital of this "South Slav" nation, was captured by Soviet and Yugoslav troops in October 1944. Tito took over the government and in a Communist-style election in November 1945 officially deposed King Peter and secured monolithic rule. Although Tito broke with the Soviet Union in 1948 and was expelled from the Cominform, he proceeded with the complete Communizing of his country.

The Germans evacuated Albania in November 1944, and Communist leaders, the "Anti-Fascist Committee of Liberation," moved to throw out all non-Communist personnel from the government. By January 1945 a Communist "Peoples Republic of Albania" was established.

Hungary presented a more difficult situation. In late 1944 Soviet troops occupied part of that country, and backed a provisional government in which political leaders specially trained in Moscow were given important positions. On November 4, 1945, a coalition government carried out the first postwar election in central and eastern Europe. The Small-Holders Party received a clear majority of votes, 57 per cent, while the Communist party got only 17 per cent. So the Communists had to use the well-tried method of coalition with other parties until strong enough to take over by force. Another election in August 1947 gave the Communists only 22 per cent of the votes, but all other parties so divided the remainder that the Communists gained control. A peace treaty allowed Soviet troops to remain in Hungary—and there they remained nine years later to beat down the freedom fighters in the streets of Budapest.

Soviet troops entered Romania in August 1944 and the following March a "popular front" government was established under sponsorship of the Soviet Union. Although the Communists had only a minority of members of the government, with Red backing they were able to seize control.

In September 1944 the Red army entered Sofia, Bulgaria.

Tightening their hold upon the government of this country at the close of the war, Communist political leaders brought about a rigged election in 1946 to insure their control. In November 1947 they executed Nicholas Petkov, the anti-Communist leader, and by December 1949 had so completely seized power that an election gave the Communist party 97.7 per cent of the votes. Of course no opposition candidates were allowed.

And what came of Stalin's keeping two of his promises?

In the Far East, with victory already won by the Western Allies under command of General Douglas MacArthur, Soviet troops took over Manchuria and received the arms and war matériel of 200,000 Japanese prisoners. This vast store greatly helped the Red military leaders of North Korea and China when they began their war against the South Korean people in June 1950.

The Red forces moved from Manchuria southward into Korea to the 38th parallel. Russian political and military "technicians," well trained in Marxist ideology and methods, swarmed into North China to assist the Communist leader, Mao Tse-tung, in establishing the coalition government with Marshal Chiang Kai-shek which the American government insisted must be formed.

As to Soviet Union membership in the United Nations: Using propaganda, slander, and obstruction, along with frequent vetoes in the Security Council, the USSR has been able to hamper and thwart the people of the free world both from preventing war and from establishing a just and lasting peace.

THE COMMUNIST JUGGERNAUT ROLLS

The end of the war made unnecessary any further hypocritical collaboration with religious leaders and believers by the Soviet regime. As each government was captured for Communist control, in Europe and Asia, persecution of religion began. The Marxist atheist juggernaut, its machinery oiled by concessions of the free countries, followed good Communist tactics by tailoring and fitting the restrictions to each national situation. But its aim was the unchanging and unchangeable goal of Marxism: To eradicate religion.

We have seen how in Riga, the old capital of Latvia, the large Agenskalna Baptist Church was permitted to function until 1961. With its cross and steeple cut down, its sanctuary was appropriated for a television station. But Agenskalna was an exception. Throughout the Baltic lands from 1944 forward religious leaders and believers of all faiths felt the ever-increasing restrictions of the Soviet rule.

All Roman Catholic schools were closed. Protestant schools were either closed or transformed into State schools, with emphasis on the teaching of Marxism. Ministers of all faiths were obliged to attend indoctrination courses where they were urged to work for the destruction of "capitalist thinking" and other counterrevolutionary crimes.

As in the Baltic countries, so it was in all the areas of the eastern European corridor as they fell prey to the iron grasp of control by the Soviet Union. Hand in hand with political domination marched the cruel, relentless persecution of religion in all its forms and programs.

High taxes were assessed against church property. Worship was restricted to the church edifice and heavy penalties were dealt out for propagating the faith on the outside. Priests and ministers were forbidden to visit country parishes or organize religious activities beyond their own congregations. Agents of the secret police were always in attendance at religious meetings, taking note of all worshipers and of everything said and done in the services.

In Poland, for example, as early as September 1945 the provisional government rescinded the concordat with the Vatican which had been in effect for more than twenty years. Two months later a renegade priest, L. Matuszewski, was named Minister for Propaganda. One of his first steps was to promulgate a new law, which transferred the right to perform marriages to the civil courts. In 1946 the government officially recognized a "Polish National Catholic Church," with top administration entirely in secular hands. At the same time the regime sponsored the creation of the "Association of the Godless" with a propaganda organ cynically named *Glos Walnych* ("Free Speech"). From 1948 forward, numerous Polish religious leaders were arrested, churches were closed, schools secularized, and sacred rites which had been observed for centuries were prohibited.

In Hungary, the Catholic primate Cardinal Mindszenty summarized the major persecutions against the faithful of that country that accompanied the first Marxist control enforced in the fall of 1945, in a pastoral letter with these eloquent, moving words:

We must regret that the matrimonial bond has been weakened by the Provisional Government which in our opinion had not the right to act thus and in doing so has contravened the will of the people. . . . As regards the redistribution of land it has been presented as a means of destroying a certain class among the citizens, and the agrarian law has been put forward as a penal measure. Is such a motive in conformity with justice and the natural law? We do not find fault with the redistribution of land but with the spirit of vengeance shown in this instance. More dreadful still is the number of people who have been sent to prison through provincial tyrants' abuse of power or for paltry reasons. For intervening to prevent the dissolution of a Catholic association in his village a priest, who has been a victim of tuberculosis for many years, has been sentenced to hard labour. Another has been treated in the same way for preaching on the Feast of St. Stephen. The prefects of police have declared that priests who oppose the present rule will be deported to Siberia.*

THESE FACTS ARE INDISPUTABLE

For the peoples of the free world who cherish their heritage of religious faith, the lessons of the war years and postwar period are clear and plain. As they stand face to face with the Marxist enemy of all things spiritual they must decide whether to heed those lessons or to ignore them at the peril of finding themselves the victims of what every Soviet dictator since Stalin has called "the inevitable triumph of atheistic Socialism."

In their opposition to religion, Marxist leaders may modify their tactics of battle but never their aim and purpose, which is to bury religion, along with all liberties and loyalties contrary to the monolithic dictatorial State.

Tactics used in the conflict with religion may vary to fit any given situation, to apply to any church group, to be adapted in any area or at any time. Is there war? Then the true Communist enlists church people, using their patriotism as a tool to win a Marxist victory. Is it peace? Then let believers in religion proclaim peace: the peace approved by the dictatorship, of course.

Do nationalistic sentiments stand in the way of the proletariat revolution? Then eradicate them, as with all obsolete bourgeois ideas. On the other hand, can nationalistic sentiments aid the "re-education" of the people in their duty to the State? Then use them, in such manner and for so long a time as they may be of use.

Another lesson—and one which many people of religious faiths find it difficult to comprehend: There is no such thing as *honor* in Communist thinking, from the Kremlin masters down to the lowliest local commissars. Honor such as would impel the keeping of a solemn agreement does not exist in Communist thinking. It is in the same category as any other "bourgeois sentiment," such as *truth,* which has value only if it advances the interests of the revolutionary State.

The fact that agreements involving the lives and fortunes of millions of people were made by Stalin and his associates only to be broken gives the true Marxist no concern whatever. Loss of face? The true Communist has no face to be lost! He has only the urge to accomplish his mission to aid the Communist Party program at home and abroad.

Coexistence? No greater example of coexistence between Marxists and believers in human freedom could ever develop than that which made temporary allies of the leaders in the USSR and those of the democracies during World War II. No greater challenge could ever be found for collaboration between the Soviet Union and all other nations than the common task to create a just and lasting peace. There can be no greater opportunity presented a country and its government than to be an important member of the United Nations.

Fate presented these challenges and opportunities to the rulers of the Soviet Union during and after the greatest war in history— and God grant, the last great war. They were either spurned by these rulers or prostituted by them for prestige and power through the extension of the Marxist world revolution.

As we shall now see, they chose to forge iron links that make up the chains of political, economic, and social domination for the peoples of their Communist empire.

CHAPTER NINE

THEY WEAR COMMUNIST CHAINS

In December 1948, shortly after the Communist party of Bulgaria seized control of that country, two Roman Catholic priests, Kupen Michailoff and Gabriel Belorejdoff, returned to Sofia after eight years of study in a seminary in Rome. A local religious publication made the mistake of mentioning this bit of news, with the pictures of the young men.

Soon afterward the priests were arrested by the Communist authorities and held for "questioning." Catholic leaders visited the jail where the priests were imprisoned but were refused permission to see them. Alarmed at what seemed to be gross violation of promises made by authorities that there would be freedom of worship in the new regime, several Protestant ministers also attempted to intervene in behalf of the young priests.

All such visitors were blandly assured that "justice" would be done. The charge? "Counterrevolutionary activities," answered the authorities. Where? When? In what manner?

Here the answers became vague. The priests had had no opportunity to engage in activities hostile to the government.

"But they must be spies, or they would not have been out of the country for so long a time," the commissar in charge of the matter declared.

Later it was learned that under the "questioning"—presumably torture—the priests had "confessed" to some anti-Communist activities that went on in the Vatican during the war. Since the Holy See was the target of raucously hostile propaganda in all the

100

newly formed Communist governments, the arrest of the young priests became clear. Michailoff and Belorejdoff were sentenced to long terms in an unnamed concentration camp, and were never heard of again.

The binding of the chains of persecution upon believers in Bulgaria was typical of the whole story of the campaign to eradicate religion in eastern Europe.

The Bulgarian "People's Constitution," issued on December 6, 1947, with hypocrisy typical of all Communist constitutions, guaranteed "freedom of conscience and religion," and "separation of Church and State," but in the same clause it forbade "political organizations with a religious basis." Education became the sole responsibility of the State, smashing with one blow all schools sponsored by religious bodies. Protestant and Catholic ministers were harassed by being deprived of ration cards, constantly shadowed by secret police, called into "security headquarters" to answer vague rumors and unfounded charges. An intense propaganda drive was launched to discredit religion and to enlist the people in atheist organizations.

In February 1949 the National Assembly passed an act "On Religious Denominations." It was a sweeping law, which stands as a model summary of the restrictions that the new Communist regimes used to choke the breath out of religion. As usual, its first article affirmed freedom of conscience and worship. Then followed the nullification of this promise in almost every subsequent article.

The act declared that the Bulgarian Orthodox Church "may be considered as a people's democratic Church," meaning the group through which the government would extend its control over religion.

COMPLETE DENIAL OF RELIGIOUS FREEDOM

Other articles developed the theme of absolute dictation by the State.

Because of their significance in Marxist ideology we present the most important articles:

Article 9: Every denomination must have a directing body responsible to the State. Ministers of religion may remain in office, be dismissed, or changed only after receiving the *nihil obstat* of the Ministry for External Affairs. Ministers of a religion having foreign economic relations may be nominated only after being approved by the Ministry for External Affairs. On entering office they shall make a solemn promise of loyalty to the Government.

Article 10: Only Bulgarian citizens may be ministers of religion or fill ecclesiastical offices. They must be men of good conduct, inspiring confidence, and not deprived of those rights set out in Article 30 of the Penal Code.

Article 13: Ministers of religion and other ecclesiastical functionaries who violate the law, offend against public order or ethical standards, or oppose the democratic institutions of the State, may be immediately suspended from the exercise of the office on the proposal of the Ministry for External Affairs. This measure must be applied by the directing body of the denomination in question immediately the Ministry for External Affairs gives intimation of its decisions. Should the religious authority fail in this matter, the minister of religion shall be suspended by an administrative measure.

Article 16: The directing bodies of the different denominations are bound to send in due time to the Ministry for External Affairs for its information pastoral letters, encyclicals, circulars, and other official publications. The Ministry can forbid the circulation of or the execution of the directives contained in these letters, circulars, documents, or other official publications, should it deem them contrary to law, public order, or recognised ethical standards.

Article 19: Because of the supreme authority of the State and of its official organizations the different religious associations may organize no ceremonies or solemnities which have not had the previous and express approval of the Ministry for External Affairs.

Article 21: The formation of religious associations, their organization, and the printing of religious books are subject to the general laws and to the particular ordinances of the administration. The education and organization of children and youths are specially reserved to the State, and are in no way the concern of the denominations and their ministers.

Article 22: The denominations may not open hospitals, orphanages, or other like institutions. Works of this kind in existence when the present law comes into force are to be taken over by the Ministries for Public Health, Labour, and Social Welfare. Their property, movable and nonmovable, shall become the property of the State.

Article 24: Religious denominations may have relations with other denominations, institutions, organizations, or persons situated outside the country, but only with the previous approval of the Ministry for External Affairs.

Article 25: Denominations or their orders, congregations, missions, etc., having their administrative seat outside the country may not open houses in the People's Republic of Bulgaria. All those now in existence shall be closed within a month of the coming into force of this present law.

Article 30: Whoever organizes political associations with a religious basis, or in any way whatsoever (by word or writing or action) uses the Church and religion to engage in propaganda against the authority of the State is liable to imprisonment and other severe penalties.

Both Roman Catholic and Protestant leaders denounced the Bulgarian Law on Religious Denominations as a complete denial of religious freedom. In answer, spokesmen for the Communist regime took to the radios and to publications to condemn the churchmen in harshest terms. Then with boundless effrontery to the intelligence of every Bulgarian believer, including those of the favored Orthodox faith, the authorities declared that there was indeed freedom of worship as guaranteed by the constitution, if only believers would omit politics from their religion!

In early February 1950 arrests and imprisonment of ministers and priests got underway in earnest. Father Danian Glhiulov, superior of the Capuchins in Sofia, was arrested and after nearly two years in prison was finally brought to trial and condemned to serve an additional term of twelve years. The decision of the "people's court" which assessed the twelve years sheds light on the type of charges made against religious leaders by Marxist dispensers of "justice": Two years were for "defamation of the Bulgarian government"; one year for having defamed the government of the Soviet Union; two years for "bad conduct in prison"; seven years for acting as a spy for the Vatican and for "capitalist Powers." No punishment for the real offense—that of being a courageous religious leader!

No Higher Loyalty Permitted

The plight of the Bulgarian religious leaders under the Communist regime illustrates this basic fact:

Communism considers religion its greatest, most persistent enemy because religion calls for allegiance to a Power higher than government.

"Thou shalt have no other gods before me," a sacred commandment given to Moses by our Creator, stands as a barrier against a believer's complete dedication to Marxist ideology. For that ideology itself is a god—all powerful, all embracing, brooking no permanent opposition.

The Bulgarian priests, like religious believers everywhere, owed allegiance to God and their Christian faith. They looked also for spiritual guidance and leadership to the Roman Pontiff. These loyalties automatically made them "enemies of the State," to be dealt with as criminals.

"I am the way, the truth and the life," said the Master. Those who follow him place themselves in a spiritual realm that communism cannot possibly accept. To the true Marxist there is only one "way"—the Marxist way of dialectic materialism which recognizes no spiritual realm whatever. To the dedicated Communist "truth" can mean only the statement or idea, true or false, that supports the Marxist cause of world revolution. To the power-hungry person steeped in the dogmas of atheism there is only one "life"—the life entirely subservient to Communist control under a Soviet-type government.

In the selected works of Lenin will be found an angry ranting against religion, an enemy he never really understood but actually feared and therefore vastly hated. The polemic contains these terse words:

"Religion is a kind of spiritual gin in which slaves of capitalism drown their human shape and their claims to any decent life."

Like lashing out at ghosts in an attic with a broom, the Marxist religion-fighters flailed away at the believers with whatever club was handy, hoping to deal religion a fatal blow. In the predominantly Roman Catholic countries of eastern Europe the attack often centered upon the Pontiff. The *Teachers Gazette* of November 26, 1949, published in Leningrad, presented the typical criticism expressed in the official press in those early days of the Soviet Union's captivity of its small neighbor countries:

"A particularly reactionary role is played by the Vatican, the head of the World Catholic Church. The Pope, together with the complex machinery of the Catholic Church and the Catholic clergy, is a direct instrument of American imperialism in the struggle again against democracy, communism and the Soviet Union, and its preparations for a new world war."

In Yugoslavia, Dictator Tito established one of the most totalitarian regimes in the entire eastern European region. His refusal to come under the domination of the USSR did not modify by one whit his program to destroy the personal, civil, and political rights of the Yugoslavian people, and his vigorous hostility toward religion.

Upon seizing power, the Croatian Red, indoctrinated and trained in Moscow, took complete control of churches and religious organizations. He allowed only one youth group, his Communist-sponsored People's Youth of Yugoslavia. He permitted only one women's society, the Anti-Fascist Women's League. He appropriated for his own propaganda use the direction of all newspapers and radio facilities.

R. H. Markham, authority on the fate of religion in Marxist eastern Europe, has described the situation in Yugoslavia under Tito's early control:

> The Yugoslav must march in communist parades and shout for Tito. He must sing for Tito. He must attend meetings and various courses for Tito. He must subscribe to communist literature. Children are mobilized by communists to work or sing or march or play football during hours of church services.
>
> Every textbook from the primer up is based on atheistic Marxist materialism. Children are instructed from infancy to scorn God and ridicule Christianity. There is a special drive against religious liberty. Hatred, fanatical narrowness, scorn for faith, blind atheism, are pressed upon the population by every means.*

THE COURAGEOUS LEADER SPEAKS

To observe how communism marshalls its mightiest weapons against loyalty to God and religious faith we go to Hungary. The people of that country, divided as to church affiliation into about 68 per cent Roman Catholic, 26 per cent Protestant and 5 per cent Jewish at the close of World War II, earnestly resisted the restrictions upon the practices of their religious faith by the Communist regime. As of 1945 there were 2,265 Catholic parishes and 4,012 priests. Large estates were owned by the Catholic Church, furnishing the means to carry on extensive welfare and cultural activities of value to the entire nation.

From the time the Red military forces entered Hungary until the Marxist leaders had a firm hold on the government, Communist agents infiltrated Catholic congregations and organizations. Many were elected to parish councils. These agents showed great respect for religion, until the signal came to fasten the chains.

"Agrarian reform" measures deprived the Catholic Church of most of its estates. This program was followed by severe restrictions upon all the Hungarian religious press. For the Catholics it meant the practical elimination of 1,500,000 copies of various publications, and for Protestant and Jewish worshipers at least half a million copies used in church services and for propagating the faith. The reason given by the authorities?

"Sorry—but there is a shortage of paper! No paper can be made available except for *necessary purposes.*"

Shortage of paper became, and remains, the one standing excuse for the elimination of religious publications, and for preventing the production of Bibles, hymnbooks and all other printed media for use by believers in all Communist areas.

In 1946 all religious associations not authorized by the regime were ordered dissolved. About 4,000 Catholic organizations were thus suppressed. Many of their leaders were imprisoned and the church property confiscated.

Again the Catholic primate, Cardinal Mindszenty, issued a vigorous protest. Mincing no words, Mindszenty accused the authorities of unwarranted attacks upon religious institutions, schools, and worshipers. Fearing the power of this courageous leader among the masses of people the regime ignored his protest and refrained, for the time, to take any direct action against him.

When the rigged elections of August 1947 consolidated the power of the Communist Party in Hungary, the opposition of religious leaders, Catholic and Protestant, was the only obstacle to complete control of the people. There stood the Catholic cardinal, Mindszenty; and the foremost spokesmen for the Protestant groups, Bishop Lajos Ordass, primate of the Lutheran Church in Hungary; and Dr. Alexander Haraszti, outstanding physician and surgeon of Budapest and president of the Union of Hungarian Baptists. All three churchmen rallied the faithful in their denominations to stand up for the rights of freedom of worship under the new constitution.

Vice-Premier of the government was Matayas Rakosi, a Hungarian thoroughly indoctrinated in Marxist methods, the real spokesman of the Soviet Union in the government. Rakosi attempted to induce all religious leaders "to join in supporting peaceful co-existence between the Hungarian people and the Russian Army," as he called it with marvelous lack of tact. At the same time he ordered new restrictions upon the churches. These brought another forthright declaration of protest from Cardinal Mindszenty, who concluded his lengthy statement with these words:

"So long as we continue to be the target for accusations that lack all real proof it is impossible for us to accede to the demand contained in the Government's appeal. When however reparation has been made for the outrages inflicted on the Church and when we have received an assurance that we shall be allowed the free exercise of our religious activity, then we shall be ready to give our unreserved collaboration."

The Cardinal followed this with a detailed account of the restrictions placed upon religious teaching. Soon afterward, Minister Rakosi told a meeting of his Party functionaries that the problem of relations between church and State would be solved "in one way or another." The Soviet satrap orated:

The Hungarian democracy has for three years tried every means to incorporate the Catholic Church in its reconstruction schemes but without success. . . . From now on we need to show no tolerance but rather unbending severity in our treatment of spies, traitors, traders in illegal exchange and Fascists, who hide behind the robes of priests . . . such as are led by Mindszenty. Our program demands that order should reign in his domain too, and if we cannot establish order by means of a reciprocal agreement, very well then! We shall obey the will of the people and establish it by the strong arm of the State!

Here was an unintended but excellent exposition of the hidden meaning of co-existence with communism. Now there seemed to be only one way to deal with the trouble-maker Cardinal Mindszenty. On December 26, 1948, he was arrested.

Brought to trial in February 1949, the Cardinal was accused of espionage, treason against the regime, illicit trading in money exchange, and "plotting against the State." Religious leaders who tried to come to his defense were also arrested, and some were deported with no public hearing whatever.

Most ghastly aspect of the trial was the confirmation of some of the accusations by Cardinal Mindszenty himself. After forty days of "questioning" he appeared at the trial a completely broken man, gaunt and shaken in body, his mind and spirit shattered by the tortures he had endured. He "admitted" that many of his statements and actions had branded him as an enemy of the government.

Cardinal Mindszenty was sentenced to imprisonment for life. The Communist press continued to heap fuel upon the fire of accusations against him. In a steady barrage of condemnation, official propaganda declared the verdict to be "the will of all Hungarians who work for peace."

The antireligion campaign moved vigorously forward. In the issue of *Szabud Nep* of June 6, 1950, Jozsef Revai, Minister for Popular Culture, declared:

"A People's Democracy has no need of religious persons for they not only do not fulfil their vocation but actually sabotage the aims of democracy. They must therefore, as soon as possible, be put where they will be unable to harm the interests of the People's Democracy."

When the mighty, historic, tragic surge for liberation from the Communist yoke moved the Hungarian people to revolt in October 1956, Cardinal Mindszenty was freed from prison. The tanks and cannon of the Russian troops blasted their way back into Budapest and slaughtered the freedom fighters. With hope of freedom extinguished, the Cardinal took refuge in the United States Legation.

A FEARLESS BISHOP STANDS FIRM

Many other names could be mentioned, names of courageous men who placed loyalty to God and spiritual service to humanity above that demanded by the Marxist oppressors, in those trying postwar days in the captive countries. These religious leaders' steadfast devotion to duty wrote illustrious pages in the history of this period of Communist persecution of the faithful.

From the beginning of the Nazi occupation of Czechoslovakia, Bishop Josef Beran, of Prague, was harassed by Hitler's agents, who demanded that he bring the Nazi teaching of Aryan supremacy into the schools. Bishop Beran refused to do this and publicly condemned the program. He stood against all other attempts of the alien occupiers to control the church under his charge. When arguments and threats failed to move him, in early 1942 Beran was arrested and imprisoned in the infamous concentration camp at Dachau, Germany. He spent three long years there, forced to clean the latrines and perform the most menial tasks. He cheerfully swept the floors, worked in the prison potato fields, all the while encouraging his fellow prisoners to pray and hope for liberation. A severe attack of typhus brought him almost to death's door.

Freedom for Beran and other survivors of Dachau came with the advance of the American forces as they moved across Germany and into Czechoslovakia. The Americans reached Prague before they were ordered far back to the line agreed to by the Soviet command, thus permitting the Red army to take over the victory so dearly won.

Pope Pius XII named Josef Beran archbishop of Prague in 1946. So great was Beran's fame as an opponent of the Nazi occupiers that the Communist leader who entered with the Soviet troops in preparation for the seizure of the government, Klement Gottwald, came to honor the archbishop at his installation.

With the Communist takeover, persecutions against all religious organizations, especially against the predominantly Roman Catholic Church in Bohemia and Moravia, began in earnest. In February 1948 Slovakia was also brought under Red control.

True to the formula of repression and harassment, the Marxist rulers, led by this same Klement Gottwald, outlawed the Catholic press. The parochial schools were closed or secularized. A commission of "patriot priests," carefully selected by the authorities because they were willing to collaborate with the government, drew up a "corrected" version of the catechism. Over the protests of true Catholic leaders, the false catechism, glorifying the "people's revolution," was made required study in all schools.

Catholic action groups and organizations of all kinds were suppressed. Church hospitals and charitable institutions were "nationalized." Church properties were confiscated, leaving the parishes impoverished. By 1949 all religious functions outside the place of worship were prohibited, while inside the church edifice only such ceremonies as were approved by the authorities could be held.

Against this steadily increasing harassment of the church and its ministries, Archbishop Beran spoke out, clearly and fearlessly. He led his priests in drafting a memorandum, addressed to President Gottwald, which stated:

"Today we have a further and undeniable proof that the government has launched an all-out campaign against the Church, using all the means at its disposal, in the fact that orders and precise instructions to that end have been transmitted to the police authorities in the provinces and districts. We know that these orders are only the first phase of the final and decisive blow."

Beran was correct in his estimate of what lay ahead. Gottwald quickly formed a Communist-front "Catholic Action Committee," which he could use as a puppet for propaganda purposes. Beran denounced the group as false to the faith and as collaborators with the atheist regime.

On June 15, 1949, Gottwald's secret police raided the episcopal palace in the absence of Archbishop Beran, seized his papers and documents, and installed a commissar in his office with order "to keep a strict watch" on all matters pertaining to the church. On his return Beran protested this arbitrary action.

At the archbishop's mass on the following Sunday a large group of hoodlums, recruited by secret police goon squads, entered the cathedral. Undaunted by this intrusion, Beran launched into a sermon in which he began to explain why he owed his highest allegiance to God, to his church, and to his religious ministry. The hoodlums opened up with shouts, whistling, and catcalls. The archbishop's voice could not be heard over the disturbance so he ended the sermon and retired. That evening he was placed under house arrest.

Still unterrified, Beran drew up a letter to be read in all Catholic churches of Czechoslovakia on the following Sunday. It denounced the persecutions and restrictions that the Gottwald regime had placed upon religious worship. The letter declared that there clearly was "a systematic persecution of the Catholic Church in Czechoslovakia, well prepared and methodically administered."

Alexi Cepika, minister of justice in the Gottwald cabinet, came with several police agents to admonish Beran and to give him his choice: He could either cooperate with the government or be imprisoned.

When the minister had finished his threats, Archbishop Beran rose from his desk, unlocked a closet door and picked up a bundle of tattered clothing.

"Gentlemen," said the prelate, "here are the rags I wore in Dachau prison. I am ready. Let's go!"

Imprisoned in Prague, Archbishop Beran was at last silenced. St. Vitus Cathedral remained silent too. In 1951 Beran was taken from the country to a secret prison elsewhere. His faithful followers, beaten into submission but worshiping and praying in secret, heard nothing about him for ten years. In 1961 came news that Josef Beran was still alive. He was allowed to go into "retirement" as the "former archbishop," at Caritas Institute, outside the city of Prague.

Was Archbishop Beran the man the late Pope John XXIII named a cardinal *in petto*—in his heart? Many of the Catholic faithful think so.

CHAPTER TEN

MANY SHOW INDOMITABLE COURAGE

As the iron curtains of Communist control came down upon the borders of the nations from the Baltic to the Balkans, the people of that whole hapless area were not allowed to forget the man whose master plan was enslaving them in his expanding Marxist empire. In all public buildings, on billboards, and hanging from ropes at all official ceremonies was the picture of the grim, mustached Joseph Stalin. He was usually flanked by the pictures of Lenin and the national Communist leader.

"Founders of Our Socialist State." "Saviors of the People." "Stalin Our Benefactor." The slogans extolled the glories of the revolutionary leaders. But they could not create respect and affection for the chief boss of the monolithic Soviet dictatorship. Stalin became the most hated man on earth for about 69 million people of eastern Europe.

All Stalin's local Communist quislings understood that their task of forcing acceptance of complete Marxist control included the suppression and final extermination of all religion.

A story went around—secretly among believers, of course—about the disappointment of the Politburo that religion had not curled up to die at the behest of Stalin's slave-drivers. Something had to be done to empty the churches and start everybody on the happy road to atheism. So a psychological expert was called in by the bureaucrats and was given the problem. With a pledge that he would have immunity for anything he said, he declared:

"Empty the churches? That is easy. Just take down all the holy pictures in the places of worship, and substitute the picture of the Great Leader, Stalin. Nobody will attend worship any more!"

Some national religious leaders had already experienced suffering for their faith. Such a one was Lutheran Bishop Lajos Ordass of Hungary, whose name stands today as a symbol of indomitable faith and personal courage for the entire religious world.

Ordass was born in 1901 in the Torzsa district of what is now Yugoslavia. He grew up the son of a professor who taught in a Lutheran country school and planned to educate his boy for the ministry. Lajos was a student in the University of Budapest when World War I ended. The treaty of peace draw new boundaries for eastern Europe. He found himself in one country while his parents were in another.

The theological faculty of his seminary was moved to Sopron, in western Hungary. Cut off from further support from home, the young ministerial student earned his livelihood as best he could. He won a scholarship which enabled him to go to Germany to continue his studies. However, inflation made the scholarship almost worthless and Lajos worked in the coal mines to support himself.

Lajos Ordass was ordained in 1924 and after serving as an assistant pastor for two years he managed to study in Sweden for two terms. He returned to Hungary and devoted much time and energy to organizing Sunday-school programs for Lutheran congregations and translating religious literature from Swedish and Norwegian publications.

During World War II Pastor Ordass frequently came into conflict with and spoke out against Nazi infiltration into the churches. He tried courageously, but failed, to mobilize all Hungarian religious bodies against persecution of the Jews.

Ordass Takes the Offensive

More than 60 per cent of the Hungarian Lutheran church buildings were destroyed in World War II. Many people lived in conditions of extreme poverty with church activities severely curtailed. Many small Lutheran congregations were scattered in towns and villages. At the close of the war Pastor Ordass began the task of visiting as many of these as he could to encourage the members to rebuild their spiritual lives. His task was made all the more difficult by an exchange of about 40,000 Slovaks in Hungary for approximately the same number of Hungarians in Czechoslovakia.

Because of his organizing ability and dedication to his work, Ordass was elected bishop of the Budapest diocese and in late 1946 was made primate of all Lutherans in Hungary. Bishop Ordass represented his church at the first assembly at the Lutheran World Federation in Sweden in 1947 and was elected vice president.

Already he had encountered the determined opposition of the Communist leaders in Hungary. At the Federation meeting in Sweden the bishop delivered one of his memorable sermons on the text, "Work While It Is Yet Day." He indicated that he knew what lay ahead of him and his ministry in his homeland. Many of his friends begged him not to return to Hungary, but he refused to desert his post. After a short tour of churches in western European countries Bishop Ordass came to the United States to arrange with American Lutheran leaders for children's relief in his war-torn homeland.

Soon after the Communist seizure of the Hungarian government, Bishop Ordass was called before the authorities. They ordered him to dismiss the lay collaborators in his church organization, obviously so that these religious leaders could be replaced with Communist agents. They ordered him also to advise those who listened to his radio services to support the new "Socialist" regime.

The bishop flatly refused both these directives. So the Communist authorities appointed a number of lay collaborators and forced the pastors and congregations to admit them to the church councils and activities. They shut off the power from his radio station, abruptly ending that service.

The next step in the harassment of this determined religious leader was the order to incorporate the principal women's group of his church, the Evangelical Women's Association, with the Communist Women's Federation. On several occasions Magda Joboru, the woman commissar dealing with such matters, visited Bishop Ordass and tried hard to convince him that he should conform peaceably to what she called "this progressive step." Again the bishop refused.

When all the church bodies of Hungary were ordered to accept the "nationalization" of their schools, Ordass stood in the forefront of opposition with Catholic and other Protestant leaders to oppose the move. Matayas Rakosi, Vice-Premier of the Communist regime, angrily threatened to stop all support of schools. Ordass publicly announced: "Our churches cannot in good conscience abandon their schools. We can be made to do so only by force."

As in all other areas taken over by Marxist governments, some church leaders threw in their lot with the new regime rather than stand up to be counted in opposition. Among the Hungarian Lutherans, Pastor Samuel Mihalovics, of Ber, jumped on the Communist bandwagon and warned Bishop Ordass to do the same. Pastor Laszlo Dezsery, a student pastor in Budapest, signed up with the party authorities and volunteered to bring the Lutheran Church into "socialist enlightenment"; now Laszlo Dezsery is editor of the "official" Lutheran paper, *Uj Harangszo*.

Far from being influenced by such advice, Bishop Ordass took the offensive against his tormentors. He drew up and presented to Vice-Premier Rakosi a list of requests which he maintained were essential to any semblance of freedom of conscience and worship. They included: Complete freedom of preaching; continued control of parochial schools by the churches; liberty to teach religion outside the schools; the right of every church to carry on social work including management of its hospitals and orphanages. At that time the Lutheran Church in Hungary had under its charge 74 institutions, including 12 orphanages.

The Communist authorities ignored these requests, but at meetings held in Lutheran churches all over the country during March 1948 Bishop Ordass' views were enthusiastically upheld.

GOD IS UNCHANGED

On Pentecost Day, May 16, 1948, the authorities announced that all church schools in Hungary were to be nationalized. Immediately the press began a vigorous propaganda barrage calling on the people to support the move. The church schools were branded as "hotbeds of ignorance, with no true educational value." The dominant Roman Catholic Church staunchly opposed the move, while all the Protestant bodies joined them in speaking out against the secularization of the schools.

Near the end of June the law went into effect. Communist agents went throughout the country using black paint to cover and obliterate the names of churches over the schools.

As vice president of the World Lutheran Federation, Ordass had applied for permission to attend a meeting of this organization in Amsterdam. He received word that his application was denied, and furthermore, he was warned not to go far from his home.

Near midnight on August 24, 1948, as Bishop Ordass was working at his desk, the police arrived and arrested him. He was held twenty-four hours for questioning, and given the "privilege" of resigning as bishop. He refused the offer. Again on September 7 he was given twenty-four hours in which to resign. Again he refused, and the next day he was herded off to prison. Janos Kadar, Minister of the Interior, personally signed the charges: "Illegal financial transactions, defraudations, and other serious political crimes."

At the bishop's trial another charge was pressed against him. He was accused of "consorting with the chief enemies of the Hungarian People's Republic." The prosecution referred repeatedly to his leaving Hungary to visit capitalist countries, and especially condemned him for visiting the United States, where he had won the support of American Lutheran churches for his child-feeding program. Bishop Ordass spoke these words in his defense:

"When I returned from that journey which has been discussed so frequently in the course of the accusations made against me, I immediately turned to my church authorities with the expressed desire that not only publicly but privately they would desist from all expressions of gratitude toward the services which I had successfully completed by the will of God." The bishop further declared: "The Hungarian Lutheran Church does not look for the suffering of martyrdom, but it is not afraid of it and does not shrink from it!"

Every day during the trial the Lutheran churches of Budapest were crowded with worshipers who came to pray for their beloved bishop. The court sentenced him to two years in prison, deprived him of his civil rights for five years, and fined him 3,000 forint. After twenty months the bishop was released and went into forced retirement.

Lutherans the world over never ceased to work for the rehabilitation of the persecuted bishop. After eight years—and the uprising of the freedom fighters in the streets of Budapest—vindication and restoration came to Lajos Ordass. Preaching his first sermon in eight years in October 1956, the bishop said:

"If nothing is constant in this world, God is unchanged; and to Him that which was sin yesterday remains sin today, and that which was holy yesterday remains holy today."

But what of the future for Ordass? With the intensified attack upon religion now underway in every area of Communist captivity it is likely that this leader will again be the victim of the ruthless enemy of all spiritual things.

In China's Red Paradise

Would China under Communist rule be "different" in its treatment of religion from that of other Marxist governments? Millions of devout people in the free world hoped so, as the troops of the Communist warlord Mao Tse-tung pushed relentlessly southward during the latter months of 1949. After all, many hopeful commentators reasoned, this was a movement in a backward country for "agrarian reform" long overdue. Surely the Communist leaders in China would revert to a coalition-type government as soon as they had driven the corrupt Generalissimo Chiang Kai-shek from power.

What such hopeful but mistaken persons failed to understand was this simple fact: Any Marxist regime has as its ultimate goal the complete, unqualified subjugation of the people in every aspect of their lives, including the final eradication of their religious loyalties. There can be no halting of the program so long as an advance in Communist control can be made; there can be no yielding of any Marxist principle except for temporary expediency.

So with the advance of the Communist forces across China, the nation that had survived eight years of aggression and war from Imperial Japan, rode Mao's political commissars. They were well briefed in the arts of "re-educating" a whole population to understand the glories of the Communist revolution and the workers' paradise it would bring. In that summer and fall of 1949, as Nationalist President Chiang Kai-shek was pushed off the mainland to find refuge in Taiwan, Christian missionaries in China, representing many faiths, saw the handwriting of doom on the walls about them. They feared that with the Communist seizure of the government their days of service in China were numbered. They were right.

China had been a favorite mission field for Catholics and Protestants alike, since the great country with its teeming population had been opened to the commerce of the outside world in the early nineteenth century. Its people predominantly Buddhist, China had been an outstanding challenge to hundreds of young men and young women to find their spiritual lives by losing them in religious service in that far-away country.

As a result of their efforts, at the beginning of the Japanese attack in 1937 China had thousands of Christian churches, hospitals, and schools. Many of these were under the ministry and control of nationals, as all denominations with mission work in China followed a program of teaching and training Chinese converts to take over their own religious worship and the administration of their institutions.

William L. Wallace of Knoxville, Tennessee, was just such a young man as the many who had answered the call to that mission field. Son of a physician well known and respected in Knoxville, Bill Wallace felt impelled to study medicine in order to be a missionary-surgeon. He was graduated from the medical college of the University of Tennessee at Memphis in 1932. Young Dr. Wallace did his internship at Knoxville General Hospital and remained at that institution for surgical residency.

In China's ancient city of Wuchow, 200 miles up the West River, the Stout Memorial Hospital stood as a monument to a Southern Baptist medical missionary a generation before. One day in the fall of 1934 the hospital's superintendent, Dr. Robert

E. Beddoe, wrote a letter to Dr. Charles Maddry, secretary of the Baptist Foreign Mission Board at Richmond, Virginia, in which he said:

We have a long and noble history here at the Stout Memorial Hospital, and Southern Baptists can be proud of what has been done in the name of the Lord Jesus Christ. But we are in danger of losing that position that has been so hard won, and neglecting grossly the responsibilities that are ours in this desert of suffering and heathenism. Without a surgeon, this hospital is operating in a definitely limited capacity, and its potential as a teaching institution and an influential lighthouse for all China is going unrealized.

We must have another missionary doctor, a surgeon who can come in and do things I have not been able to do since my eyes gave way so many years ago. I repeat. *We must have a surgeon.* I appeal to you, in behalf of all the suffering which you yourself are aware of here, find us a surgeon.*

LET US ALL BE FRIENDS

By an astonishing coincidence Dr. William L. Wallace at the Knoxville General Hospital wrote a letter to Dr. Maddry that arrived almost in the same mail as Dr. Beddoe's from China. In it Bill Wallace told of his education and present position, and said:

Since my senior year in high school I have felt that God would have me to be a medical missionary, and to that end I have been preparing myself. . . . I must confess that I am not a good speaker nor apt as a teacher, but I do feel that God can use my training as a physician. As humbly as I know how, I want to volunteer to serve. . . . I will go anywhere I am needed.

Within a few months Dr. Wallace was on his way to China and to the hospital at Wuchow. Like all missionaries in a strange land, he had to master the language and become acquainted with the customs and needs of the community. His years of service in China can be summed up thus: He was an efficient, tireless physician and surgeon, totally dedicated to the task of physical healing and of impressing his patients with the importance of their religious faith. His fame as a surgeon brought people in need of treatment from as far away as hundreds of miles. He performed operations that many of his patients were persistent in believing were miracles. He became one of the most respected and best loved of any man of any race or calling in that area of China.

Bill Wallace made friends and worked closely with all the missionaries of his area. He had many a Sunday dinner with the Christian and Missionary Alliance group at their compound in Wuchow. The nearby Catholic Maryknoll Mission had long depended upon the Baptist hospital for their medical services. Now to the surprise of the priests and their associates at the mission Dr. Wallace came often to their quarters to follow up his Maryknoll patients' care and well-being. He refused all their efforts to pay him. "Let us just be friends in the Lord's service," he would say.

In the fall of 1943 the governor of Kwangsi Province, H. Wong, was brought to the Stout hospital suffering acutely from a ruptured appendix. The high official had been treated at a government hospital, but the doctors there, fearing loss of face if they should lose such an important patient, sent him to Dr. Wallace. Peritonitis had set in, and the case seemed hopeless. Wallace performed the operation, then brought in a cot so that he could stay close by Governor Wong's bed. His skill and attention saved the governor's life—and spread the doctor's fame further over China.

By the time the Communist advance reached south China many missionaries, Catholic and Protestant, had been transferred to other and safer fields of duty. But Dr. Bill Wallace, now superintendent of the Stout Memorial Hospital, insisted he must stay. He felt that his medical services were so badly needed that even the Communists would appreciate his work. In this he mistook the cruel hatred of Marxist leaders for any person who gains the esteem of his fellow men because of unselfish service in the name of religion.

Persecutions and harassments took the form of exorbitant taxes on the hospital, needless inspections, and accusations against Dr. Wallace and his staff for being "Yankee spies." Under threats to close the hospital, Wallace was forced to send ten nurses in uniform to take part in a "spontaneous parade" to show his support of the new People's government. The doctor and his staff watched with horror as the "trials by mob" took place. They saw the revolting spectacle of landlords and other property owners brought out on public platforms with their hands tied behind their backs. They heard the accusations read, such as "enemy of the revolution," and the howls of the mob for punishment. They witnessed the surge of the crowds upon the accused as the hapless victims were beaten to the ground and often to their deaths.

From the time the North Korean rulers, well equipped with military supplies from the Soviet Union, began the aggression against their brothers in free Korea and the United States and the United Nations intervened to defend the Republic of Korea, an intense, vitriolic campaign was carried on against all things American. The people of the United States were called Yankee dogs, imperialist wolves, capitalist exploiters.

On the evening of December 18, 1950, Dr. Wallace made the rounds of his hospital wards with his head nurse, Miss Everley Hayes, who had joined his staff as a missionary from Missouri. As they checked the patients the doctor noted that a young Communist soldier whose appendix he had removed was making good recovery. Dr. Wallace made some notations for his nurses and retired.

DR. WALLACE FINDS HIS LIFE

At 3 o'clock that morning there was a loud banging on the hospital gates. An attendant cautiously approached the gate.

"Open up! We have a sick man here who needs help!" a voice called out. The attendant opened the gates—to be confronted with the bayonets of Communist soldiers. Some of the armed men quickly fanned out over the hospital grounds while others entered all the dormitories of the staff members. The doctor's personal attendant wakened him with the bad news, just as a squad of the troops burst into his bedroom. He was forced to dress quickly and marched to the hospital reception room, where all the personnel were herded.

The officer in charge of the raiding party told Dr. Wallace that he was under arrest for treasonable activities, including the hiding of firearms in the hospital. He denied the charge and his voice was drowned out by the cries of his staff members that the accusation was a lie.

"He is our friend! He is a friend of the Chinese people! He has treated our sick! He is like a father to all of us!" chorused the voices.

"You will soon see!" declared the officer with a devilish grin. "Search his room!"

Several soldiers hurried away, taking the personal attendant with them. One of them pulled up the mattress of Dr. Wallace's bed, reached under, and pulled out a pistol.

"But Dr. Wallace never had a gun!" the attendant said. A sharp blow across the mouth silenced him.

When the officer placed the gun before him, Dr. Wallace denied he had ever seen it. His words were wasted as the raiding party put everyone under arrest.

"We know that you are the principal spy for President Truman and the Americans here in south China!" the officer shouted.

Dr. Wallace was imprisoned, along with several of his staff. Daily, and some days and nights hourly, he was brought to the interrogation room. He heard the accusation, shouted over and over, that he was an imperialist spy. With fiendish cruelty his captors told him that doctors all over China had gathered evidence against him for illegal and obscene operations, and were demanding his punishment. When exhausted, he would be returned to his small bare cell.

At his public trial Dr. Wallace was brought before a small table piled high with guns, radios, opium, and other articles which the prosecutors accused him of stealing. He heard the charges shouted at the small group of people who had assembled.

"He is a spy! He is an incompetent surgeon! He has maimed and murdered our Chinese people. He has performed obscene operations. Should he be punished?"

Dr. Wallace looked down into the grim, immobile faces of the people before him, and saw a sight that enraged his tormentors. Not a fist was raised. Not a voice was lifted against this man who had been the friend and doctor to everyone there. Every person remained silent.

Back to his cell—and to days and nights more of questionings and attempts to force the doctor to confess to crimes he had not committed. The story of what happened then has been graphically told by his biographer, the Rev. Jesse C. Fletcher, who obtained much of his information from Nurse Everley Hayes and from two Catholic priests who were imprisoned in nearby cells:

The Communists plainly intended to brainwash their victim into an open confession, to have him repudiate publicly all that he was and all he had stood for. They thought their goal was within reach, but the tough spirit would not capitulate so easily, and his protests rang through the night.

The guards, driven by fear or perhaps guilt, came to his cell in the night with long poles and cruelly thrust them between the cell bars to jab the doctor into unconsciousness. Somebody figured wrong. For one night the battle was over, and though no one heard Bill Wallace cry "It is finished," he offered up his spirit and brought his ministry and mission to a close. Quietly his soul slipped from his torn body and his exhausted mind and went to be with the One he had so faithfully and unstintedly served through the years.*

Next morning the guards announced that Dr. Wallace had taken his life. They brought the two priests from their nearby cells to show them that the body of the doctor was hanging from a beam by a quilt—a feat he could not possibly have managed by himself. The priests were asked to certify that Dr. Wallace had committed suicide. This they refused to do, writing out a statement describing how they had found him, and nothing else.

Bill Wallace had found his life by losing it in loyalty to the holy service of healing, and finally by giving it up in martyrdom for something the Communists can never conquer: a living religious faith.

CHAPTER ELEVEN

COMMUNISTS ARE CHAMPION HYPOCRITES

At a time when this writer * was serving in Congress as a Representative from Missouri a man came to my office and told my secretary that he wanted to set me straight in regard to freedoms in the Soviet Union. I asked my secretary to show him in.

The man had read of a speech I had made in which I had pointed out the loss of freedoms by the people living under Marxist governments. I had mentioned specifically the loss of freedom to worship and of liberty to work at times and places of one's choosing.

I must say that I was intrigued by the visitor's arguments, and I listened intently and patiently.

"You are wrong!" he declared. "Actually, there is greater freedom in the Soviet Union than in the United States of America, for in America people attend church because they are forced to do so by social pressure. Also, in the United States and other capitalist countries a man must take almost any job just in order to keep alive."

"And how does that differ from the situation in the USSR?" I asked. His reply was a masterpiece of the "double-think" of the true Marxist disciple. He responded:

"There is greater freedom of religion in the Soviet Union than here in America because the Soviet State guarantees freedom of conscience and worship and there is complete separation of

* O.K.A.

124

church and State. As for labor, a worker in the Soviet Union is free to work anywhere the government assigns him."

I thanked the visitor for this information. I did not argue the matter, for I had already learned that the opinions of the dedicated Marxist are not subject either to reason or change.

Perhaps the Marxist-oriented visitor had in mind statements such as appeared in the publication *Soviet World,* issued in November 1945, which contains these words:

"In our countries there exists for the workers the full freedom of criticism of the work of any organization or undertaking. The Soviet Union guarantees to all its citizens extensive rights. The most important of these is the right to work—a guarantee which it is impossible for any capitalist country to give."

For a non-Communist person the maddening thing about Communist thinking is the impossibility of determining whether or not the Marxist actually believes his own propaganda. Can it be possible that the dedicated Communist loses all conception of the difference between truth and falsehood? One thing is certain: the genuine Marxist will *use* truth or false propaganda with equal facility, strictly on the basis of which will best advance the cause of the Communist world conspiracy.

"Freedom to work wherever the government assigns him." "Freedom of conscience and worship—the constitution guarantees it." Those words condense a huge volume of Communist ideology: The State is supreme. The person has no unalienable liberties as an individual. He receives only such liberties as the all-powerful State doles out to him. He "enjoys" those freedoms permitted by the State only on conditions laid down by the government. *This is freedom, Communist style.*

THEY BLOW HOT OR COLD

One of the most despicable tactics of the Marxist hypocrites in their program of the extermination of religion is to loosen the screws of persecution for a time in order to deceive believers into thinking some change for the better has come about, or some permanent softening of the hostile attitude of the atheistic Reds. This has been going on since the days of Lenin, and reached its height during World War II when Stalin found it necessary to win the collaboration of church leaders, at home and abroad, for the war effort.

Since the close of World War II Communist rulers have frequently found it profitable to ease up on religious leaders and organizations and shift to a period of false "coexistence." Assuming an attitude of righteous tolerance, the Marxist dictators try to entice the peoples of the free world to believe that the Communist regimes have become less cruel, less severe, more amenable to human liberties, and especially to the practice of religion. Of course this is always the means to the end of enlisting peoples of religious faith, particularly in the enemy "Imperialist" (non-Communist) countries to support some policy that advances the cause of world revolution.

So it was in 1954 that Soviet authorities decided the time had come to shift to a period of coexistence with religious organizations. Propaganda poured out steadily, directed at the free world, to promote the image of the Soviet regimes as tolerant and especially interested in building world peace. In a resolution of the Central Committee of the Soviet Communist Party, signed by Nikita Khrushchev and reported in *Pravda* for November 11, 1954, local officials in all areas of the Russian Communist empire were given instructions to ease up on religious persecutions. The resolution included:

> Propaganda which is scientifically atheistic, used in a profound and patient manner and employed judiciously among the faithful, will eventually succeed in liberating them from their religious errors. On the other hand every administrative measure or illegal attack against the faithful and the clergy will turn only to our disadvantage and will definitely strengthen their religious prejudices.

In less than a year it became evident to Khrushchev and his Kremlin associates that the matter of coexistence with religious groups had gone much farther than they had planned. Accordingly, in September 1955, Khrushchev issued a statement that contained these words:

> Each citizen can do as he wishes with regard to religion; profess whatever faith he likes; frequent his churches. . . . But that does

not at all mean that communism has modified its fundamental attitude toward religion. We repeat as heretofore that religion is the "opium of the people" and that the greater number of those who will be awakened from their pipe-dreams, the better it will be for progress.

Since that time, many similar pronouncements have issued from the Kremlin, proof that true Marxists never change their "fundamental attitude toward religion."

The statement that there is freedom of worship in the USSR and in all other countries with Marxist dictatorships is repeated time after time by Red propaganda experts whenever there is need to answer queries from concerned foreign sources or to quiet criticisms of anxious religious leaders outside the Soviet Union.

In an attempt to support this falsehood, a few churches in strategic places are permitted to hold services and also are encouraged to bring visitors from other lands to be in the worship services. The more important the religious leaders among the visitors, the better!

Perhaps the most outstanding example of this hypocrisy is the Baptist Church of Moscow. Rarely a Sunday but important men and women from the United States and other free countries are escorted by "interpreters" (usually members of the secret police) to this church. Always the visitors are impressed with the throngs of people who crowd into the 700 seats and stand along the walls, and with the fervor with which they sing and pray. They are impressed also with the sincerity of the pastor, the Rev. Jacob Zhidkov.

The Marxist stage managers of this show do not explain to the impressionable visitors that this is the *only* Baptist church allowed to hold services in all Moscow, a city of more than five million people. They never point out that if freedom of religion were permitted, hundreds of such places of worship for people of all faiths would be crowded with believers too.

Pictures may be freely taken by the visitors to this and other churches used as show places in the Marxist empire, and many sermons and speeches to the people "back home" are illustrated with the slides showing these devout believers freely worshiping in the Soviet Union.

"I know there is freedom of religion in Russia, for I worshiped in this very service. No one stopped me!" is the theme of many of the returned visitors, to the great delight of the propaganda workers in Moscow who receive the clippings from their diligent agents in the Soviet Embassy in Washington.

Biggest tragedy of all in this piece of blasphemous hypocrisy is the fact that the worshipers *are* devout believers. They did not crowd into that Baptist church to help the Marxist duplicity. Pastor Zhidkov *is not* an agent of the secret police. This man of God, and thousands more like him, are doing a most difficult work under handicaps that would try the soul of a saint. Added to the crushing burden of his restrictions is another: he knows very well that his church and his ministry are being used by the authorities for their own devilish purposes, but he cannot lift his voice in protest lest it be stilled by persecution.

GREATEST HOAX ON EARTH

The most monstrous example of hypocrisy in the entire modern world is the announced guarantee of freedom of conscience and worship in the Soviet Union and in every Marxist country, including Red China and the Communist colony that was once free Cuba.

Of course, the constitutions of the Red regimes all say that there must be freedom of religion. Since the constitutions of all the captive countries of eastern Europe were written under direction and by dictation of the Kremlin, it is understandable that they should have similar wordings or at least express the same false ideas about religious freedom. Let us note again Article 124 of the Soviet constitution:

"In order to insure to citizens freedom of conscience the church in the USSR is separated from the State and the school from the Church. Freedom of religious worship and freedom of anti-religious propaganda is recognized for all citizens."

Now for similar examples of the double-talk of Communist ideology:

Hungary: "The Hungarian People's Republic guarantees freedom of conscience of its citizens, and the right to the free practice of religion. In the interest of the assurance of freedom of conscience the Hungarian People's Republic separates the Church from the State."

Romania: "Freedom of conscience and freedom of religious worship is guaranteed to all citizens of Romanian People's Republic."

Yugoslavia: "Freedom of conscience and religion is guaranteed to all citizens, with separation of Church and State."

East Germany (German Democratic Republic): "Every citizen enjoys full freedom of conscience and religious belief. The unhindered practice of religion is protected by the Republic."

Poland: "The government of the Polish People's Republic, which recognizes the principle of religious liberty . . ."

China (People's Republic of China): "The people shall have freedom of thought, speech, publication, assembly, association, correspondence, person, domicile, moving from one place to another, religious belief, and the freedom of holding processions and demonstrations."

Cuba: "The profession of all religions, as well as the practice of all cults, is unrestricted. . . . The Church shall be separate from the State, which cannot subsidize any cult."

Close on the heels of these supposed guarantees are words that prove them false. We have noted how a provision in the Lenin constitution of the USSR—still in effect—adds as the right of every citizen "and freedom of anti-religious propaganda." Under that cover the State marshals all its power to persecute and harass religion.

Actually, only freedom of worship is pretended to be assured. In other words, the church or synagogue may do nothing but conduct services (so long as the building is not closed as "surplus"). Only *antireligious* propaganda is permitted, meaning that there can be no propaganda *for* religion, such as instructing young people in religious principles or publicly propagating the faith. At the same time, antireligious propaganda is subsidized by the vast resources of the State and party.

Science and Religion, the official atheist periodical of the Soviet Union, published a most revealing article in its issue of May 5, 1960. In a lengthy discussion entitled "Against Infringements of Soviet Legislation Covering Religious Observances,"

Communist authorities disclosed the true extent of religious suppression currently practiced in the USSR despite the assertions about freedom of worship. The discussion spelled out in detail many restrictions on church affairs.

"Soviet legislation does not forbid the priesthood to read sermons in churches, mosques, etc.," the article declared. But the discussion went on to make clear that all sermons "must have a purely religious content." And what is a "purely religious content"? Here is the official answer to that question: "The pulpits of churches must not be used for political and other statements unconcerned with religion and in contradiction to the interests of the Soviet State."

In the same Article 84 of the Romanian constitution guaranting freedom of conscience is the sentence, "The organizing and functioning of religious denominations are regulated by law." The word "regulated" covers every activity of every religious organization in the country. All heads of denominations, bishops, vicars, pastors, and other officials of religious groups in Romania must "take the oath of allegiance before the Minister of Religious Affairs before entering upon the discharge of their duties."

Here are some of the words of that oath: "As a servant of God, a man and a citizen, I swear to be faithful to the People and to defend the Romanian People's Republic against enemies, foreign and domestic." Anyone who is not completely loyal to the Communist regime and willing to advance its cause is an enemy.

PAST MASTERS OF DECEIT

In the same Section 41 of the constitution of the Soviet Union's colony of East Germany which guarantees "freedom of conscience and religious belief" is this stipulation: "Institutions of religious communities, religious activities and religious instructon may not be misused for the purposes contrary to the constitution."

Although in Poland there is a measure of freedom not enjoyed in other eastern European countries, because of an accommodation between the government and the predominant Roman Catholic Church, all property, finances, income, and expenditures are under strict control and administration of the government.

An executive order of the Polish Minister of Finance on February 20, 1962 gives detailed instructions for all church officials on keeping their accounts and makes the account books open to the Minister of Finance at all times to ascertain "whether the above-mentioned religious legal entities function in accordance with the Law on Associations." And suppose some bureaucrat in the ministry decides the functioning has stepped out of the strict line of party collaboration? The account books can be very quickly closed—along with the church or other religious organization.

In Red China the constitutional provision for freedom of religious belief contains words that make a mockery of such a guarantee by stating that every citizen has the duty "to defend the Fatherland, to observe the laws . . ." Any act of religious worship can be used for a trumped-up charge of failure to observe the laws.

Whatever the wordings of constitutions and laws of Marxist governments may be, the interpretations and implementations are the important thing. The guarantees are always so limited in practice that they can be enjoyed by believers only on a strictly controlled basis. Without exception, every Red regime interprets the right of antireligious propaganda as license to move firmly forward in the crusade to eradicate this greatest enemy of atheistic dictatorships: religion.

Hundreds of examples of the "interpretation" of freedom of religion can be cited, from reports of disciplinary actions in party papers. Take note of these few, in communities of Hungary:

A farm leader was expelled from the party and his job because his son, under eighteen years of age, went to church. A member of the local housing committee was given a heavy fine and relieved of his job because it became known that he and his family had decided to enroll his daughter for religious instruction. Another worker was expelled from the party and "severely disciplined" because his wife had their child confirmed in a church.

The laws of the Red tyrants that still hold Hungary in their bloody hands are striking proof of the duplicity of Communist statements about freedom of religion. Explaining the Marxist control of that hapless land, Janos Beer, a Budapest official, declared:

"Freedom of conscience includes that subjective right of the citizen that he may freely profess any religion, may freely practice it within the limits of the security of the State and social order, and may equally freely profess and preach his anti-religious belief."

This very definition gives a striking example of the discrimination against religion. *Professing* one's religious belief is free— because, obviously, thought cannot be controlled by the government. But *practicing* religion is permitted only within the limits defined by the "security of the State and social order." And those limits need not be defined by law; they can change to suit the occasion. The preaching and propagation of atheism, meanwhile, is not only expressly permitted but is supported by every means at the disposal of the government.

Consider that additional huge hoax, the "separation of church and State." In all Communist countries this principle is used *not* to prevent the State from intervention in church affairs and to free the church from government influence, but rather to permit the total domination of religious organizations by the Red regimes. Again quoting the official party line as expressed by Hungarian Janos Beer:

"The separation of the State from the churches as a constitutional guarantee means that no denomination may perform, even with special authorization, governmental functions. This does not exclude that they may not support in their own sphere of activity the solution of the most important government problems."

Put into plain non-Communist speech, this means that while religious groups have no right to interfere, or even criticize, the political life of the country, *they are expected at all times to collaborate with the government and to promote the Marxist goals of their rulers.*

"The Real Nature of Communism"

On June 3, 1963 during an intensified drive on religion in Hungary, the foremost atheist propaganda publication of that country, *Vilagossag,* candidly expressed the party policy of using the churches when they can be of service to the revolution:

The starting point and main purpose of our policy toward the churches is to promote the increased participation of the working masses—including also the religious people—in the building of Socialism. This demands that we should display tolerance toward the religious people as well as the churches. . . . But it is obvious and natural that the relation of State and Church cannot stagnate at a mandatory minimum—at the benevolent political neutrality of the churches. According to our party and government the important criteria of the effectiveness of cooperation are the positive steps taken by the churches in the interest of the working masses.

During the crisis between the United States and the Soviet Union in October 1962 over the atomic-capable missiles installed by the USSR for the Marxist puppet Castro in Cuba, Khrushchev used every possible propaganda device in an effort to forestall the truth of this clear threat of military aggression from becoming known to the world in general. Proving as nothing else had to that moment the subservience of the Russian Orthodox Church to the Red dictatorship, the hierarchy of that dominant religion dispatched an urgent message directly to President Kennedy:

"As lovers of peace, we implore you not to stir up conflict on the Island of Cuba. We urge your government to make no moves that would endanger the friendship and continued cooperation of the Union of Soviet Socialist Republics in the cause of international peace."

Soon after this message from the churchmen reached the White House the President was sitting in his office, confronting Andrei Gromyko, veteran administrator of Foreign Affairs for the Kremlin. Gromyko assured the President that no offensive missiles had been installed in Cuba. A few days later Khrushchev himself had to admit to the whole world that the missiles were there, and that he had an agreement with President Kennedy for their removal.

It is quite certain that it never occurred to the dictator to apologize to the Orthodox Church leaders whom he had used as duped mouthpieces to cover his enormous and dangerous duplicity.

The late J. Edgar Hoover, director of the U.S. Bureau of Investigation, who knew a great deal about the dishonesty and duplicity of Communist leaders, made this telling point:

If members are forced to present the Party's views, they are instructed to stress, as Lenin did, that religion is a "private matter" for the individual, and to pose as "tolerant." Doesn't the Party's constitution say that a person is eligible for membership "regardless of religious belief"? The object here is to dull the vigilance of the noncommunist mind and to make religious belief appear as something minor, secondary, and inconsequential.

When tactically expedient, the communists even liken themselves to the early Christian martyrs suffering persecution for attempting to aid mankind. . . . A *Daily Worker* writer, reviewing a movie in which the background was laid in the early Christian era, says: "Some interesting parallels can be found between the persecution of the Christians shown in the film and the political jailings in the United States today."

Behind these deceptive tactics, however, can be seen the real nature of communism. For the member, religion is *not* a private affair. No tolerance is allowed. He cannot be a Marxist and adhere to religion. The Party is today desperately working to mold atheistic materialism as a weapon of revolution, a revolution which, if it is to succeed, must first sap religion's spiritual strength and then destroy it.*

During his visit to the United States in 1959, Nikita Khrushchev made several references to God and to Christ in his rambling, bumbling speeches and press statements. In view of this top Marxist's complete dedication to atheism and to the eradication of religion, such references should be recognized as the "deceptive tactics" mentioned by Mr. Hoover.

At a banquet in San Francisco on September 23 that year, Khrushchev declared: "We want to build a society under which every man will be a brother of his neighbor as was preached by Christ. . . . We have taken a lot of Christ's precepts, regarding for instance love of one's neighbor and others."

Several times during his trip the Soviet dictator explained his idea of coexsistence thus: "You have to live with the neighbors God gave you—not with the neighbors you would like to have."

Whether the current crop of Communists are willing to live in peace and brotherhood with the neighbors God gave them can be measured, now and in the future, by their willingness to grant true freedom of religion to these who really believe in God.

CHAPTER TWELVE

MARXISTS ARE GOOD DOUBLE-CROSSERS

On February 14, 1956, at the opening of the twentieth Communist Party Congress in Moscow, Nikita S. Khrushchev, Chairman of the Council of Ministers, top man in the dictatorship that struts before the world as the government of the Union of Soviet Socialist Republics, made a speech. It was a seven-hour report of his stewardship as keeper of the faith and practices of the regime that holds the 220 millions of peoples of Russia in subjection and that holds by the throats 122 million other peoples of the once-free nations of eastern Europe.

"Our party is more monolithic than ever!" trumpeted Khrushchev. Just how more monolithic it could become after its creation by Nikolai Lenin from the blueprint of Karl Marx and after its refinement in tyranny and cruelty under Joseph Stalin and Khrushchev himself, the rotund Chairman did not explain.

Khrushchev went on to warn against "a lack of confidence toward the workers in the agencies of governmental security," and added: "Our Chekists in their overwhelming majority are honest workers devoted to our cause."

All went smoothly in that twentieth Communist Party Congress for eleven days. Then Khrushchev dropped a verbal atomic bomb that crashed into the hearing of the monolithic regime's satraps and lackeys, shook them to their innards, and reverberated throughout the news media of countries all over the free world. It was Khrushchev's famous denunciation of his former sponsor, teacher, mentor, friend, and erstwhile saint, the late Joseph Stalin.

In his speech Khrushchev laid at Stalin's door about all the black and foul deeds in the books of political and personal villainy. He characterized Stalin as a calloused murderer, a sadist, an opportunist, a man who sacrificed even his closest associates as well as anyone who might have been remotely suspected of opposition to this evil man's will.

Sources close to Khrushchev later let it be known that the wily Chairman knew it was a calculated risk to keep his speech a secret from the public, but felt he could accomplish this by strict censorship. Thus he hoped to gain his ends among his own Communist associates without exposing himself as a liar, an ingrate, and a heel for knocking from a pedestal the man who made him what he was that day. As it turned out, some member of the Council himself was only too glad to expose the exposer. He double-crossed the double-crosser by letting out the full text of the lengthy speech "debunking" Stalin.

Informants in a position to know declare that Khrushchev's anger at this disloyalty knew no bounds. To be exposed to the world as the man who tore the mask of respectability from the face of Stalin, the national hero, was just too much. To have denounced the man who was linked in public thinking as an equal with Marx and Lenin, the saints of the Communist revolution, proved that all the good things Khrushchev had said about his sponsor Stalin in the past were lies.

But the speech had been made, and there was nothing Khrushchev could do but swallow his words. Nothing, that is, but proceed with the necessary follow-up gestures of removing the body of Stalin from its honored place next to that of Lenin, changing the names of dozens of cities and streets, buildings and parks, from "Stalin" to something else; knocking down hundreds of statues of the grim hero now turned villain, and otherwise tarnishing the name of the man who had while living already fully tarnished it in the minds of his millions of victims and others who understood his murderous tyranny.

THE HOLE IN THE MARXIST ARMOR

Plowing through the dreary rocks and stumps in the rough field of Khrushchev's speech to that party Congress, one finds no references to two of the most important "crimes" of Stalin: First, Stalin's mass murder by starvation of millions of peasants who resisted losing their property and their liberties by the "agrarian reforms." Second, his program of persecutions and strangulations to eradicate religion from the lives of the Russian people.

The reasons are clear for Nikita Khrushchev's omission of these items in his famous denunciation. As we have seen, in his capacity as a young and ambitious Communist bureaucrat in the Stalinist regime during the early 1920s Khrushchev did nothing to oppose his master's policy of mass starvation. His title "the butcher of the Ukraine" was not an honorary degree. He earned it, by his assistance to Stalin in the bloody purges of the 1930s.

Khrushchev had no intention during his early tutelage under Stalin, and has had no intention since, of abandoning the process of eradicating what he considers the superstitions and illusions of religious faith.

The famous Khrushchev speech, a colossal example of the Marxist double-cross, stands for all the world to see as proof that no one is safe under a Communist slave regime, whether official or plain citizen. It proves that the cruelty and terror and suffering forced upon innocent people under Communist rule can be quickly turned against those who have enforced it.

If Khrushchev can uproot Stalin and throw him out of popular favor as one would throw a dead cat into the alley, then Khrushchev's successor can do the same to him—probably without even putting him in tomb to be gawked at by curious tourists or honored by statues. If Stalin was bad, so were all those associated with him. If his policies were bad during his lifetime, then they are bad now and will continue to be, however much the Soviet tyrants may sugar-coat or decorate them.

Discussing Khrushchev's speech, the Rev. Dr. Charles Wesley Lowry, learned student of Marxism and thoughtful writer, declared:

Khrushchev has done us, if we will but use our eyes to see, a large favor. He has given the Soviet peoples and all peoples a tremendous gift. In ingenuously exposing and diagraming the black, infernal wickedness of Stalin, the incarnate spirit for a fourth of a century of the workers' paradise, he holds without knowing it a mighty magnifying mirror up to the presumption and iniquity of man. He shows with unconscious dramatic skill what absolute hypocrisy is. He discloses the hideous reality of "the lie in the soul." He uncovers the mystery of ungodliness in its most ancient and its most modern form.

This mystery finds ultimate expression only when absolute power, which always means the power of the state, is institutionalized and is placed without check of human hands. Our forefathers understood this and were wont to call the state Leviathan or "second God." Absolute power in this sense corrupts absolutely; and it corrupts not only the tyrant who wields it but the colleagues and subordinates around him who must obey and await his commands. It is the appalling fate of our generation that it must learn in the harsh and bitter school of historical experience the meaning of absolute corruption allied to the most efficient and technically advanced organization of tyranny which the world has ever seen.*

THOSE NICE WORDS: COEXISTENCE AND COLLABORATION

Since the promises of "freedom of conscience and worship" in all the constitutions and laws of the Marxist governments are themselves a massive betrayal of believers of all faiths, so are all programs for coexistence and collaboration with religious denominations, groups and individual leaders. In every Communist country a policy of coexistence with religion by the government has turned out to mean a period of watchful tolerance while preparations are being made by the regime for new and bigger restrictions and suppressions.

Coexistence with communism, in the religious field as well as in social, economic, and political matters, means that the trusting groups and individuals are but calves being fattened for the slaughter.

As for collaboration, Marxist rulers cunningly entice church leaders to support what seem to be common ideals and aims, such as "betterment of the People," "disarmament," and "world peace." Without exception religious groups that have given their leadership and sponsorship to such cooperative efforts have found themselves drawn more tightly into the net of governmental control. Whether they have gone in voluntarily or under pressure of the monolithic State, the result is the same. They must support the policies of the regime, or suffer the consequences.

Collaboration with Marxist authorities, on any level of activity, by any church group, as with any organization created for human betterment, catches the collaborators like insects lured into the webs of the Red spiders.

Let us note one captive country as an example of all: Bulgaria. The Bulgarian Orthodox Church embraces more than 80 per cent of the population of that nation. In addition, there are four minority denominations, which counted, according to an estimate made in 1956, 930,000 Muslims (Turk-Muslims and Bulgaro-Muslims), 56,000 Roman Catholics, 28,000 Protestants, and 6,000 Jews.

As we have noted previously, all religious denominations are completely controlled by the State. The Bulgarian Orthodox Church has been made a "National Church" with the status of a legal entity but with all its properties expropriated or nationalized. All religious organizations in Bulgaria must register with the authorities. There is absolute censorship by the police of all religious pronouncements and materials.

The Red regime admits that its aim is to do away with all religion in the nation, in due course of time. Meanwhile it shamelessly exacts from the religious groups full collaboration on countless matters of public interest.

Throughout December 1949 all churches and synagogues were required to hold special services in honor of the 70th birthday of Joseph Stalin. The ruthless Soviet dictator was extolled by bishops, priests, pastors, and religious leaders generally as "the liberator of our nation, the savior of our People, the preserver of the peace of the world."

During the aggressive war of Red China, made with Soviet Union backing in military experts and war matériel, against the

Republic of Korea in 1950-1952, the official organ of the Bulgarian Orthodox Church, *Tsurkoven Vestnik,* beat its editorial drums with "Let Us Help Korea" themes. The "Korea" to be helped by the churches was *not* the victim of wanton aggression but the Red aggressors themselves.

When the Soviet Union and Red China's Mao regime joined hands to grind out their propaganda lies, almost in the same wording, to convince peoples of the world that the American and other United Nations forces resisting the aggression in Korea were using "germ warfare" against both military personnel and civilian populations, the Holy Synod of the Orthodox Church dutifully issued denunciations of the alleged act, to be read by priests in all services.

At feast days and numerous occasions of religious significance, and particularly at Christmas time, the Orthodox hierarchy is required to issue statements denouncing the horrors of atomic war and mentioning the "hundreds of thousands of victims" of the atomic attacks at Hiroshima and Nagasaki, Japan. Priests are instructed to follow these pronouncements and to emphasize them in their services.

The highest bishop of the Bulgarian Orthodox Church, Patriarch Kyril, made a congratulatory speech on February 11, 1957, at the opening of the 4th Congress of the Fatherland Front Organization, in which, according to *Tsurkoven Vestnik,* he stated:

> In regard to this task, the servants of the Bulgarian Church have been rendering and will continue to render full cooperation for the success of the Fatherland Front. . . . This organization of all the citizens of our country truly reflects the national feeling of love and devotion to our liberator, the lofty Russian nation; to all Soviet Peoples and their great Fatherland, the Union of Soviet Socialist Republics.

During the Cuban missile crisis of October 1962 Patriarch Kyril sent a telegram to the 17th Session of the United Nations General Assembly, similar in wording to messages sent to the U.N. from church leaders in all the captive eastern European countries, stating:

"The imposed United States blockade of Cuba seriously endangers the peace of the world. . . . In the name of all the faithful Christians of our country, we and the Holy Synod of the Bulgarian Orthodox Church persistently urge the United Nations Organization to invoke its charter and stop the aggression against Cuba."

Despite this embarrassing double-cross of the Patriarch by Khrushchev in the Cuban matter and the Soviet dictator's admission that his regime had placed the aggressive missiles in the island at the United States' doorstep, Archbishop Kyril continued to allow the prestige of his church to be prostituted in the cause of "peace" —Khrushchev style. In a speech in Sofia on January 28, 1963, before the Plenum of the National Committee in Defense of Peace, the Patriarch said:

In spite of the expressed will of the nations, war has not been suppressed and peace has not been assured. This has been especially apparent in the recent crisis in the Caribbean Sea. This crisis, which had threatened the world with rocket and thermonuclear war, has been averted, thanks to the Soviet government and personally to its Chairman, Nikita S. Khrushchev. . . . To the government of the Soviet Union and also to its Chairman Khrushchev have been expressed the deserved gratitude and appreciation.

And what have the Bulgarian believers received in return for all their leaders' cozy coexistence and active collaboration with the Marxist representatives of the "lofty Russian nation"? The Orthodox Church has been kicked in the teeth with the closing of at least 60 per cent of all its places of worship. The Roman Catholic Church has been practically outlawed. Only a few Protestant churches still survive. This is payment—in Communist coin.

SUPPORT THE REGIME—OR ELSE

In all the captive nations, pressure upon religious leaders and believers of all faiths to support the Soviet puppet governments has been constant and intense. In East Germany, for example, an "East German Christian Democratic Union" was organized by the Red colonial administration headed by Walter Ulbricht for the express purpose of collaboration with his policies. The Reds have been using this false-front organization especially to enlist Christians in the program of making that part of Germany permanently Communist.

In October 1962, according to a Religious News Service report from Berlin, the Christian Democratic Union adopted a resolution urging all believers in the Soviet Zone to work for "greater action and creative cooperation to build up the Socialist order in East Germany; to promote the fight against political clericalism, and to stress the promising aspects of Christianity in Socialism."

The resolution stressed the great importance "to make the friendship of the Soviet Union a heartfelt concern of all Christians and to win them for membership in the Society for the Promotion of German-Soviet Friendship."

The resolution complained that contacts between the Communist party and "nonpartisan" Christians continued to be insufficient, "a situation which must be quickly remedied through the cooperation of church elders among our party members." It emphasized that among Protestant circles "there are symptoms of a critical attitude toward our State and its Socialist policies," and particularly toward "progressive" clergymen and the Communist youth dedication services.

This same cry was taken up all over Soviet-controlled East Germany. It merged into a campaign for German Christians to support the Soviet proposals for a peace treaty for Germany, which would in effect make the Soviet Zone a permanent colony of the USSR, including all the city of Berlin, and leave all western Germany open to ultimate Communist rule. The Christian Democratic Union plugs for the Soviet policies on disarmament, as quickly as its leaders can shift with every shifting Soviet move at the Geneva conference tables. But they remain constant, as do the USSR spokesmen who use the windy, futile discussions on disarmament for propaganda purposes, in their demands. They will have only the type of disarmament that would weaken the defenses of the free nations and permit the continued build-up of the military power of the Communist bloc.

Soviet propaganda experts, meantime, pound away at the theme, for consumption outside their colonial empire, that there really is no religious persecution in the USSR. Peter Kolonytsky, chief editor of *Science and Religion,* principal atheist publication in the

Soviet Union, wrote an important official article for *Izvestia* to mark the 45th anniversary of Nikolai Lenin's decree on Separation of Church and State. In this article Kolonytsky bolstered his argument that there is complete freedom of religion in the Soviet Union by the often-cited fact that the churches are always crowded with worshipers. Also, he declared, in the last few years fifty delegations of church leaders had visited the USSR, "and not one person has found any religious persecution here!"

As proof that no religious persecution is to be found in his country, Kolonytsky played up the fact that "no person in Russia asks about religious beliefs, and no one is obliged to report about going to church." He went on to charge that there is no real freedom of belief in capitalistic countries, because "only the dominant religion" enjoys such rights as freedom of worship. He charged also that in the "imperialist and war-mongering nations there is no freedom to be an atheist."

In support of his astounding assertions the writer quoted the Rev. Dr. W. A. Visser't Hooft, General Secretary of the World Council of Churches, as having said that religious congregations can worship and function freely in the Soviet Union. Actually, the World Council leader, who visited the Soviet Union in 1959, had discreetly described the situation of religion there as "very complicated." He had added: "Every moment in a Communist country the Church exists in a situation that is not at all Christian, but based upon another ideology. Moreover, there is active anti-religious propaganda. Given these known facts, we were impressed by all this [Russian Orthodox] Church is and does." *

DOUBLE-CROSSING BOTH SIDES

With straight faces the propaganda artists of the Soviet Union will play both sides of the religious street to further the cause of Marxism. This happened in January 1964, when ridicule of religion reached a high pitch in anticipation of the new drive for atheism in all Communist countries.

While the Moscow radio stations were following the ridicule line, stations in East Berlin and East Germany generally were spouting propaganda to show the compatibility of communism and

Christianity. As monitored by listeners in the free world, a station in Moscow was saying, "Religion makes people unhappy and divisive," and at the same time an official broadcast in Red Berlin was saying, "We should always bid Christians a cordial welcome on every level of public and social life, and meet them with respect and friendship."

What made the difference in the approach? In Germany it was an effort to overcome bitter resentment among people of East Berlin and the captive Soviet Zone against the Ulbricht regime for restrictions upon travel at Christmas time from the Soviet sector to the West.

Other broadcasts disclose the hypocrisy of such programs. For example, Moscow Radio said: "Clergymen never work for unification of working people; they teach their followers to divide people according to religious belief." Berlin Radio was saying: "The daily living and working together of Christians and Marxists in our State demonstrates that their basic interests coincide. Those interests are the preservation of peace and the building of a just society."

In Russian broadcasts the Red regime ridiculed all Christian clergy. In East Germany, however, the Communist government was intent on showing the clergy's participation in civic affairs, claiming that some 50 ministers served on city and town councils. The Red broadcasts cited Christians as good citizens eager to aid the State, because "more than 15,000 Christians have been elected to various local councils. Thousands of Christians are mayors, and some are ministers of State."

From Moscow came broadcasts that complained that while communism is doing everything possible to make Soviet people happy in their lifetime, religion is falsely persuading them that man's happiness does not depend upon himself or people around him but on God. In the series of Moscow broadcasts some old scarecrows were dusted off, such as the charge that "baptism of the young has caused hundreds of deaths from pneumonia."

The crowning insult to the intelligence of the German believers came in one of the Berlin broadcasts with the question: "Why do Christians teach in our schools?" and the answer: "Because Christianity and the humanist aims of communism are not antagonistic and religion here has been freed from being misused by the exploiters of the people. A Christian at last enjoys in the communist State a true chance to make the message 'Peace on Earth' a tangible reality!"

Equally insulting to persons of the Jewish faith are propaganda articles and broadcasts that come in a steady stream to brainwash the Russian public as to the treatment of Jews in other countries. Aaron Vergelis, a convert to atheism, presented a sample of this in a lengthy radio "news and editorial" discussion from Moscow Radio. This man, who is the editor of *Sovetish Kheyruland,* the Yiddish-language publication of Moscow, had visited the United States for some weeks. He declared that conditions under which American Jews lived were deplorable. He described the miserable "ghettos" in which they are forced to live. He said that anti-Semitic literature is circulated widely, defaming the Jews and their religious faith. And he added:

"What worries me is this: Why does the American press have to lie about Soviet Jews? Why do they have to invent stories about anti-Semitism in the USSR? The worst of it is not that they lie, but that most Jews and the American people (*sic*) believe the lies for lack of any true information about our glorious Soviet Union."

In Red China, as might be expected, the double-cross of religious believers was more candid and direct, in its first phase. From the time of the seizure of power by the Mao regime in late 1949 until January 1951, persecutions of leaders and members of all faiths were carried on with ferocious violence. The Vatican was accused of setting up a counterrevolutionary spy network among Catholic priests, nuns, and communicants. Protestant groups were for the most part charged with being in league with American "imperialism" and spies for its "reactionary" activities. Thousands of devout men and women paid with their lives for their "disobedience" in not at once denouncing their bourgeois superstitions and proclaiming the glories of the atheist People's Revolution.

In 1951 the Red regime began its second phase of treatment of religion. It set up its own "religious" organization in order to close out gradually all remaining resistance to Communist "re-education." The government sponsored a "Movement of Triple Independence," called the "Three-Self Movement." It stipulated that henceforth religion would follow (1) Self-Government (Tse-Chih), (2) Self-Support (Tse-Yang), and (3) Self-Propagation (Tse-Ch'uan).

Actually, the movement was a most clever way to bring all religious groups under Marxist control, as the purposes of the program made clear. The founders declared it was their aim:

"To promote the establishment of a truly Chinese Church, and to administer the New Church; to undertake and actively advance the indoctrination of priests and members through the study of Marxism. . . ."

THE GREAT LEAP DOWNWARD

Specifically, "Self-Government" means that church groups can no longer administer their own affairs, but must turn them over completely to the officials of the Communist-sponsored movement. "Self-Support" means, in the astonishing "reverse-think" of Marxist language, that religion will no longer be permitted to support itself but will be supported—if at all—by the government. "Self-Propagation" means that all nonnational preachers, missionaries, and other religious workers are out. No more foreign devils in Chinese religion! And of course all sermons and publications must be adapted to the cause of the People's Revolution.

Faced with the pressure of conforming to this whited sepulcher of Marxist treachery, many Christian missionaries who had not left Red China by early 1951 withdrew from the country. Many national Christians resisted as best they could, but for the most part they went underground in quiet loyalty to their faith.

Countless numbers were swept into the current of collaboration, made easier by the recognition by the regime of "Patriot Priests," "Patriot Pastors," and other "patriots" willing to conform to the New Church and support the Three-Self Movement. Father Gerbier, a French missionary who remained at his post until 1954, relates the words of a Communist official who was an apostate Christian, as reported in *L'osservatore romano* for January 31, 1955:

We consider Chinese priests as a social value, which, far from wanting to destroy we want on the contrary to retrieve. In general they have a good education and are accustomed to severe discipline. . . . Once we have freed them from their foreign preceptors, we hope to retrieve the priests easily and use them with profit in the social field. We shall send them to re-education camps to change their brain. . . . And when this is changed, those priests will become ardent promoters of the new order. Their first task will then be to change the brains of the faithful who like themselves have gone astray after Christ.

Chairman of the Three-Self Movement is Dr. Y. T. Wu, a religious leader who became a Marxist and found it easy to follow the broad way and the wide gate leading to collaboration with Red China's atheist rulers. Dr. Wu studied under the Rev. Dr. Reinhold Niebuhr at Union Theological Seminary in New York. He is perhaps China's outstanding example of how religious spokesmen can be used by Marxist dictators to lead the believing sheep into the Red barns of captivity. He constantly denounces the devout and dedicated men and women of many Christian faiths who came as missionaries to China, calling them representatives of "imperialist societies." Dr. Francis P. Jones, long-time missionary in China until 1951, author of *The Church in Communist China,* quotes Wu as saying:

"As to how much innate evil there is in man's nature, what percentage of man's total nature it amounts to, and whether it can ever be eradicated—such metaphysical questions as these we have no time for. Let the anti-Communist Western theologians impale themselves on the horns of their own dilemma." Dr. Jones comments: "As for him (Wu), the Communist government looks so good that there can be no problem of church-state relationships."

It is quite certain that this man, claiming to be a Christian leader, would never have been selected for the head of the Red-sponsored Three-Self Movement if the Communist government of China had not looked "so good" to him.

One of Dr. Wu's associates in the Three-Self Movement is Kiang Wenhan, who also studied under Dr. Niebuhr at Union Theological Seminary. He is secretary of the Shanghai YMCA.

The extent to which such leaders of Christian activities can be drawn into the net of Communist collaboration and support is in evidence in all of Kiang's writings. He affirms that the Red regime of China is a good government, and that "the higher standards of living and morality" among his people have made for improved opportunities for religion. Dr. Jones quotes Kiang's explanation of his attitude toward the Mao dictatorship:

We do not oppose the People's Republic, because a government which serves the people ought not to be opposed. We admit that it would be a compromise of Christian principles were we to be complacent toward a government which was aggressive abroad and oppressive at home, but it is not a compromise when we support a government that is truly peaceful and conciliatory abroad, and earnest in its attack on poverty and exploitation at home.*

Whether Kiang would include the Red Chinese sanguinary aggressions in Korea, Tibet, India, and southeast Asia as "truly peaceful and conciliatory abroad" is not known. But it seems certain that this religious leader does not care to stand up for religious principles to the extent of suffering for them.

We can never forget the man who was serving as janitor in a little Methodist chapel in the heart of Hong Kong, when we visited that city of opportunity and stagnation, of hope and despair, in 1955. This Chinese was a doctor of philosophy in education, and had been a well-known and honored teacher in an institution of higher learning in Shanghai. He had escaped just ahead of what would have been certain death on false charges of "spying for the American government"—actually for being active in a church that had been the spiritual home for many Americans living in the city. Pausing in his humble task of cleaning and dusting the interior of the little place of worship, he told us sadly:

"Yes, I had to leave. I would rather be a janitor in this chapel all the rest of my life, and enjoy my mental and spiritual freedom, than to live in luxury under a godless tyranny!"

CHAPTER THIRTEEN

YOUTH MUST BE CAPTURED

One Sunday morning during the second session of the Ecumenical Council in Rome in autumn 1963, on invitation of a Catholic bishop from one of the eastern European countries now held captive by a puppet Soviet regime, we visited a small seminary on the outskirts of the Eternal City. The Bishop was holding services for the twenty boys, average age about sixteen, who were there studying for the priesthood. Some of the lads were sons of refugees from Marxist persecution.

"We must save our youth for religion," the Bishop told us earnestly. "It will be difficult, but it must be done if faith is to survive. I know personally how the Communist authorities have stepped up their campaign to prevent all religious influences from reaching our children and young people. It is their hope that they can create a whole generation of atheists, and thus strengthen their crusade to bury the whole free world."

In West Berlin we talked to Dr. Friedrich Wunderlich, bishop of the Methodist Church in Germany, who is permitted to perform his spiritual duties, on a strictly limited basis, in East Berlin and the entire Soviet Zone. "Our youth are the special target of the Marxist crusade against religion," the bishop declared. "In scores of ways the atheist leaders make it difficult for young people to attend worship. They harass the parents, deny religious youth their right to a higher education, and force young people to work or attend Communist lectures on Sunday. The Red regime expects to win its political and economic goals by weaning children away from religion."

Professor John Allen Moore, of the Baptist Theological Seminary at Zurich, Switzerland, who has contacts with religious leaders of many faiths in the Soviet captive countries of eastern Europe, summarized the matter for us in these words:

"It is clear that Marxist regimes all over the world have decided that the most effective way to eradicate religion is to capture the youth for materialistic atheism."

Worshiping in a Protestant service in one of those captive countries in late 1963, we noted only one boy and one girl under eighteen in the congregation. About 75 per cent of the worshipers were mature or elderly: from sixty years old and upward. The remainder were young adults. The pastor of that church commented sadly:

> Our authorities know that the older believers will soon be gone, so the elders do not matter any more. "Let them die! We'll capture the youth!" the Communist leaders say. And I must tell you American friends: This is the greatest challenge that believers, of all faiths and creeds, face in this life-and-death struggle to preserve religion and with it human freedom.

Youth early became a target of the Marxist rulers in their attacks upon religion. In 1921 Nikolai Lenin established in Petrograd a "seminary" to teach atheism as a special project for the Komsomol (Communist Union of Youth). Members of this group were pressed into antireligious meetings and conferences. Parades burlesquing religion were organized regularly, particularly upon feast days and other occasions of religious significance. Every possible effort was made to mock and humiliate religious believers in the eyes of young people.

"Children are the monopoly of the State," Lenin declared. His dictum has been faithfully parroted by every Communist leader since.

Time after time in Marxist publications the determination of Red leaders to create future godless generations has been given expression. "A young man or woman cannot be a Communist youth unless he or she is free of religious connections. If a Communist youth goes to church or engages in religious superstitions he cannot remain in good standing with the People or the party," said *Komsomol Pravda* (*Young Communist Truth*) in a series of articles in October 1947, preparing youth for atheism in the eastern European countries.

The recently announced campaign to eradicate all "vestiges" of religion in the Soviet Union and all other areas of Marxist rule betrays the desperate situation faced by these devotees of dialectical materialism. Religion is the only enemy they have not been able to subjugate and control. Private property has been all but abolished; production, transportation, distribution, sales, social and cultural life: all have come under the yoke of monolithic governmental control. But religion remains a force that all the bludgeonings of persecutions and restrictions have failed to exterminate.

"Therefore," say the Marxists, "let us strike its roots—in the minds of the young!"

The campaign to strike the roots of religion is a club with these three cruel spikes:

1. *Prohibitions and restrictions upon religious influences affecting children and youth are being intensified.*

From the beginning of the Communist regime in the Soviet Union to the present, all Marxist governments have attempted to enforce this rule: Children and youth under eighteen must not attend religious services or receive religious instruction.

In Article 59 of the constitution of the USSR the matter is spelled out thus: "The performances of religious rites and ceremonies is restricted to believers themselves; and the proselytizing of new cadres of working people, especially children, to become adherents of a church is punishable."

A section of the Soviet Law on Cults is worded: "The teaching of religion is prohibited in all state, municipal, and private schools as well as in boarding schools, kindergartens, etc."

The most effective stroke to implement this policy was the closing of parochial schools of Orthodox, Protestant, Catholic, and all other faiths, and the reopening of those selected for Communist use under ownership and control of the government. How the complete secularization and control of education was accomplished was well illustrated in Poland, a predominantly Catholic country, after the Communist seizure. It is described by Dr. Albert Galter thus:

Every religious influence was eliminated from the schools. Gradually prayers were abolished. The time for religious instruction was reduced, and in the higher schools it was suppressed. Religious feast days were replaced by Party demonstrations. A campaign was organized to have the crucifixes removed from the classrooms. Within the schools every activity was forbidden to the religious associations. Whenever possible more direct action was taken against religion by means of antireligious school organizations, whose role it is to take an interest in workers' children, "so that they may be educated in the Marxist spirit." *

As though to prove that all Marxist methods to crush the liberties of the people follow the same pattern, Fidel Castro in Cuba canceled the "officialized" status of Catholic schools, then placed more and more restrictions upon them until full nationalization was completed in 1961. Meanwhile, Protestant schools were gradually given the same treatment.

A Castro decree of February 23, 1959 required that all teacher appointments made since 1955 be voided, so that the vacancies could be filled by persons friendly to the Revolution. An act of July 29, 1959 gave "exclusive jurisdiction to the Minister of Education," not only to select all textbooks, but also to sell them or make them available free to all schools.

"With complete ownership and control of the schools, with employment only of teachers loyal to Communist ideology, and with textbooks all slanted to praise and support the Marxist line, the Reds have it all their way in shaping the thinking of children and youths, including indoctrination in atheism," a former Cuban school administrator, now a refugee, told us.

The Law on "Registration for Religious Education" in Hungary says, "Religious education shall be given as a freely elected subject in the general schools and the general high schools." But so many restrictions are placed upon such registration that the words "freely elected" become a huge farce. The actual operation of the law is characterized thus by Dr. William Solyom-Fekete of the Library of Congress Eastern European Law Division:

Although the wording of the Decree may lead to the conclusion that it promotes religious education, *actually almost every one of its provisions lends itself for the opposite purpose.* The Decree places religious education and religion teachers under the censorship of government agencies by requiring teachers and supervisors to obtain special permission from the local councils. It bans every kind of religious education in churches or on other church premises. It does not forbid the exercise of "friendly persuasion" against parents by school principals, employers, Communist party secretaries, and other authorities in regard to the mistake that parents are shown to be making if they decide to enroll their children for religious education. There are various indications showing that, as a result, religious education in schools is practically nonexistent.*

Every conceivable roadblock is erected by Red regimes to prevent the participation of young people in religious activities, whether in churches, in the homes, or in the communities. After the uprising of East German workers on June 17, 1953, the Marxist puppet dictator Walter Ulbricht declared: "Youth must be forced to embrace a politico-scientific, fundamentally systematic outlook on culture, and more especially the natural sciences, against the reactionary influences of the Church and the Clergy."

In Ulbricht's drab and dreary Soviet satrapy today, the right to give children religious instruction is "guaranteed," but such instruction must be given only during the very early hours of the morning, and under other conditions almost impossible to be met by normal family life. Parents and pastors who give religious teaching must reckon with frequent interruptions and humiliations from school authorities, nearly all of them card-carrying Communists.

One of the Protestant pastors in East Germany told us of his experience in applying for a permit to hold an Easter procession.

"Why do you want to hold this procession?" the local commissar demanded to know.

"It is a part of the celebration of Easter," the pastor answered.

"Rubbish, Comrade! Now, will there be children in this procession?"

The pastor said he supposed so. The commissar exploded in anger. "You know that children under eighteen are not allowed— I mean not encouraged—to receive religious instruction! Outside the church it is strictly forbidden. I'll recommend your application, provided no children under eighteen are included."

The pastor said he would have to accept that condition and asked how soon he might receive the permit.

"It may take quite some time," the bureaucrat answered. "You see, it will have to be approved by higher authority."

Some two weeks later the pastor returned to the bureau and inquired about the permit.

"Ah, Herr Pastor," the smiling commissar greeted him. "I am so sorry, but our bureau chief has gone on his spring vacation. He will not be back until after Easter!"

2. *A massive campaign of education and indoctrination in atheism is under way.*

Throughout the worldwide community of Marxist empires, a positive program to teach atheism to the impressionable minds of children and youths has been launched and is now in full swing. The campaign is relied upon as a most important factor to eradicate the "vestiges" of religious belief among future generations.

Purpose and hope of the program was well stated by Wladyslaw Gomulka, President of the "People's Republic" of Poland, on November 13, 1962, in an address to the Polish National Congress of Lay School Society, representing 12,000 institutions and 250,000 members. Gomulka said:

"Teachers must concentrate in the years to come on winning all parents to harmonious cooperation with schools and to the ideas of Socialist education, based on the firm foundations of the nonreligious scientific world outlook and secular morality."

At this same meeting Witold Jarosinski, an official in the Polish Ministry of Education, told the delegates: "The Communist party attaches much weight to the activity of the Lay School Society and to the present Congress. The party expects early results from the work of the Society in freeing the minds of children from religious superstition."

To further the intensified drive to capture the youth for atheistic communism in the USSR, an Institute of Scientific Atheism has been established in the Academy of Social Sciences of the Central Committee of the Communist party. According to the March 2, 1964 issue of *Pravda,* the Institute will have these important duties:

"To co-ordinate and conduct research work in the field of

atheism, train cadres of the highest quality, elaborate upon the actual problems of scientific atheism, convene All-Union scholarly conferences and creative seminars, and organize contacts abroad with atheistic institutions."

Stripped of its Marxist verbiage, the Institute is being used to train teachers to teach atheism, and to see that education in atheism is pushed to the ends of the earth.

Today in all Soviet Union universities and colleges, selected students in the departments of history and philosophy specialize in "the problems of scientific atheism." Moscow and Kiev universities, for example, have departments of "scientific atheism." Principles of both the Jewish and Christian faith are "analyzed and exposed."

The "ideological department" of industry and agriculture (meaning propaganda training courses in those subjects), under direct supervision of the Central Committee of the Communist party, have been directed to organize permanent courses for training lecturers and writers on atheism, and for teaching instructors in atheism in high schools and seminaries.

A course of studies on "Principles of Scientific Atheism" has been introduced in the higher Correspondence School of the Central Committee, in the Central School of Communist Youth, and other party schools. The plan calls for special emphasis upon Communist youth organizations, since their members are to be used as "training cadres for political education." To be sure that no group is neglected in atheist training, the directive dealing with the new atheistic training program states:

It is desirable to organize seminaries for workers and activists of the party, Soviets for central and local administration, Communist youth organizations, and trade unions; also courses for teachers, physicians, workers in kindergartens, teachers of vocational training schools, journalists, administrative workers, chairmen of women's councils, members of house committees, and councils of pensioners.

The modernized program of atheist instruction consists of twenty-four lessons and twelve lectures, a seminar, and an examination: a program accorded the most important subjects in Soviet high schools. One should bear in mind that Russian high school students do not automatically continue through high school. They must secure passing grades, and failure will oust them from school. The importance of atheistic training to the Red authorities and the need for students to be expert in knowledge of atheism are pointed up by the fact that if a student fails in the exam on atheism he is dropped from the school.

Recruiting of students for "atheist clubs" has been stepped up during recent years. The Young Atheists Club in Moscow lists 1,000 members. The clubs sponsor lectures on atheism, excursions to atheistic museums, and most important, according to the youth journal *Komsomol Pravda,* the clubs "protect young people from religious poison."

A NEW MEANING FOR CHRISTMAS

Departments of education in all the colonies of the Soviet Union have faithfully followed the party line and established similar training facilities and personnel for the intensified drive to replace religion with atheism. Communist teachers are trained to present religion to the children and youth as superstition, prejudice, and "reactionary treason against the People's government."

A report from Sofia, Bulgaria, discusses the methods used in that country to teach atheism as a regular subject in all schools: "One typical slogan in a first-grade textbook reads: 'God—who is that? Can you see him? Can you hear him? No. Is God dressing you and feeding you? No. It is not God. It is the Communist party.'"

The Red regime of Romania, through the "Society for the Dissemination of Science and Culture," has published a new series of brochures for use by teachers and parents in denouncing religious beliefs and extolling atheism. Here are some of the titles: "Adam and Eve, Are They Our Ancestors?" "When and Why Did Religion Appear?" "The Origins of Christianity." "The Anthology of Atheism in Romania." "The Bible in Pictures." All these publications, slanted toward impressionable youth, are veritable blasphemies and caricatures of Holy Scripture and history.

To make their hold on youths more secure, Red governments generally have increased the time children must stay in school.

In East Germany, for example, according to a report from Berlin by Religious News Service, many schools now operate on a nine-hour daily schedule. When Ulbricht's puppet regime, through his Ministry of Education, announced the extended school time, Protestant and Roman Catholic leaders joined to express grave concern over the measure. They pointed out that under the new system pupils would remain the entire day under the influence of Marxist-Leninist ideology. Says the Berlin report:

"Church leaders said the full-day education schedule would deprive the young people of any possibility of an independent development outside of Communist indoctrination and would destroy formative influences of the home. Protestants and Catholics denounced the plan as atheistic in character and a violation of freedom of religion and the rights of parents."

To eradicate all references to religion in family and community life, religious holidays have been abolished in Communist countries, except in areas where too much resistance was expected, and there they have been "converted" into national holidays.

In Hungary, for instance, St. Stephen's Day became "Constitution Day," on which the glories of Communist "guarantees" are celebrated, with emphasis upon programs and special lectures for school children. Christmas became the "Feast of the Pines," and in the celebration the Christ Child is never mentioned.

In the USSR and some of the captive countries Christmas was traditionally celebrated on January 7. Every imaginable effort is made to wipe out from the minds of children and youth all ideas that Christmas has any religious significance. In fact, the actual celebration has been moved back to the January 1 holiday. Instead of Santa Claus, the gifts are distributed by *Ded Moroz:* "Grandfather Frost." Dressed much the same as the European St. Nicholas and adorned with the same white beard, he is rather an awesome character to Russian children. When he is mentioned at all in Soviet storybooks, this Soviet Santa Claus is represented as a good fellow who inspires and requires "hard work" from Soviet children. At gala children's performances, boys and girls from families that can afford the tickets see *Ded Moroz* in person at the beginning of the show. He lectures them on good Communist behavior.

Through Soviet planning, the whole Christmas season in the USSR has been turned into a gay holiday period completely devoid of any religious meaning. January 1 is the focal point of their festivities. By January 7 the fancy decorations have been torn down, the "Christmas" trees carted away, and the drabness of Soviet life has returned to homes and communities.

There is no room in the Marxist atheistic State to give any meaning to the observance of Christmas, or to any other day of religious significance.

SOAP OPERA AND OTHER TECHNIQUES

Religious ordinances of all faiths are constantly held up to ridicule by every possible medium of information and propaganda in Communist lands. Observance of the Feast of the Passover is frequently referred to as a cloak "to cover speculations by Jewish reactionaries." An important item in the intensified drive to keep religion from youth is the secularization of marriage, impressing upon young people that there is no religious significance to it. Civil marriage rites are required by the authorities in all Marxist countries, even though a couple has been united in church or home by a minister of religion.

Baptism is castigated as a menace to health. A broadcast from Moscow Radio on January 24, 1963 declared that "thousands of babies die of pneumonia every year, due to this senseless and dangerous rite." The broadcast mentioned the high incidence of weak hearts and weak lungs which result from baptism. It cited fantastic "statistics" to prove that in the time of the Tzars the life expectancy of Russian people was only 32 years, "due to religion being widespread." Now, so the commentator asserted, "life expectancy in our glorious Soviet homeland is up to 69 years—largely because of our health services and the fact that fewer baptisms take place."

Moving pictures, radio and television programs are used constantly in the USSR and Marxist colonial areas to educate youth in atheism and to portray religion as the enemy of the people. *Komsomol Pravda,* organ of the Young Communist League, resorts to soap opera techniques to spread its propaganda. It uses a film studio in Moscow to make antireligious short subjects to be shown before feature films in movie houses.

Here is a typical plot, used in one of these "shorts": The "hero" is named V. Myashnikov, and his wife Masha. They live in a small town in the Ural mountains. The husband is quite happy until he begins to suspect "something religious" in his wife's frequent visits to her mother, who is an evangelical believer.

Myashnikov's suspicions, so the story goes, are confirmed when he cleans the house in anticipation of Masha's return from the hospital, where she has given birth to a fine, healthy baby. He finds a Bible and a golden cross hidden behind a wardrobe. Here is ample evidence of the "criminal activities" of his wife!

The plot develops quickly. Masha takes the baby to her mother's home. She returns to report that the baby has contracted "inflammation of the lungs." Myashnikov is convinced that the baby's illness is the result of christening—and how often have the people been warned that pneumonia follows baptism! To make matters worse, Masha takes the baby to her pastor for a blessing, instead of taking the child to a hospital. Two days later the baby dies. The story ends when Myashnikov sues for divorce on the grounds that religion has ruined their family life.

The studio producing the atheist films, called the Scientific Film Organization, acts on the principle that it is vital that atheistic movies be seen by believers and not just by those converted to atheism. Among its "shorts" running from ten to fifteen minutes are comedies ridiculing superstitions the producers claim are associated with religion. One tells of a young priest who gave up religion after the Soviet Union's scientific achievement in sending a man into space. Other films, written as comedy, "expose" the activities of the Jehovah's Witnesses and various Pentecostalist sects, all of which are outlawed in the Soviet Union.

A steady stream of books for young readers, sponsored by the Academy of Science, criticizes and pokes fun at Jewish ritual. It assails the "reactionary essence of Judaism," and tells how Judaism has been "adapted to capitalist conditions." The books give similar treatment to all other cults, usually selecting for heaviest ridicule some major theme sacred to the particular believers.

In response to a book defaming the Jewish faith, protests arose from Jewish leaders in many areas of the free world. In answer to the protests, Moscow Radio beamed an English-language broadcast to the United States. The commentator declared, presumably with a straight face: "No one in the USSR is persecuted because of his race. No one is persecuted because of his religion. No one is imprisoned because of his faith. Jews are treated like all other people and some hold very high government posts or are generals in the Army."

Perhaps the low point in the depths of ignorance concerning the nature of religious belief was reached in the drive to win youth to atheism when *Komsomol Pravda* officially admonished the entire school system in the USSR to *use the Bible* in the war on religion. The proposal's author, Ivina Kichanova, said she felt that high schools should promote detailed studies of the Bible among students.

"By exposing the Bible to young people, they will learn its superstitions, illusions, and reactionary nature," she confidently wrote. "Thus we can win the cause for atheism."

In late 1972 (as these words are written) the condition of the people of Jewish faith in the Soviet Union is tragic indeed. Steadily, during the last decade, the noose of persecution has been tightened around their necks. All their synagogues have been closed, and they are allowed no cultural life because, the Kremlin says, Jewish religion and culture are "anti-Socialist."

The most recent persecution is the ransom demand of all Jews in the Soviet Union who desire to migrate to Israel. The "fees" required for visas to leave the country range from $5,000 to $25,000.

The result of this blatant persecution has been to shut off nearly all migration to Israel. The Kremlin excuse is that educated Jews are needed in the Soviet Union. The true reason is the regime's paranoid desire to hide the fact that anyone, of whatever condition or religious faith, would voluntarily seek to leave the Soviet "workers' paradise."

CHAPTER FOURTEEN

PUNISHMENTS AND REWARDS ARE READY

Whether the Marxists win the youth of their world to atheism depends upon the intelligence, skill, and vigor with which their crusade for ungodliness is opposed, in their own homelands and colonial empires, and throughout the free world.

We of that free world must decide upon a pattern of campaign, as clear in its purpose and as definite in its details as the crusade of the atheists. We are approaching that in this study. Meantime, the third cruel spike in the atheist club to bludgeon religious influences away from young people is this:

3. *Under Marxism, religious youth are punished; atheist youth are rewarded.*

Often a youth club is constantly harassed, which gives children and young people to understand that religion will handicap all their future activities.

Let us go (only in our thinking, of course) to the Workers' Paradise which Fidel Castro promised the people he so deplorably betrayed.

The lusty singing of the Spanish version of "Onward, Christian Soldiers" by a school busload of young people in Havana traffic one Sunday evening drew the attention of the police. With sirens howling they surrounded the bus, directed it to pull over to the curb, and entered to look the youths over and to ask why all the noise.

The young people were students at the Baptist Theological Institute of Western Cuba. Their spokesman told the police they

161

had taken part that day in services at a suburban church and were merely singing together as they rode home. And he added: "To express our joy as Christians."

"No more of that noise!" ordered the senior officer, as he motioned the driver to proceed. The police stayed on the bus until it reached the students' quarters. Then the officers made a thorough search of the dormitory and classrooms of the institute.

That was in 1961. From that night forward the seminary has been under constant surveillance by Castro's police and secret agents. The police demanded and obtained the names of all the young people enrolled at the institution. It is certain that the students are blacklisted by the authorities, and will be barred from entering any of the professions in the impoverished domain that was once free and prosperous Cuba.

The standard punishment given young people in all Marxist countries for attending worship or practicing religion in any form is forfeiture of the privilege of a higher education. This effectively blocks entry into teaching, law, engineering, and all other choice professions. It is the stoutest club held by the fanatical Communist atheists over the heads of children and their parents alike in the campaign to let religion die out with the elders. It will be depended upon increasingly in the intensified antireligious drive to create a godless generation, a population freed from religious "illusions" and thoroughly indoctrinated in Marxist atheism.

To further this crusade, Communist authorities pressure parents into preventing their young people from taking part in the ceremonies and ordinances sacred to believers. An outstanding example of this flagrant violation of freedom of conscience and worship is the outlawing of the sacrament of confirmation of youth and its replacement with a statist secular ceremony.

YOUTH: "CONFIRMED" IN ATHEISM

In East Germany the rite is called *Jugendweihe* (Youth Dedication). It is the formal dedication of youth to loyalty to the Communist government, and by inference, to atheism. All East German youngsters between twelve and sixteen years of age, of whatever faith their parents may have held or may still cling to, are supposed to go through the pagan ritual. About 88 per cent of all youths in this age bracket took part in the *Jugendweihe* ceremony during 1960. Failure to do so marked the youths—and their parents—for increased restrictions and harassments.

The ceremonies are colorful affairs, with hundreds of youths, boys and girls, massed before gaily decorated stands filled with the Communist dignitaries. Bands and orchestras play stirring music of Wagner or Beethoven. The young people raise their hands and recite the pledges. The most significant sentence in the Hitlerlike oath that takes the place of Christian confirmation is this:

"I swear to serve with all my heart and soul the cause of Socialism!"

Discussing this ritual, Dr. Adolph Schalk of Berlin informs us:

While both confessions, Catholic and Evangelical, have forthrightly condemned the ceremony and have forbidden participation in it, the greatest heroism is required on the part of parents to resist the "polite request" of party leaders to send their children to *Jugendweihe* ceremonies. Not only do they stand to lose their jobs if they do not comply, but their children are denied admittance to all schools of higher learning and all opportunities for advancement.

In one six-month period, more than 1,600 Protestant and Catholic teachers fled East Germany (before the Wall) to avoid making the moral compromise of encouraging their pupils to participate in *Jugendweihe*. Many lay leaders who actually did encourage youngsters to abstain, paid for their advice by spending several years in prison for "Interfering with the development of youth." *

Professor Bernhard Nuener, Director of the East German Central Pedagogy Institute, early in 1964 announced, with complete candor, that the Communist party attaches very great importance to the *Jugendweihe* ceremony because "the fourteen-year-olds of today are the builders of socialism and communism of tomorrow, and therefore must be brought into the fold of Marxism at an early age."

In all other captive countries of eastern Europe there are officially sponsored movements and organizations to take the place of former church activities for youth and to keep them from religious influences. The Romanian regime, for example, organized the "Young Pioneers," a regimented youth group that takes up so much time there is none left for any effective religious instruction at home. The combined efforts of government and the schools almost completely monopolizes the time of young people under Red regimes.

When Ghana, a West African nation, became independent under the late President Kwame Nkrumah, a Marxist dictator, a "Young Pioneer Movement" was established, teaching that Nkrumah had taken the place of God. A decree called for Young Pioneers to be set up in all public and private schools of the country. Young people belonging to the movement were taught such phrases as "Kwame Nkrumah does no wrong" and "Kwame Nkrumah never dies," along with ideologies that are plainly Marxist inspired.

Bishop Reginald R. Roseveare of Accra, head of the Anglican diocese in Ghana, has characterized the Young Pioneers Movement as a godless organization. In an address to the synod of his diocese, the Episcopal prelate said the movement was a shock to all true believers in religion, for its leaders were teaching that Nkrumah was a redeemer and was immortal. The leaders of Methodist and Presbyterian churches in Ghana have joined with Bishop Roseveare to protest to the government the decree forcing the organizing of the Young Pioneers in all the country's schools.

Steadily, methodically, the campaign to replace religious ceremonies and sacraments with atheist-slanted substitutes moves forward in Marxist countries. Always it is accompanied with threats of punishments for parents and children who do not conform, and implied favors for those who do. *Pravda* significantly refers to the program as "the implementation of Socialist forms of celebration of family events." All matters of religious significance affecting the families of believers are being secularized with prescribed "Socialist" forms.

A "Palace of Weddings" in Moscow furnishes a convenient and State approved place where marriages can be performed by a civil authority, without the "reactionary" influence of a superfluous priest, minister, or rabbi. Since its completion in 1959, so *Komsomol Pravda* reports, an average of about 16,000 couples a year have availed themselves of the Palace of Weddings, "in keeping with the spirit of the scientific age."

The March 1964 issue of Moscow's publication *Trud,* the Soviet trade journal, announced plans for the building of a "Palace of Baptism." Author of the *Trud* article was I. Bogdanov, Secretary of the Leningrad Industrial Region, who deplored the lack of such a facility in the past. He declared that the building will furnish a needed place to provide for "atheist christenings," without realizing, we suppose, the contradiction inherent in those two words.

FORWARD ON COUNTLESS FRONTS

Indoctrination of youth in atheism is the very heart of the intensified antireligious crusade in all Marxist lands. From 1959 the "seven-year program" to eliminate religion was pushed with new vigor. It slowed down with the coexistence policy adopted by Nikita Khrushchev, despite the almost frantic efforts of Communist authorities, led by Khrushchev himself, to pass the word to all the godless faithful that there simply can be *no ideological coexistence* with capitalist war-mongers, especially in matters of religion. Today the antireligious program moves forward on countless fronts, in varying degrees of severity.

The November 29, 1963 issue of *Pravda Vostoka,* the principal Communist organ in the Uzbek "Republic," reported that three Protestant women missionaries had just been sentenced to prison for two years in the town of Namangan. They were convicted of "organizing secret meetings of an unregistered Sect." Specifically, the most "criminal" of the three was charged as follows: "She had her granddaughter transcribe and distribute the texts of songs from books published in Tzarist times, so-called Baptist hymns, by means of which the character and world outlook of the girl were influenced."

In early February 1964 the puppet Red commissars of Leipzig, East Germany, demolished the tower of the famous *St. Johannes Kirche* which had survived the heavy bombing of World War II. The reason? So many young people were being told about the old church that had stood so long as a symbol of religious faith in that city. A report of the razing of the tower added: "Police barred all photographers from the demolition scene."

Youth in the armed services are not overlooked in the new

program of punishments for those that profess religion and rewards for good atheists. The Ulbricht Reds in East Germany bitterly denounced authorities of the Republic of Germany for agreement with church leaders to furnish chaplains for the defense units. "One more indication that the imperialist governments are preparing for war, and are exploiting religion in their warmongering!" scolded the Communist press.

A report from London to Religious News Service, dated February 20, 1964, states that personnel of the Polish armed forces are deluged with massive antireligious propaganda. In all military units of the country, the report disclosed, antireligious study courses are required. A government-sponsored atheist society has branches at all military centers, with young personnel in administrative charge who realize very well the advantages of cooperation with the program so far as their advancement is concerned. *Bandera,* official organ of the Polish Navy, during the twelve months of 1963 published 147 articles attacking religion. Especially vitriolic were the attacks upon the Second Ecumenical Council of the Vatican in Rome.

While the Soviet Union is far along in the program of eradicating religious influences among its children and youth, reports indicate that older young people, established in the professions, who attend worship are systematically hounded and harassed.

In May 1962 *Science and Religion* complained that "a university diploma is no guarantee of the atheism of its owner." To support the charge, this atheist organ published an article by a writer named N. Barykin, who drew particular attention to a physician in Kuibyshev, a large industrial community on the Volga River. The writer accused the physician, Dr. Nikolay Shmurov, of being "an ardent evangelical" and very active in a local church.

Barykin said that when he tried to interview the physician, Dr. Shmurov rebuffed him with the remark, "We have nothing to talk about. You are an atheist, I am a religious believer." The writer said that when he persisted in trying to find out how it was possible for a doctor to combine his scientific knowledge with a belief in religion, the physician again rebuffed him. Barykin conceded that the doctor "works well and it is difficult to reproach him for any professional blunders."

"But how is it possible to cure people in the daytime and go to church in the evening?" the writer asked, in wonderment.

WANTED: GOOD ATHEIST SCIENTISTS

The numerous rewards for becoming active supporters of the Marxist regime, which means good atheists as well, are very tempting. Most outstanding, since the space age began with the launching of the first Soviet sputnik, are the promises of scholarships for budding scientists and engineers. To become an astronaut is now the crowning ambition of millions of boys—and girls—in the USSR.

At a great rally of the Komsomol, Russia's youth corps, in Moscow in July 1963, Sergie P. Pavlov, first secretary of the militant youth organization, assailed educators and others for ignoring their duty to stamp out religious ideas among young people and to teach "active atheism." He warned against youth being drawn "into religious nets, such as are set by Orthodox, Catholic, and other sects," by such activities as hikes, singing popular songs, and playing games. Such things were more dangerous than arguments by religious leaders, Pavlov said.

Then to clinch the idea that being good atheists can lead to great honors, the First Secretary introduced the woman astronaut, Valentina Tereshkova: "And she is an active member of the Komsomol!" he declared, as a great ovation to this famous young woman began.

A choice reward for students willing to adopt Marxist principles is offered youth in parts of the free world still underdeveloped, in the form of scholarships for four years of specialized study in Communist countries. Asian and African students are the choice target of this project.

Typical of the treatment accorded such students was that recounted by a young Nigerian, Audu Kwasau Abashiya, who was given a scholarship for study in Bulgaria. Arrangements were made by the Nigerian Trade Union Congress, a pro-Communist organization. Abashiya is a Protestant believer and received his primary education in a mission school. He attended the Federal Science School at Lagos, Nigeria, for his premedical courses. With several other Nigerian students he reached Sofia in March 1962.

One year of study under Bulgarian Marxist tutors was all he needed to be surfeited with Communist indoctrination and with the discrimination he and his fellows met because of their race. He left Bulgaria, he says, "Because I did not want to live in a country that asked me to denounce my own country and where black people are not treated like white people." After leaving Bulgaria, Abashiya related in Vienna:

From childhood my ambition was to be a medical doctor. The Bulgarian language took me three intensive months of study, but meantime I had to learn about Lenin, Marx, and Engels too. This was only the beginning of my Communist indoctrination. My faculty warned that to know Lenin's teachings is a necessity for all good doctors.

Public lectures were arranged for me to condemn my government, which I rejected. I was taken on tour to speak bad of my government and the Western powers in Nigeria. The Communist leaders were not happy when I told the people of the number of universities, hospitals, and factories we have in Nigeria. Radio Sofia wanted me to broadcast only about British and American exploitation in Nigeria. The Communists do not like to hear that a free country has any universities and hospitals.

We used to stop medical classes to see Russian professors and cosmonauts who gave us lectures on the success of communism. Textbooks for our subjects had been out of print for ten years, so we had to borrow from other graduates. Those of us who went to the American legation library were called "imperialist agents." Bulgarians who came with us were called "Fascists."

We had to spend so much time on political indoctrination and classes on Marxism-Leninism that little was left for medicine. We were told that only Communist scientists could be *good* scientists. Six hours a week were thus spent on Communist propaganda, and in the evenings, instead of being allowed to study medicine, we had to hold discussions on communism again.

As a Christian I was in the habit of attending services every Sunday. In order not to get the pastors of the churches into trouble, I had to go from one to the other so that my constant attendance in one would not be noticed by the secret police.

After attending the all-African Student Conference in Belgrade last August, we Nigerians felt the necessity of founding a federated union in Bulgaria of all the national unions of students. The Bulgarian government at first agreed. Later we discovered that the officers would be imposed on us by the government, so we refused and elected the ones we wanted. This brought about the arrest of our leaders. We decided to quit Bulgaria—having learned the true nature of communism! *

Recruiting Young Women for "Literacy"

How a Marxist government "substitutes" secular activities for religious callings is well illustrated in Fidel Castro's darkest Cuba. Many dedicated young women taught and worked in the church-related schools and orphanages of that island before this despot came to power. When such institutions were closed by the bearded ruler, along with the great majority of the churches, these young women were thrown out of employment.

The hope for new, interesting work was held out for them by an official announcement that the government would sponsor a special project. It was described as "a campaign for literacy." Numbers of young women, preferably in their early twenties, would be needed as instructors and supervisors, Castro's education ministry announced.

The response was most gratifying. Educated Cubans have long hoped that every child and youth in the nation could have elementary education. They knew that many people in the rural districts, and especially in the mountain areas, had little or no opportunity to go to school. It has been recognized in Cuba that much of that island's poverty could be eliminated if all the people could be taught to read, write, and cipher. So hundreds of young women answered the call for teachers to help in the campaign for literacy. Here, they thought, was a humanitarian project designed to enlist the best-educated and most high-minded citizens of the country.

All volunteers were asked to report on a certain day at a convenient headquarters in their own communities. They were registered and interviewed, then told to return home until they were given further instructions. Two or three weeks later they were ordered to report to a transportation center to go to Veradero Beach, a resort area with excellent hotel facilities, for two weeks of orientation as literacy teachers. With enthusiasm, small hordes of well-bred, idealistic young women reported for training.

The training center was well chosen. Deluxe accommodations and exhilarating atmosphere caused the volunteers to feel they were selected for a great crusade on behalf of their fatherland. Then came the first shock for all of them. Instead of studying techniques for teaching the illiterate, the eager volunteers were pressed into indoctrination courses in Marxist materialism. It was apparent that the instructors were dedicated Communists. Many had studied in Soviet training centers. The more sophisticated young women recognized that they had been duped and on one pretext or another they went home.

Those who remained were taken in groups, always supervised by a Communist military leader, into the more remote and lonely areas of the country. There they had to endure more Marxist indoctrination. The leaders had two responsibilities for them: to watch for counterrevolutionary attitudes, and to destroy all attachments to a former way of life.

Before long there appeared at the camps a number of "assistants" in the program: young men who were dedicated Communists. The young women were encouraged to make close friendships with these willing helpers. In strange surroundings, far from home, and under constant dosages of Communist theory, many of the lonely young women found themselves overwhelmed with ideas of free love.

The term "campaign for literacy" soon became synonymous with the word *prostitution*. Very few of the volunteers ever taught anyone to read and write. Many returned home pregnant. Thus blackmailed into identifying themselves with the Communist movement, large numbers of these young Cuban women suffered disgrace among their families and the friends in their communities.

THEY OFFERED A CHOICE

A church leader referred us to a young immigrant from an eastern European country whom he called Joseph Bensz, an engineer, who could tell us about life behind the iron curtain. In response to our questions about the treatment of young people who practice religion in his native land, Joseph said:

"Well, let me illustrate the matter by telling you of my friend in the old country. I'll call him Jon, to protect him and his family. His case is typical of all others relating to youth under Communist regimes."

Joseph related that Jon's parents were devout people, and despite harassments because of their church attendance they continued to worship in the only Protestant church open in their town of about 150,000.

Jon was their only child, and a "normal" lad. During the first term of his secondary schooling he led his class in math and science courses. He wanted to be an engineer, and his teachers encouraged him in his ambition. Without thinking too much about it, Jon's parents took him occasionally with them to church. One day they were visited by three members of the scholarship committee of the local schools.

"You have a smart boy there, your Jon," the committee spokesman began. "We have our eyes on him. What career would he like to follow?"

"Oh, he wants very much to be an engineer," replied the father.

"Very well. We shall be glad to recommend him for a scholarship." The parents thanked the men heartily. This was glad news for them. Since engineers rank high in the Communist nations, it would be a good life for Jon. As the visitors rose to go, the spokesman said:

"By the way, Comrade. We have been informed that your son has been seen in church with you. We are sure you did not realize the seriousness of burdening him with religious superstitions—that is, if he is to be an engineer and be of use to our People's government. We trust that you understand that the scholarship depends upon your taking proper action."

At this point Joseph paused in his narrative, and we asked him what the parents decided to do. He was silent for a moment, then replied:

"They decided to leave it up to me. *I* was that young man." He told us more about his family, and continued:

I decided to accept the scholarship. In due course I was apprenticed to an engineer on a freighter steamship—the hardest, dirtiest kind of work. I did not mind the hard work, but I grew sick and tired of the daily Communist indoctrination and their silly, lying propaganda. Always they denounced the Church and the United States. That is why I took the first chance to escape. Now I am both an engineer and a free man!

CHAPTER FIFTEEN

ATHEISM'S BATTLE IS INTENSIFIED

"We will bury you! Your grandchildren will live under communism!"

So said Nikita S. Khrushchev, during his visit to the United States in 1959. Did he really mean that "we," the Marxist camp of atheistic governments, would preside at the burial (after the demise, we assume) of "you," the governments of free and democratic peoples?

Apologists for communism were quick to declare that the Soviet visitor was "speaking allegorically," and what he really meant was that the Marxist system would successfully compete with the "capitalist" system.

"He couldn't have meant that communism would bury our way of life after he saw with his own eyes the productivity, good wages, and high standards of living in the United States," one wishful commentator wrote.

Another deep thinker on public affairs gave out with this puerile comment: "Surely Mr. Khrushchev could not have meant what he said since he was so pleasant during his visit. Why, if one would place a white wig and whiskers on him, with a red suit, he would look just like Santa Claus!"

Let heaven be thanked that persons blissfully ignorant of the true nature, purpose, and methods of the Marxist worldwide conspiracy do not constitute a majority either in official or private life. Why should not Dictator Khrushchev have been pleasant on his visit to the United States? It was a supreme moment in his life. It brought him out upon the stage of international affairs with the full light of favorable publicity playing about his head. It put all his captive peoples on notice that their captor was an honored guest in the country he brands with every breath as his chief enemy. There he was, foremost in the news of all persons of the globe, being wined and dined, and fawned upon by many important citizens, some of them educators and industrialists, products of the American freedoms that the Communists plan to bury.

Let no person in his right mind assume that Khrushchev was not in firm, deadly earnest in his remark about buying the free world. He did not use allegories and oblique references when speaking about non-Communist governments and peoples. He reverted to his true self during that visit when in the United Nations he took off a shoe, pounded the desk, cursed, and otherwise acted like an atheist Marxist barbarian.

All Communist dictators have had, and still have, this abiding unchanging aim: to overcome the "capitalist" governments and impose the rule of the proletariat revolution upon them, in whatever time may be necessary, by whatever means available now and in the future.

The only change the American visit may have made in the opinions of Dictator Khrushchev was to extend the time it might take to prepare the capitalist world for burial. His impressions doubtless prompted him to borrow some of the hated capitalist methods of production, particularly in agriculture, since he saw a people rolling in surplus foods while his own slave-driven peons were hungry.

One other change in Khrushchev's attitude soon became apparent: since it would take a longer time than formerly thought needed by Marxist global planners to soften up the capitalist world and—as Lenin said—let it "drop like a ripe plum into the Communist basket," a policy of coexistence was called for. A breathing spell was needed, to allow time to consolidate gains and overcome the effects of setbacks.

Coexistence with the enemies of Marxism—for how long? A decade? A century? It does not matter how long to the Marxist leaders. The true answer is this: so long as it takes to strengthen the Communist bloc and weaken the free nations. Certainly Khrushchev had in mind when he visited the United States, and still remembers, the cynical remark of his tutor, Joseph Stalin:

"Give the stupid capitalists the shovels and they will dig their own graves!"

They Made Considerable "Progress"

By the year 1957, Marxist leaders had chalked up a measure of solid success in their relentless program of choking religion to death. In the Communist homeland of Soviet Russia, in the quisling regimes of the captive countries, and in Red China, atheism could measure its success by the following score card:

State control over churches and religious organizations was complete. Official agencies were well established to hold the administration of religious affairs in a firm grip. In the USSR it is the Council for Cults, in Czechoslovakia the Government Bureau for Church Affairs, in Bulgaria the Directorate for Religious Denominations. Whatever the name and country, the Marxist State had unquestioned authority over religion and could set the conditions for its functioning.

From 1957 there have been few changes in the basic legal status of religious bodies, so let us move to the present tense and note in outline the major items in the suppression of religious freedom:

Registration required of all religious bodies. This naturally follows State control. Registration includes the designation of the congregation, often with a complete roster of members with their addresses, ages, and occupations, for the constant scrutiny of the secret police. The executive officers of all religious organizations must be nationals, which makes impossible hierarchical administration and extension of programs of spiritual concern into other lands. Thus churches are *dependent* upon the State. They exist constantly under a Sword of Damocles. At the whim of a commissar the sword can fall with the revocation of the permit to use the building of worship—the usual method for closing a church or synagogue.

Ministers and responsible officers must be licensed. Here again is a provision necessary for complete State control of religion. Priests, ministers, rabbis: all must carry cards permitting them to hold divine services. Sermons, pastoral letters and circulars, reports and recommendations, all are censored. Thus the minister serves at the will and pleasure of the regime from local bureaucrat to top control agency of the government. One "mistake," such as a remark in a sermon critical of official policies or actions, can mean immediate and permanent forfeiture of the license.

Church finances are strictly controlled. All money for the support of the religious body, received and expended, must be accounted for to the authorities, in every Marxist country. Generally the support of religious bodies must depend upon irregular collections. This prevents orderly budgeting and planning for adequate financing. "Regular membership fees are prohibited and their collection is punishable," says the code for the USSR Ministry of Cults. Churches are heavily taxed, and the power of taxation is an executioner's ax always handy.

In several countries, as in Czechoslovakia, the government even pays the salaries of priests, ministers, and other church officers. This makes firm the general prohibition against creating any funds to assist needy members or to propagate the faith in any manner. Congregations cannot own, buy, or sell property. No money can be sent out of the country for missionary or other religious purposes, nor may endowments for charitable purposes be created.

Individual believers are objects of discrimination. "We took our children out of Sunday school and church services when I learned I would lose my job if we didn't," a workman in a town under Communist rule told us, and his remark expresses the situation clearly. Uniformly, religion is prohibited to young people under eighteen. Any parent who ignores this rule is under constant suspicion of disloyalty. Any youth who defies this provision cannot get higher education, nor enter the professions and public services. "Practicing" religion elsewhere than in places of worship is forbidden. In some countries, believers cannot change their denominational membership without official permission.

BETTER TOOLS TO BURY RELIGION

Despite the "progress" in restricting religion to such extent that it was supposed to die off, religion did not die in the Marxist lands. It remained alive in the churches and synagogues still permitted to function, with worshipers crowding in to the services. It remained alive in the resistance of priests and ministers of all faiths who faced death rather than sell their souls to Communist cooperation. It remained alive in the hope of liberation from Communist enslavement that anchored the souls of the faithful to the solid rock of spiritual consolation.

In the late 1950's the Kremlin despots decided to face up to the problem. Religion simply refused to be buried. "So let us find better tools with which to bury it." said the Marxists, in effect. An intensified drive against religion was decided upon. It was heralded by a vigorous discussion in the Soviet publication with the innocent-sounding title of *Questions of Philosophy,* and contained these words:

"The broad expansion of antireligious propaganda is also hampered by the mistaken view held by a certain section of lecturers that religion will die out of its own accord. Religion is NOT dying out of its own accord. On the contrary, there is a partial revival of religion as a result of the relaxation of our struggle against it."

The challenge to step up the attack upon religion was dutifully taken up by propaganda organs in all the Soviet Union. The problem was turned over to a squad of planning experts. After nearly two years, in ponderous bureaucratic fashion the masterminds came up with a scheme for the new campaign to eradicate religion. It was built around two major projects:

First, a campaign of antireligious "information," based to a large extent upon slander and defamation of religious leaders, in order to discredit all persons connected with religion.

Second, renewed persecutions of the more "criminal" (meaning more anti-Communist) religious leaders and groups, but with enough restraint so as not to create sympathetic reactions among the faithful.

The renewed crusade got underway in the early summer of 1959. The attacks upon the characters of priests, ministers, rabbis, and other outstanding advocates of the faith was particularly odious. Since charges could not be openly based on the practice of religion, for fear on the part of authorities of being accused of persecution of religion, the atheist masterminds dragged out all sorts of laws and regulations which they used as pretexts for arrest of clergymen and lay workers.

Often the charges were for despicable offenses. Immorality, sex perversion, theft of church money, embezzlement: these ranked high on the list of antireligious weapons. The plan was shaped to destroy confidence in *all* religious leaders and faith in all sacraments and rites.

The charges of immorality began in July 1959 when a former Orthodox priest in Stalingrad (now changed to Volgograd), was induced by the authorities to betray his church and sacred calling. The priest wrote an open letter to Bishop Sergius of Astrakhan accusing him of appropriating hundreds of thousands of rubles for his personal enrichment. Added to this false charge was this defamation: the Bishop had "lived in sin with adopted daughters and nieces selected for him by a local monk." On July 3 the story was given prominence in the Ukrainian newspaper *Pravda Ukrainy.* On July 11 it appeared in the central newspaper *Sovetskaya Pravda* and two days later it was broadcast over the Moscow Home Service radio. The Bishop was arrested and sentenced to hard labor.

FROM THE CLOTH OF VICIOUS PROPAGANDA

The new drive against religion resulted in countless such attacks on the ministry for "immoral practices." *Soviet Lithuania* on October 10 carried an article describing the "scandalous life" of the monks at the Catholic Monastery of the Holy Spirit in Lithuania. Father Superior Antoni and Deacon Veniamin were denounced for homosexuality. Another priest was reported to have kept a diary of his many seductions.

On April 17, 1960, *Trud* levied a charge of homosexuality at the Russian Orthodox monastery at Zagorsk. "We have accidentally come into possession of the correspondence between two monks. The letters cannot be printed because they are one mass of indecent expressions," said the *Trud* writer. He stated that in the cells are priests "who have abandoned all worldly things, but carry on drunken orgies and disgusting debauchery. A former novice, who ran away from this plague spot, writes that the priests drink and engage in debauchery in their cells all night."

Although the publishers of such tales knew that they were falsehoods cut from the whole cloth of vicious propaganda, they sent them along to the public in steady streams. In just one single issue of *Science and Religion* (No. 10, 1961) articles appeared that accused religious leaders of Roman Catholic, Protestant, Orthodox, and Jewish faiths of widespread theft at a seminary in Leningrad; plying adolescent young people with vodka and instructing them in depravity; being interested in "lining their pockets at the expense of their congregations," and the usual charge of homosexuality. In addition, presumably to bring in leaders of minority religions for the character assassinations, the defamers called the sheiks attending Muslim pilgrims to the Mount of Suleiman "ex horse thieves, robbers, and housebreakers."

The campaign of slander and defamation was augmented by severe persecutions whenever Communist leaders felt a point could be gained by terror and religion could be further suppressed. From sources within the Soviet Union we have gained accurate accounts of numerous such cases of persecution. These are typical:

On November 11, 1961, *Leningradskaya Pravda* reported the trial of three Jewish leaders, G. R. Pecherskiy, N. A. Kadanov, and Y. S. Dynkin, for "maintaining criminal relations with some employees of an embassy of one of the capitalist states, receiving anti-Soviet literature and spreading it." The capitalist Embassy was the office of the Israeli government in Leningrad. Clearly, the purpose of this action was to prevent any further contact between the community and the Israeli personnel. Pecherskiy was sentenced to twelve years in prison, Kadanov to seven, and Dynkin to four. The account of the trial mentions that Dynkin's "frank repentance and his own condemnation of his criminal acts" caused his lighter sentence.

Extracting repentance and self-condemnation is quite an art

with the secret police. The process includes all-night interrogations, the degradation of solitary confinement without toilet facilities of any kind, statements that others associated with the accused have already confessed and told the whole story of the crimes, and other physical and mental tortures little more refined than those of medieval dungeons.

The fate of Mikhail Artini, a preacher of the Innokentiy sect, is typical. He was sentenced to twenty-five years in prison in 1953 for "unauthorized sectarian activities." After five years he was released upon condition that he make a full confession, which of course was written out for him to sign. Here is the heart of it, as reported by *Sovetskaya Moldaviya* on July 14, 1962:

> For a period of sixteen years, I have failed to benefit society in any way. I have planted neither one sapling nor one bunch of grapes and have inserted not even one stone into the buildings which have been built by the hands of the Soviet people. I ate someone else's bread and preached a parasitic way of life. I renounce my religious convictions and urge all those who still are going astray to follow my example. I have the trade of a tractor driver. After serving sentence I shall sit on the tractor and work honestly in order to wash away this dirty, shameful stain.

The Archbishop Was a "Parasite"

On January 14, 1962, *Pravda* "exposed" two priests, Father Povilonis and Father Burneykis, on a charge of "speculating." *Pravda* called them "swindlers in black soutanes" and accused them of receiving donations from their parishioners to build a new church in Klaipeda. The case was well publicized, for the authorities were determined to stop the building of new churches. *Izvestia* reported that "step by step the trial uncovered the dirty affairs of the clergymen and their hirelings." Father Povilonis was sentenced to eight years in prison and Father Burneykis to four.

A most flagrant case of cruelty was the sentencing of Archbishop Andrey of Chernigov to nine years in prison because of his "parasitic way of life" (he owned a home, given him partially by his parishioners). "Naturally," said *Sel'skaya Zhizn* for April

4, 1963, "Soviet justice cannot leave the crimes of the Archbishop unpunished."

An Orthodox priest and scholar, M. Sevast'yanov, was sentenced to "five years' exile to an especially reserved place," because, according to *Sovetskaya Rossiya* of April 8, 1962, "this rogue and inveterate idler was caught in the library of the Moscow State University" doing religious research.

THE SABBATH IS OBSOLETE

Minority religious groups have been given savage treatment under the program of eradication. In June 1961 a new Soviet law prescribed the death penalty for "economic crimes": an act passed especially to strike at the financing of religious organizations. As of January 1964, a total of 181 persons had been condemned under this act, and of this number 97 were Jews. Typical of the victims was Rabbi Benjamin Gavrilov of Leningrad, executed on a charge of "speculating in currency and gold, particularly in swindling-ring activities." Only three synagogues survive in Moscow to serve that city's half million Jews, and only about 40 synagogues serve all the 2,268,000 Jews of the USSR.

There are approximately 30 million adherents of the Islamic faith in the Soviet Union. Violent propaganda attacks have been launched against these Muslim faithful, a sample of which is found in the June 12, 1962 issue of *Turkmenskaya Iskra:*

"From the beginning of the rise of the Islamic religion all actions of the 'holy' prophets of Allah were conditioned by profit motives, the struggle for power, and the pursuit of wealth."

Many Islamic leaders have recently been imprisoned, and several executed, for being what *Turkmenskaya Iskra* calls "the most thorough charlatans, living off the offerings of the faithful, dealing in roguery and unscrupulous machinations."

According to the Institute for the Study of the USSR at least two thousand places of worship, representing every faith struggling to maintain itself under persecutions in the Soviet Union, were nailed shut during the three years following 1959. Only about ten thousand are still open as of mid-1964.

Corresponding numbers of closures have been enforced in all

the captive areas. Dr. Armins Rusis, authority on Baltic affairs, reports on recent "conversions" of church property for secular and antireligious purposes in Latvia:

The altar was removed from Riga Cathedral in 1962; seats were turned to face the other way, and the sanctuary was made into a concert hall and antireligious museum. The Adazi Church has been converted into a club and dance hall for a collective farm, Burtnieki Church into a grain-storage house, and Dublti Church into a museum. Elksni Church is now a barn used by the local collective farm. Ludzas Church is a cinema hall, and the chapel at Rozeni is a club, dance hall, and cinema. All crosses have been pulled down by tractors, and all religious symbols removed.

One tragic item in the drive against religion is the official abolition of Sunday as a day of rest and of worship, and of Saturday for faiths that consider it the Sabbath. This policy has long been in effect in the Soviet Union. Since 1960 the Red regimes of the captive countries have followed suit. The process is described for us by Dr. Ivan Sepkov and Johannes Klesment of the U.S. Library of Congress, in their recent study of religious affairs in Bulgaria:

According to Resolution No. 825 of November 16, 1963, of the Council of Ministers, Sunday was declared to be a regular work day and a day of the week was designated as a day of rest. Under the pretext of saving electric power, the day of rest is different in the different administrative districts of the country. This change became effective as of December 1, 1963, just before the greatest religious holidays. This decision may well completely paralyze church life, and those who had the courage to attend church services on Sunday will be deprived of that possibility since they cannot absent themselves from their jobs for that purpose.

Jehovah's Witnesses, Seventh-Day Adventists, Mennonites, and various other small sects have all felt the keen edge of the sword of Marxist persecution. A favorite device to trap their leaders is by the "antiparasite" laws which *Pravda* describes as needed "to intensify the struggle against those who avoid socially useful work and lead an antisocial and parasitic way of life." On such a charge, in February 1963, two clergymen and 17 young lay leaders of an Evangelical sect in East Germany were sentenced to prison.

An edict by the Red regime of Estonia, where the great majority of the people are affiliated with the Evangelical Lutheran Church, brands ministers as "obscurants" and "enemies of the people." Estonian clergymen are forced to pay rent on their apartments at rates from six to eight times the usual tariff. Excessive school "fees" are levied upon the children of ministers, to make up for the lack of their parents' "contribution to the Socialist State."

The Red Chinese regime, busy creating its own monolithic Socialist "Three-Self Movement" church, paid no attention to the new efforts of the Soviet bloc heads to abolish religion. But Fidel Castro fell dutifully into line, screaming his hatred for religion in numerous speeches and edicts. On March 13, 1963, in a two-hour broadcast over Havana Radio, the bearded Cuban lackey lashed out at three Protestant sects which he said were "agents of the imperialists" and "enemies of the revolution." Those singled out for attack were Jehovah's Witnesses, Evangelists of Gideon, and the Pentecostal Church.

Employing the usual tactic of Marxists—accusing the enemy of plans or methods employed by themselves—Castro called these sects "a vanguard for penetrating Latin America."

"They are very subtle," Castro continued. "They work through youth to eradicate illiteracy. . . . They use religion to preach against voluntary work on the Sabbath, telling people not to pick cotton or cut cane on that day. . . . Do the imperialists think we are idiots to permit this? We aim to stop it!"

As though to prove his support of the intensified drive to exterminate religion, in October 1963 Castro ordered the execution of three Protestant clergymen. Their crime? Attempting to escape, and helping others attempting to escape, from his atheist paradise. In mid-August, Miami-based Cubans led by the Rev. Vincente Concepcion, a refugee, sought to bring 29 Protestants, men, women, and children, into the United States. Their two boats were noted by U.S. aircraft and Navy launches. They were also spotted by Cuban boats and a helicopter. In desperation the refugees beached their boats on Anguilla Bay, a British possession in the Bahamas.

Cuban soldiers and sailors invaded British land in an attempt to capture them. Despite this gross violation of international law, and despite the fact that both British and American military personnel witnessed the invasion, neither the British nor the Americans made any attempt to rescue them. Ten of the Cubans escaped, but 19 were caught. Those captured included the Rev. Antonio Gonsalez, pastor of the Evangelical Church at Pinar del Rio; the Rev. Pablo Rodriguez, pastor of the Church of God of a community outside Havana; and the Rev. Jose Durand, pastor of the Gideon Church, at Florida, Camaguey. Labeling these ministers "yellow worms," Castro personally supervised their execution.

THE MONASTERY IS CLOSED

A dispatch dated November 13, 1963, from London gave a detailed report from several Church of England clergymen who had visited Byelorussia, mentioning the severe persecution dealt the monks of the famed Pochayev Monastery, at the hands of the Soviet secret police. This Orthodox institution was founded in the twelfth century by St. Olaf, whose revered relics are still preserved there. It is located in the area of East Poland that was torn away from Poland and given to the Soviet Union at the demand of Dictator Stalin with the agreement of Prime Minister Churchill and President Roosevelt.

To visit Pochayev Monastery was a tradition among Orthodox faithful for centuries. After World War I and the restoration of the independence of Poland as many as 33,000 persons a year were counted among its visitors. In August of every year there was a great feast, bringing hundreds of worshipers to the Monastery and to the small town nearby.

In Washington, D.C., we visited the Rev. Dr. Arkady Moiseff, now pastor of St. Nicholas Orthodox Church of that city, a refugee who left his native Poland in 1952 and who knows intimately the story of the Monastery. He told us:

I have worshiped at Pochayev, an ancient symbol of my Church in Poland. Soon after the Russians seized our area of Poland the restrictions on religion began. The Reds are determined to prevent new converts to religious faith, and to accomplish this they must prevent young men from becoming priests. That is why they close seminaries and monasteries.

In 1959 the great August feast days were cancelled by the authorities, because they were considered "a waste of time." People were forbidden to take guests into their homes who came on pilgrimages to Pochayev. At night there would be inspections of homes by the police. Any family harboring a visitor had to turn him over for prison.

Then came direct action against the Monastery personnel. The Soviet MKD (secret police) took over the institution and began arresting the monks on charges that they were "parasites" and criminals. Some bureaucrat hit on the idea that they were all crazy, or they would not be there. So most of the priests were declared insane and sent to asylums or concentration camps. Finally the institution was closed entirely, and many of its buildings demolished. But I can tell you this: the spirits of the victims still hover over the sacred soil of the Pochayev Monastery.

While every possible means of censorship was used to prevent news of Pochayev's destruction from getting to the outside world, still the facts became known. Angry church leaders of many faiths have protested this and other antireligious atrocities. In a sort of lame answer, *Science and Religion* in late 1962 commented:

"We do not encroach upon a man's religious convictions. Belief in God is his affair. But we cannot reconcile ourselves to people, who by making use of their positions and their disrespect for public organizations, drag more and more people into the nets of religious communities."

CHAPTER SIXTEEN

COMMUNIST CURTAINS
SHOW CRACKS

"Freedom! Freedom for Hungary at last! Down with the Soviet occupiers!" Such were the cries that sounded over the streets and among the buildings of downtown Budapest on the morning of October 23, 1956, as crowds of young men rushed upon the headquarters of the bureaus that controlled all the life of the city.

"Death to the Russian invaders!" As the crowds grew, augmented by more young men and young women—most of them students—the shouts rose louder and angrier. Surging about the principal office of the Soviet-controlled administration, several of the youths gathered missiles and smashed the windows. Some whipped out pistols and began firing into the building.

Completely surprised by the attack, and especially by its fury, Prime Minister Matayas Rakosi, cruel puppet satrap of the Soviet rule in Hungary, called for the Russian-trained Hungarian militia to put down the rioting. From their barracks these soldiers came rolling up in their Red Star trucks.

The amazing battle of the Hungarian freedom fighters had started. The days that will live forever in history as the time of unforgettable infamy for the Soviet Union had begun their bitter hours.

Let us hear briefly the story from Niklos Gigler, who as a twenty-year-old student was one of the leaders in that tragic struggle for liberation. He escaped after the fighting and is now an honor graduate student in an American university:

The whole idea started with that speech of Khrushchev to the Communist party Congress in February. For months we students on the campuses had talked, debated, and pondered what the Big Red had said. He said Stalin was a murderer and tyrant. If Stalin was out, why not Rakosi too?

Our original plan was not for a rebellion, but to lay certain demands before the government. We wanted freedom to study without the constant Communist indoctrination. We wanted to choose our own way of life and our careers. Some of our young people were sons and daughters of religious parents. We were sick of seeing our priests and ministers persecuted, our churches closed, our younger brothers and sisters hounded and punished for attending worship.

The uprising was triggered by Rakosi's refusal even to receive a grievance committee of our students accompanied by several prominent business men of Budapest. He threatened to have us all deported. Anger began to spread all over the city. The uprising was spontaneous. It was like touching a match to a dry field. Resistance spread like a fire from one person to another. Everyone knew it was the one chance to drive this foreign Communist government out of Hungary.

Well, we tried. I can never forget how we fought, some with bare hands, and those hours of victory, when the Russians slunk out of the city, completely beaten. I confess I cannot forget also that we waited in vain for help from those we trusted in the free countries. But this we did: *we cracked the iron curtain and let in the light of truth on the true nature of communism!*

Let us now hear Dr. Alexander Haraszti, outstanding physician of Budapest, President of the Hungarian Baptist Theological Seminary, a leader of the Protestant groups of this captive nation in opposition to Marxist persecutions of religion:

My wife, who is also a physician, and I had built up a very respectable practice in Budapest. Because of my religious activities we were constantly watched by the police. We defied the Rakosi government by taking our five children with us to worship. I am sure I would have been arrested and perhaps deported had there not been such a need for doctors in the city and country.

We knew that resistance was mounting against the Communists, especially since the "de-Stalinizing" began. But we were hardly prepared for the great rebellion.

Let us stand with Dr. Haraszti and his wife in their upper office at a window close to an important intersection where the hottest fighting took place.

We hear the shouting and other noises. We can see the crowds growing larger by the minute. The firing starts. The Hungarian militia-police come up in their vehicles. They deploy among the students. They try to restore order. But not one Hungarian officer orders them to fire on their people!

Overnight the Russian motorized troops come in. They line up along the sidewalks. The angry crowds push all around them, threatening to trample them to death. Now see this amazing sight: the Russian soldiers begin handing their rifles to the Hungarian people, and melting away around the buildings! Here is proof that the Soviets cannot trust their "satellite" forces, now and in the future. Some of the fighters are wounded, and they start bringing them to our office. We quickly bind up their wounds. They have won a great victory for independence—or so we think.

The Harasztis tell how an uneasy calm settled over Budapest, how everyone waited to hear recognition of the newly installed government of Premier Imre Nagy by the United States and other non-Communist countries, how no recognition nor support came, and how three days later, sure that they could crush the rebellion unchallenged, the Soviet troops came back—this time callous Orientals who coldly turned their machine guns and cannon on the crowds and mowed them down.

Again the wounded, some terribly mangled, were brought to the office of the Drs. Haraszti, and again their wounds were bound up. Because of his help to the freedom fighters, the doctor was marked for arrest and execution. He and his wife and their five children escaped, tramping through ten miles of swamps at night to the Austrian border. At Atlanta Baptist Hospital where Dr. Haraszti now is in practice, he told us:

"The fight for freedom, even in final defeat, was the most glorious victory of our time. It proved that the Communists can be beaten."

FACING AN INSOLUBLE DILEMMA

Countless cracks had appeared in the curtains of Marxist control before the greatest one of all was blasted by the bloody suppression of the Hungarian struggle for freedom. Countless other rents and holes have appeared since then. Most conspicuous of all are those caused by the vigorous resistance to atheism of religious believers and their determination to keep their unalienable, God-given right of free conscience and worship.

The "seven-year plan" to eradicate all "vestiges" of religion, which began in 1959, ran less than three years when it became plain to Red leaders that it was hopelessly behind schedule. Despite brutal persecutions and severe restrictions, more people than ever were turning to religious worship, most of them secretly, but many openly. Especially was this true in Hungary and Poland. The crusade to make all young people militant atheists bogged down before the uncooperative attitudes of youth ranging all the way from passive indifference to active rebellion.

It is clear that in their antireligion campaign Marxist rulers are facing an insoluble dilemma:

On one hand is the hesitation of Communist despots, in every region where the Red flag of the hammer and sickle flies, to go all out for the eradication of religion by administrative measures. Decrees could be announced which would make all religious activities illegal. Marxist leaders fear this would bring worldwide adverse reaction.

On the other hand there is the constant, gnawing fear on the part of the top Communists that without such a direct approach, without some campaign of prompt and vigorous suppression, religion will not only survive in their monolithic empire but will grow and expand.

On both counts the Communist rulers are correct.

Direct prohibitions against all further worship would totally violate all the nice wordings in Marxist constitutions and laws about freedom of conscience. All-out suppression of religious activities would indeed bring adverse world opinion crashing down about the ears of the tyrants in the Kremlin, in Red China in Eastern Europe, Cuba, and all other areas of the captive Marxist world. The storm of condemnation might well equal that caused by the murder of the Hungarian freedom fighters.

Yet to ease up on the antireligious campaign would mean to permit the gains of Marxist atheism to begin eroding away. By its very nature, communism must be dynamic—or nothing. It can live only by growing. Communism can survive only by expanding. Its monolithic atheistic infections must spread through the body of humankind or they will be overcome by the healing processes of faith, hope, and charity.

What is the answer to this dilemma? It is certain that Communist leaders groped anxiously for the solution. A new program to eradicate religion and at the same time to maintain world prestige was imperative. In addition they were spurred by the most uncomfortable fact that His Holiness Pope John XXIII had announced the convening of an Ecumenical Council in Rome, which they knew would create worldwide interest among peoples of goodwill, and of all faiths.

Notice that the Marxist rulers were wrestling with this problem was given in May 1962 in a series of articles in *Kommunist,* which declared: "The fight against religion cannot be regarded as a short-term campaign."

The *Kommunist* writer declared that Party members should understand how "religious beliefs formed over the centuries have permeated the people's existence and have obtained the status of irrational habits. . . . Religion must be combated by liquidating its social roots and by patiently explaining its antiscientific and reactionary character."

Through countless propaganda statements and the actions of Red authorities in all Marxist lands, the current program has become clear. It involves:

First: There must be no relaxing of restrictions already in effect upon religious leaders and organizations.

Second: Persecutions and punishments are to continue, except where adverse publicity might overbalance their terror value.

Third: Far greater reliance must be placed upon the positive program of teaching of atheism, especially to win young people away from religious sentiments.

Religious Morality Must Be Exposed

The program was given impetus by a lengthy official discussion in *Pravda,* in September, 1962, obviously prepared at the direction of the Soviet government. The article called attention to resolutions passed by the twenty-second Communist Party Congress which demanded all-out efforts against religious superstition. The article declared:

"All party organizations and ideological groups must carry out scientific atheistic propaganda systematically, purposefully, patiently, and convincingly, exposing the fallacies of religious beliefs."

The paper stressed that any attempt to establish collaboration between communism and religion must be vigorously opposed. It urged that by press and radio, lectures and talks, "religious morality and the attempts of clergymen to adapt to the times must be exposed; the incompatibility of scientific communism with religion must be demonstrated so that all Soviet people can rid themselves of the yoke of religious prejudices and become active creators of the brightest and most just society on earth—communism."

The writer also warned against propaganda methods "which are often excursions into the religious history of the past but ignore Church activities of today." It urged the use of the argument that religion is a waste of time and energy since the activities and loyalties of all citizens should be directed toward building a Socialist State. It summarized:

"Prove to the deceived believers that materialism has made religion obsolete; that religion is not needed."

Collections of propaganda articles and radio talks disclose the absurd efforts of Red regimes to patch the cracks in their oppressive curtains. The featured article in the December 19, 1963 issue of *Izvestia* is typical. This is the USSR's principal newspaper, edited by the late Khrushchev's son-in-law, Alexi Adzhubey.

"Read and Heed!" was the substance of the headline. The article, written by Ivan Kostukov, bravely faced up to a new phenomenon. It is possible, declared the writer, to wreck an up-and-coming Russian's career by calling him an Evangelical-Baptist! Therefore, one should be very careful about starting whispering campaigns against persons accused of being religious believers.

The story dealt in detail with the case of Michael Odnous, identified as the chief engineer in the Ukrainian town of Krivoy Rog. According to Kostukov, this man Odnous was a serious, stick-to-business kind of fellow. Not much of a mixer; he didn't smoke nor drink.

False rumors were launched, apparently by some persons envious of his position, to the effect Odnous was a religious believer, and specifically a follower of some Evangelical sect. This of course, if true, would render him unfit to hold his job as chief engineer. Unfortunately, the rumor spread. Odnous' colleagues began to give him the silent treatment. Trade union and Party dignitaries turned the cold shoulder. The man did not complain nor ask for an investigation of his status so he could clear himself of the infamous charge that he was "one of the deceived."

In time Odnous cracked under the "nervous atmosphere" and abruptly quit his job. He was out of work for eighteen months. Personnel people ignored him, for they feared it would be too big a task to re-educate such a man into "atheistic beliefs." Now, said the *Izvestia* story, while Odnous was to blame for "capitulating" to the false charges, still the accusation should have been investigated. The writer strongly condemned the failure to check the truth about so valuable a man as a chief engineer and urged "a more careful attitude" in community comments about a person. The article did not, however, mention that to discriminate against people in employment because of their beliefs is a violation of the Soviet constitution.

KNOWLEDGE IS INSEPARABLE FROM TRUTH

It obviously has been impossible to coordinate all the amazing mixture of truth and falsehood in the propaganda efforts of the valiant fighters for atheism. Some astonishing mix-ups have resulted. Son-in-law Adzhubey has periodically attacked the Vatican and the Ecumenical Council, calling Catholic leaders "robed tools of the imperialists." His *Izvestia* ran a four-column article by U. Filonovich who cited *L'osservatore romano,* Vatican City newspaper, as "one of those bourgeois publications," which he said "falsely claim that religion continues to exist in Russia."

That seemed to follow the proper Marxist line, except that at that very time a group of Russian Orthodox and Evangelical ministers were touring the United States to prove that religion was very much alive in the USSR.

An issue of *Kommunist* pointed with what it called "justified pride" at the claim of atheist workers "that in our country the social roots of religion have been undermined. . . . But there must be improvements in atheist campaigns in the Soviet Union and for training of atheist propagandists to a much higher standard than ever to enable them to win arguments with believers." At the same time, *Pravda* was deep in proof that "the deceived" had no arguments worth considering.

The gas attacks of antireligion propaganda punctuated by artillery shells of persecution, sweeping over the terrain of Marxist rule, often catch the Fighters for Atheism in their own maneuvers. *Pravda* often gives prominent space to the constant, all-out campaign by the Presidium of the Central Council of Trade Unions for the "popularizing of atheism." Workers were urged to try to talk "deceived comrades" into accepting godless beliefs.

"The popularizing of atheism must be based on the outstanding achievements of Soviet science and the materialistic point of view," said the Presidium spokesman.

At the same time, several Soviet scientists were permitted publicly to complain that dialectical materialism, the very core of atheist Marxism, does not provide an adequate preparation for scholarship and production in the nuclear age. Peter Kapitza, a leading Soviet authority on nuclear chemistry, called for a return to "mysticism" in the education of young students. By that term he avoided any reference to religion, but his inference was clear. He mentioned the need for a new approach "to the limitless dimensions of the universe as the abode of the human spirit."

All propaganda organs of the Soviet bloc constantly play the theme of "peace." Even this noble ideal brings trouble to the Red regime from young men in the military service. From the Soviet army journal *Red Star* we learn that cadets have complained to their school authorities that they are harangued continually by lecturers who exalt the military calling, and they wonder "What's peaceful about it?" One cadet is quoted as saying:

"It is wrong to talk about the nobility of the military calling since there can be no nobility where there is constant suppression and restriction of freedom."

Jagged cracks are opening in the cultural curtains that have long held Soviet literature in bounds. The decision in 1963 to permit the publication of the book *One Day in the Life of Ivan Darrishovich* by Alexandre Solzhenitzyn was an effort to support Khrushchev's "de-Stalinization" program, but it backfired in a terrific manner. The book tells the story of life in a typical concentration camp in the Stalin era, with considerable nauseating detail.

That would seem to be a gain for de-Stalinization. But reports indicate that the book has aroused a storm of discussion about *present* "correctional labor camps," and has brought to the surface such questions as "What's different about them now?" and "Who were Stalin's helpers?" The inference, that Stalin's associates in carrying out cruel and degrading punishments (such as Khrushchev himself) have some things to answer for, strikes readers with terrific force. The Kremlin bosses are never sure just how much the people have found out.

The almost frantic efforts of Red rulers to popularize atheism reveals their concern over the obvious breakdown in their plans to make the present generation atheist and godless. In Bulgaria, for example, atheist propaganda offices have been established by Communist youth organizations in every important city and town. A "House of Atheists" in Belgrade serves as a clearing station for the antireligion campaign of Yugoslavia.

A Militant Atheist Council of Soviet Latvia was formed recently in Riga, with branches in all areas of that nation. These branches, closely linked with local urban and rural administrative bodies, supervise atheist teaching in every factory and on every collective farm. The president of the Militants took part in a meeting of the All-Soviet Atheists (an attempt to unify the work of atheist propagandists in all Soviet bloc areas) in Moscow in 1963 and reported in *Skolotaju Avise* (Teacher's Journal):

"They did not advocate peaceful coexistence with religion, but aggressive destruction of religion. 'We cannot wait until the old-time religions die out; we must fight against them,' they said. In this age of the construction of communism we must seek and apply all kinds of strategy and weapons in our fight against the darkness of religion."

While teachers are thus being instructed in every Communist area, the instructions are being knocked flat with urgent pleas by

Marxist commissars for universal higher education for their youth. As Charles A. Wells, noted commentator on religious matters, has aptly said:

An insoluble dilemma faces the Communist leaders as more of their people become educated. For education creates a thirst for knowledge and knowledge is inseparable from truth. The Communists cannot tolerate truth, for truth too often clashes with Marxist dogma. Yet educate they must to compete with the West. As the masses become better educated they will think more, be more critical, demand more—especially the right to all truth, which requires freedom. Scientists, educators, writers, and creative artists have already entered this phase of the struggle everywhere behind the iron curtain.*

THE LIGHT OF TRUTH SHINES THROUGH

To shore up the crumbling walls of the myth that there is freedom of religion in the Soviet Atheist Empire, delegations of churchmen are permitted occasionally to visit the United States and other free countries. Of course they are carefully selected for their "reliability" not to make statements that would reflect upon the Communist dictatorships or would reveal the program for eradication of religion. Always they must be accompanied on tour by one or more hard-core Communist agents to see that all goes well propaganda-wise. Yet the true believers among these churchmen are not frauds and hypocrites. They perform their missions as conscientiously as they are allowed to do. They continually face the problem of answering questions so that the rasp of half-truths will not be too abrasive upon their consciences.

Always these delegations from the USSR and captive areas disclose more truth than appears on the surface of their remarks. This was well illustrated by the visit of sixteen Russian churchmen, led by Orthodox Bishop Nikodim, who came to the United States and Canada as guests of the National Council of Churches recently. Ten were ministers of the Eastern Orthodox Church and the others Evangelical-Christians-Baptists.

The Rev. Dean Goodwin, executive director of the Division of Communication, American Baptist Convention, accompanied these visitors during most of their tour. In a keen analysis of their statements, Dr. Goodwin reports:

I listened many times in many different press conferences, interviews, discussion groups, and dinner meetings, and suddenly it struck me that these men were saying something that I had not been hearing. Then I tried to come forth with what seemed to me to be the real message from the Russian churchmen.

Take the question about religious freedom. Their answer was that the law of the USSR provides for freedom of worship. When they said that, they satisfied the Soviet authorities back home. Their questioners were usually satisfied also. They ran out and wrote in their papers that the Soviet churchmen were whitewashing the true situation by saying they had freedom of worship. But they failed to give due weight to the remainder of the answer the churchmen gave: ". . . and there is also freedom of atheistic propaganda."

That was the message: the unequal situation in which they labored. Freedom to worship is there, restricted to the church building, narrowed to singing, prayer, Bible reading, and preaching that has no social application or criticism. But the atheists can go out and use every technique of propaganda in every public way—the school, newspapers, radios, lectures, posters, etc., to teach atheism. It is an unequal situation for the churches.*

Dr. Goodwin's analysis of how the churchmen's answers crack the barriers of Soviet propaganda may be condensed thus:

Question: "How many church members have you now in the USSR?"

Answer: "Maybe 30 million, or maybe 50 million."

Meaning: *The Russian Orthodox Church which once embraced almost 90 per cent of the population in Russia can now count only 25 per cent. Evangelicals much less. A poor showing!*

Question: "How much literature are you producing?"

Answer: "We printed 15,000 Bibles and 15,000 hymnals in 1959."

Meaning: *We have not been allowed to print a Bible or hymnal since 1959! Even then we could print comparatively only a few.*

Question: "Are you permitted to build new churches?"

Answer: "We built four new churches in the last year."

Meaning: *Only four new churches in the vast area of the Soviet Union!*

Question: "What about the closing of churches by the government?"

Answer: "Many churches have become museums because they are valuable pieces of architecture; the State took them over to restore and preserve them."

Meaning: *Sorry, but we cannot discuss this. But it is obvious that when a church is closed there is no place for the people to meet to worship.*

Question: "What about those 32 Siberian peasants who sought asylum, claiming religious persecution?"

Answer (Silence by the true churchmen. One of the Communist agents speaks up): "These fanatics were practicing cruelties upon their children."

Meaning: *We churchmen cannot tell the truth about this, and we will not lie about it.*

And so in countless ways and by many people the dark enclosures of the Marxist crusade against spiritual faith and the devout faithful are cracked, and the light of truth begins to shine through.

CHAPTER SEVENTEEN

RELIGION CANNOT BE CONQUERED

Has the antireligion crusade by the fanatical atheistic Marxists succeeded in eradicating religion?

The answer is a resounding NO!

All the severe persecutions of religious leaders and devout believers during the creation of the Soviet government by the crafty Nikolai Lenin could not stamp out the fires of religious faith in the Russian homeland. All the imprisonments, tortures, executions, and banishments of priests, ministers, and rabbis by Lenin's disciple Joseph Stalin could not extinguish the lights of spiritual activities in the USSR and in the captive areas of eastern Europe.

All the continued and intensified harassments of religion in the Soviet Union, as well as in Red China and more recently in the colony that was once free Cuba, have NOT proved successful in eliminating from the hearts and lives of the people that belief in the Supreme Being and in a brotherhood of man which all Marxists call in derision the "superstitions and illusions of religion."

It must be admitted that brutal persecutions and harsh restrictions have crippled religious activities in every area of Communist control. No spiritual messages come from churches and synagogues converted to antireligious museums. Activities of the places of worship still open are hampered by strict control and censorship. The trumpets of God's spokesmen who have been forced into dependency and collaboration with Marxist governments give uncertain sounds.

Still "the blood of the martyrs is the seed of the Church," today as in all ages. Just as men and women have suffered for their faith in the past, so will they suffer for it in the present and the future, with no intention of surrendering because of hardships they must endure.

In Marxist areas today Lutheran believers fervently sing "A Mighty Fortress Is Our God!" Protestant members raise the hymn "Faith of Our Fathers, Living Still!" And devout Catholics hear the mass in solemn and joyous reverence.

The one fact looming fearfully before the conspirators for worldwide atheist control is this:

Religion can never be beaten to death by the Marxist clubs of physical and mental persecutions.

Paralleling this fact so clearly demonstrated in the past near half-century is a most meaningful one for the present. It presents an opportunity for believers in religion throughout the world, in free lands or captive:

Religion can be conquered by communism only through indifference of believers, and by their failure to mount a tremendous, united crusade for its preservation.

Reports from every area of Communist control prove that the fountains of religious faith still flow and are ready to gush forth as soon as the dams of restrictions are cut through.

Religious News Service has reported that in Central Russia, and in many areas of the Ukraine, Siberia, and Kazakhstand, for example, the Evangelical Christians-Baptist believers are growing in numbers at a remarkable rate. RNS quoted an article in *Soviet Russia* to the effect that these sects in the Smolensk area have succeeded in "recruiting" many followers, and that party officials have confessed that they have not been able to contain the religious movement.

"Secret of the Evangelical Christians-Baptist growth," *Soviet Russia* lamented, "is that the churchmen help people in need at the precise moment when their troubles have been ignored by the organizations which the State has set up to assist them." Typical, said the newspaper, is the case of thirty-two-year-old Lidia Govorun, now an ardent believer. This woman was deserted by her husband at a time when she was hospitalized. Her child went unattended and the woman went unnoticed by local officials and the labor group to which she belonged.

However, her religious friends did not forget her, so the story ran. "They cared for her four-year-old son and helped her in convalescence. As a consequence Mrs. Govorun proudly escorts her son to church services, admits possession and frequent use of a Bible, and when questioned by associates said that attendance at church 'will allow my son to grow up an honest person.' "

STAGED DEMONSTRATIONS DO NO GOOD

Despite the intensified program to replace religion with Marxist atheism, some churches and religious groups behind the iron curtains show a steady increase in numbers and influence since 1959. The combined sects in the Evangelical fellowship, which in 1960 numbered approximately 545,000 members with 5,000 churches across the vast Eurasian area, report an increase of about 10,000 believers each year.

But statistics do not tell the whole story. Actually, the observers say, the total strength of these united sects, including sympathizers and unlisted adherents, is "known only to God." The Communist party leaders reveal a great deal in the temper of their open attacks. In a survey of life in Siberia and Central USSR, one Soviet paper complained:

"Religion is coming forward in modern attire. It is no longer presenting contradictions between natural science and faith, and is even exercising a beneficial influence on social life in the Soviet Union."

"The Baptist Church at Semipalatinsk," the report continued, "has built a large house where men and women from different classes may meet." Such a scandalous action was entirely illegal and reactionary, the report declared. The writer said that authorities were trying to arouse the laborers to demonstrate in protest against this group of "the deceived."

Until recently the method of "trying to arouse the laborers" and others of the proletariat to demonstrate in protest against churches and their leaders was quite successful. Countless numbers of places of worship were closed in this way. The word would go out to party whips, who passed it on to local party workers, to round up a certain number of people to demonstrate. Often the people had no idea what they were to demonstrate against until they assembled.

"This church (or chapel, synagogue, or religious institution) is counterrevolutionary," the crowd would be told. "It is an enemy of the State. What should be done with it?"

Trained leaders were on hand to take up the cry, "It must be closed! The people demand that it be closed!" So, by "popular will," the religious facility would be closed.

But all reports from the Soviet Union, as well as from eastern European Communist areas, prove that these staged demonstrations no longer work. Too many people find tasks to be done elsewhere. Some even defy the Communist authorities by refusing to be a part of the gigantic fraud.

Apparently such was the case in Kolodno in the Smolensk region. Party leaders called a meeting of about 1,500 persons, presumably all of them atheists, to protest the activities of the local Evangelical group. A resolution was passed calling on authorities to close down their church. A mass meeting to "ratify" this action brought such adverse criticism of the proposal that the matter was dropped. The faithful still meet in Kolodno church.

"Punishments do no good for such rebellion, for there are too many to punish!" a Catholic priest from Hungary informed us. "The commissars may rant and rave, for they fear such defiance will spread. I am sure that it is spreading. And pray God that it continue to do so! It proves that religion is growing under persecution."

At the beginning of the first session of the Vatican Ecumenical Council in Rome, *Pravda* carried a series of vitriolic articles denouncing Pope John XXIII and all the institutions, works, and adherents of the Catholic Church. Some refinements in false propaganda were sprinkled through the discussions, such as the charge that the church had been in league with Adolf Hitler and supported the Nazi policies against the Soviet Union.

Still the *Pravda* writers admitted what one expressed in these words:

"Religion continues to be a strong force in the USSR. . . .

There is great need for intensified efforts against this enemy of the People's Socialist State."

Thus the Marxist propagandists made two damaging admissions: that there is a still-unconquered force of religious faith and sentiment among the Russian people; and at the same time there can be no compatibility between communism and religion.

THEY STILL MEET TO WORSHIP

It is evident that Communist thinkers approach the problem of religion from the standpoint of their own antireligion suppositions. They seem to think that religion is merely an indoctrination, and that the way to get rid of it is by counterindoctrination—using doses of Marxist atheistic dogma, of course. They do not understand that religion goes far deeper in human nature than a mere scientific formula, or ideas based upon superstition, or even having a place in which to worship. They do not understand that religion actually fills a need in human personality which all the materialistic science known to man now and in the future cannot possibly fill.

The matter is well expressed by Dr. Bela Udvarnoki in his discussion of "Christianity Behind the Iron Curtain," in words that apply with equal force to believers of the Jewish, Islamic or any other spiritual faith:

Communism approaches Christianity within the presuppositions of their own irreligion. Since Communists evaluate Christian conviction as mere indoctrination, they believe that by controlling the indoctrinators they will be able to exterminate religion!

Another fact unrealized by Communists is the difference between external organized Christianity and internal spiritual belief of Christians as individuals. Communists actually believe that Christianity will be vanquished with the destruction of church buildings or organizations.

Nothing, of course, is further from the truth. Were they to raze every church building; to close every theological school; to suppress the publication of Christian literature; were they to banish Christians to the far reaches of the earth and allocate only one real Christian per square mile, Marx would nonetheless lose the battle to spiritual forces behind the Iron Curtain.*

We have a picture, smuggled out of Vladivostok, showing a group of people meeting in the open air. It is a congregation of believers. They are worshiping on the exact floor space occupied by their church building before the Communist authorities destroyed the structure.

"The local commissars did not need that space, but were offended at the independent spirit shown by these devout people in their church activities," our informant told us. "The bulldozers appeared without any warning one night and tore the whole building away. The congregation had their permit to worship there, so they simply returned, built new benches, an altar, and a communion table, and have held their worship in the open ever since."

In new industrial areas where places of worship are not provided, believers find and attend divine services even at a distance. S. L. Schneiderman in "Behind the Scenes in Poland's Model City" gives an example of the determination of Catholic faithful to attend worship. They live in the planned industrial center called *Nowa Huta* (New Mill), a showpiece of Communist enterprise located near Cracow:

This city of about 100,000 people contains Poland's greatest steel plant, 314 stores, 112 workers' cooperative shops, 14 nurseries, 20 schools, in addition to hospitals, drugstores, restaurants, and bars. But there are no churches, not one.

A visitor to this new planned industrial city found one day to his surprise that the city was deserted. All the shops and stores were closed. On inquiring, he was told that "Today is the Feast of Epiphany. They've all gone to church in Mogila," the adjacent village.

He found the narrow road to Mogila crowded with men, women, and children in two rows, one heading toward the church, the other returning from it. The Communist leaders of Poland in 1956 built a city without churches, but they did not reckon with tradition and sentiment of the people, to whom the church is a place of refuge and a source of strength.*

Baptists number only about three thousand in Poland today, but the persistent pressure of Dr. Alexandre Kircun, executive secretary of the Baptist Union of Poland, and a congregation of believers in Hajnovka, northeastern Poland, resulted in a permit to build a church at that town. The small white edifice was dedicated on December 17, 1963, with Dr. Kircun officiating and more than four hundred believers of many Evangelical faiths in attendance.

Dr. Kircun is pastor of the Warsaw Baptist Church, its members worshiping in an edifice built in 1958-1960 with funds donated by people in many lands. He displays the new boldness of religious leaders in Marxist lands as he goes about his administrative and preaching duties. Fearlessness is not new to Pastor Kircun. He hid Jews in his home during the Nazi occupation—two of them for two years—thus saving their lives and risking his own. In early 1964 he led many Christian groups in Poland to celebrate the four hundredth anniversary of the first Bible translation into Polish.

The intensified antireligion drive announced in early March 1964 can be interpreted only as an admission that the previous campaigns have failed to produce the quantity of atheism needed to meet the Marxist norm. *Pravda*'s discussion of the matter unwittingly betrayed the fact that many of the bars supposed to imprison religion in a slow but sure death have been broken.

"Not all Soviet citizens realize that religion is an ideological enemy, inflicting harm on Soviet society," Leonid F. Ilyichev, head of the Ideological Commission of the USSR, complained. He laid down the law to Party members, trade unions, schools, youth leaders, and women. "Russian women constitute the bulk of believers in this country. Something must be done about them!" Commissar Ilyichev scolded.

In numerous statements Marxist leaders admit, unwittingly perhaps, that conquering religion is a frustrating, baffling task. Laszlo Orban, Chief of the Propaganda Division of the Communist Party Central Committee of Hungary, told the Eighth Congress of the Hungarian Socialist Workers:

Recently a certain standstill can be observed in the fight against religious ideology. Some people, improperly, interpret the efforts to normalize the relations between State and Church as requiring a restriction in the fight against religion. It is obvious that here are two different things: there is not, and there cannot be, any peaceful coexistence between the ideology of Marxism and the religious ideology. The two exclude each other. Naturally, the fight against the religious ideology also requires great caution in the future, considering that religion is such a false mental state and also that it intertwines with the moral and emotional lives of the deceived.

Moscow Radio frequently issues a stern warning against the importation of Bibles and other religious literature, labeling all such as "anti-Soviet reactionary propaganda," delivered in "devious ways" by western visitors. The American Bible Society is often blamed for such illegal acts, its chief offense being that of having "translated the Bible into Russian."

"ONE CAN STILL HEAR THE BELLS"

Party Life, an organ of the Central Committee of the Communist Party in the USSR, recently boasted that the stepped-up program of atheist teaching has resulted in some "sectarian organizations" being put out of existence, pointing to "prayer houses being closed at the demand of former churchgoers."

"However, the influence of religion continues to be strong," the paper wailed. It cited a big textile factory in the central Yaroslavl region, where "young workers went to church last Christmas." The writer added: "Many people, usually passive toward the Russian Orthodox Church, always show up for services on such occasions as Christmas and Easter."

Pravda frequently turns loose a commentator to complain: "There are still too many churches and monasteries in (such-and-such) region. Socialist solidarity can never be achieved while these symbols of reaction persist." This official organ reported sorrowfully that 20,000 lectures on atheism were given in the USSR in one year, "but still the program is not succeeding in its purpose!"

A *Pravda* correspondent in Odessa was quite specific in a recent dispatch: "One can still hear the bells of several churches ringing in this city!" he wrote. He blamed a number of sects for the distressful situation, and declared: "We must have an increased campaign to counteract this religious intoxication."

Commenting on the matter, *Pravda* editorialized: "Isn't it a weakness of atheistic propaganda that explains the abundance of such prayer houses? Wider and stronger work is required. The city must take a stand against such religious druggery."

Occasionally the antireligion propaganda assaults are directed toward individuals. Usually the net result is to lay bare the fact that increasing numbers of believers are refusing to bend the knee to atheism. *Science and Religion* in its May 3, 1962 issue discussed the matter of the growing influence of religion among doctors, citing Dr. Anna Austora, thirty-two-year-old lung specialist. The writer declared that she refused to be interrogated and protested his attempt to "poke your nose into my soul." He described also how he cornered Vera Kharchenko, twenty-four, a medical student, reported to be one of the "deceived." The reporter asked this young woman how she managed to pass her exam in philosophy, "since every Soviet undergraduate must present Marxist materialistic views on nature and religion." She positively refused to tell him.

There is ample evidence that the staged "confessions" of persons who leave the ranks of believers for the glories of atheism are now treated by the public with the contempt they deserve. An example of this species of Marxist fraud is the story told by a former member of the Ilyin-Methodist Sect, "who had the inner strength to break with the believers." He testified:

I broke with the Methodists recently, and only now do I understand how many years I squandered by belonging to the sect. I was sick in Dzhambul Oblast and the sect helped me and I became one of them. I helped to distribute their pamphlets. . . . Methodists hate all who are not with them. They forbid their members to take part in elections and to send their children to schools. Their children are not allowed to join the Pioneers and the Komsomol and are being brought up as enemies of the Soviet regime. How many young people are being crippled by such upbringing! How much young talent gets buried in the Ilyin-Methodist underground! No wonder the sect gets most of its members from among the uneducated, or those opposed to the Soviet State and criminals.

The "confession" went on with long discussions of how terrible the Methodists are. And the whole document was circulated quietly among believers in the USSR to prove the absurdity of antireligion propaganda.

The atheist drive extends to "exposure" of religious leaders in capitalist lands. Generally it is a grand mixture of some truth and more fiction. It is presented in a manner designed to heap ridicule and scorn upon the person and by inference to use him or her as an example of the venality of all persons prominent in religious affairs.

One of the best examples of this will be found in a translation of an article about the Rev. Billy Graham, well-known American Protestant evangelist. The piece is entitled "The Crusader of the Twentieth Century" and begins:

"It would seem that the gloomy times of Middle Ages and the Crusades have forever disappeared into eternity. But in assuming this we forget a contemporary crusader—Billy, as he calls himself. . . ." The article proceeds to poke fun at Mr. Graham's sermons, his methods, the converts of his meetings, his "exploiting" the Bible and other "deceits," his big business advertising, the cost of his radio talks and telecasts, his use of the "jargon of jazz." The writer declares, in good Marxist fashion:

The real reason for the success of Graham can be explained by the atmosphere of fear and uncertainty in the capitalist camp. Graham understands very well that the capitalist world is in need of new arguments which would strengthen the faith in capitalism. . . . Taking advantage of this the Crusader Billy promises calmness to people stricken by anxiety. If you will stop any pedestrian on the corner of Broadway (*sic*) and ask what is his greatest desire, he will answer that most of all he is in need of peace for his soul. . . .

The article was given wide distribution all over the Soviet Union and reprinted in newspapers of several captive countries. The result was a wave of interest in this American evangelist on the part of countless believers. To the intense embarrassment of propaganda experts people began demanding:

"When can he come to preach to us?"

YOUTH WANTS FREEDOM TO WORSHIP

At the Quo Vadis Chapel on the edge of Rome, near the ancient Appian Way where the feet of the Apostle Paul walked in the days of his missionary zeal, we found Father Joseph Hutta, a young priest, native of Slovakia. He cheerfully and reverently showed us about the Chapel. We expressed interest as to religious conditions in Slovakia, and he told us his story.

Joseph was a student in a Catholic school soon after World War II ended. He was eager to help some of his fellow students studying for the priesthood, so he shared with them some printed materials he had obtained from his bishop. He related:

Even though the materials had no political meaning, the Communist authorities arrested me for distributing counterrevolutionary literature. I was sentenced to two years at hard labor. Actually, they needed strong young men to build tanks for the Soviet Union, to use someday, they said, "to fight the imperialists," and that's the labor I was forced to do.

I was a good athlete, running the 100 meters in very fast time. So I was put on the prison track team. I won several competitions, and then was sent with a local team to a track meet in a free country. That was my chance to escape! I shall not mention where it was, for I had good help in escaping. I came to Rome and completed my studies.

I can tell you this: the campaign against religion in Slovakia—and everywhere else—will utilize every possible means to win young people away from religion. But thousands more are like me. They want freedom to worship! So long as the youth fight for freedom, the church can never be conquered.

On a walking trip about the once-beautiful and picturesque city of Prague, Czechoslovakia, in December 1963, we were shown a public park that had recently been the scene of wild rioting by crowds of young people. Our companion was a young Protestant lay leader; he told us:

It was a spontaneous uprising of students and other youth, some of them young homemakers, because they were fed up with the refusal of the Communist government to grant them the freedoms they know exist in countries not under the Reds. Several of the speechmakers at the rally here mentioned "Western freedoms," including freedom of religion and speech.

Then the police came in with clubs. The young people fought back. The ringleaders were arrested, and most of them were sentenced to hard labor on charges of rioting and antigovernment speechmaking.

Our newspaper, Communist-controlled, of course, said "Now they will find out that Western freedom is just an illusion, and that *our* freedom is founded on work for a Socialist society." Such a silly statement did not help the communists in Czechoslovakia!

The event threw a scare into the officials. Will they be able to keep the lid on the demand of the new generation for liberty? We wonder— and so do the officials.

Officials in all Communist-controlled areas are wondering if stubborn youth will prevent their eradication of religion. The matter was well expressed by Monsignor Gerhard Fittkau of Essen-Werden, Germany, who served as interpreter for the German-language press at the Ecumenical Council in Rome and who has close contacts with Catholic leaders in all captive countries:

"The principal weapon the Marxists now hope to use against religion, winning youth to embrace atheism, is being turned against them. Modern, educated young people simply will not exchange the satisfactions of religious faith for cold, hard, hopeless materialism."

In East Berlin a young Lutheran leader endorsed those sentiments. "Youths are in rebellion against atheist communism all over our Soviet-controlled zone," he informed us earnestly. " 'Why can we not have the freedoms of our brothers in the West?' They want to read Western books, newspapers, and magazines. They want to travel freely. They deeply resent the symbol of permanent slavery which is the infamous Berlin Wall. When the lid blows off—as inevitably it must—the revival of religion in East Germany will be something to behold! Freedom of religion will spark and lead a restoration of all other freedoms."

Reports indicate that in all the Soviet bloc countries, including Tito's Yugoslavia, a special task was assigned the Communist youth members on Easter Sunday, 1964. The young atheists were ordered to harass the Easter services, by infiltrating the congregations and disturbing the worship with placards, catcalls, and challenges to the ministers to prove their "superstitions."

Many youths fulfilled their mission after a fashion. But many others failed, and had to be punished.

Their crime consisted in becoming so engrossed in the beauty and solemnity of the services that they forgot what they came for.

CHAPTER EIGHTEEN

FAITH'S BATTLE CAN BE WON

"There is nothing so powerful as an idea whose time has come!" The time has come for a powerful, explosive new idea: Since communism has never been able to conquer religion, and will never succeed in eradicating it from the hearts and lives of believers, communism has met its only master.

This great unconquerable force, the belief of countless millions of humankind in a Supreme Being and in spiritual values, can turn the tide of battle against the mortal enemy of human liberties.

Communism can be conquered: religion can conquer communism!

Here is the mighty challenge and tremendous opportunity for all who believe that religion must not and will not perish from the earth: to take advantage of the obvious failures and glaring weaknesses of the Marxist governments and with definite purposes and programs move to force the restoration of religious liberties.

Every concession in this field wrested from the Communist rulers will mean an irrevocable step toward the ultimate abandonment of the oppressions and tyrannies of the Marxist systems. Every gain in the crusade *for* freedom of religion will mean a weakening of the campaign to force atheism upon all the people under Marxist slavery and then upon all the people of the world. Every weakening of Marxist atheism will be an erosion of the very foundations of Communist control. The house of Marxist rule has been built by foolish men upon the sands of atheistic materialism. Those sands will not support the structure of communism when the rains of spiritual power descend and the winds of faith, hope, and charity beat upon that house. It will fall, and great will be the fall of it.

Our program needs no legislation. It needs only the determination of people who believe in freedom. Their efforts can push open many doors of concessions to believers now living under communism and trying to worship under its cruel persecutions.

We may as well anticipate that objections to our plan will come from all Communist sources, and from apologists for communism. The voices of the faint-hearted also will be heard: those who prefer to do nothing and hope for the best. Some will caution that doing something in this life-and-death struggle for the survival of human liberties might make things worse instead of better.

Certainly we shall be told that we are mistaken about lack of religious liberty under communism, for behold, it is all written out in the constitutions of the Communist countries. All of them *guarantee* freedom of conscience and worship, so our fears must be groundless. We must be mistaken about the total menace of communism, it will be said. But we are prepared for this false-front objection to positive action. We know that the so-called guarantees mask the true intention of Marxism to bury all religion. We can no longer be satisfied with empty promises of freedom of religion. From this time forward we must have deeds, rather than words that can be twisted to mean anything the Communists desire them to mean.

There will be those pessimists, branding themselves as "realists," who will try to convince us that communism is here to stay; that the division of the world into two great power blocs is permanent, and that our best program would be to learn to live with the situation and endure it. Let us remember that every daring move made in mankind's long struggle against tyranny has been opposed by those who counseled defeat before the battle really got underway. Let us remember that all liberties have been won by those brave enough to commit to the cause of freedom their lives, their fortunes, and their sacred honor.

LET THERE BE RELIGIOUS LIBERTY!

What should be our first goal in the mighty campaign to conquer communism? Nothing less than for every Communist country to grant actual freedom of religion. If not all at once, then gradually—but surely.

In addition to permitting religious services within the walls of the place of worship, which is generally the extent of religious "liberty" in Marxist lands, these freedoms must be allowed:

1. *True freedom of conscience and worship.* The drive to eradicate religion, officially sponsored and now intensified in all Marxist areas, must cease. Individuals must be free to follow religious convictions and affiliations without any restraints or punishments. Ministers of religion must have the right to use and apply the sacred ordinances and symbols of their faith. Children and youth must be free to take part in worship and other religious activities, without persecutions and discriminations.

2. *Freedom for ecclesiastical administration.* Pastors, priests, rabbis, and all other religious leaders must be unrestricted in their spiritual ministrations, both inside and outside the place of worship. Administration of the financial affairs of religious organizations and the control of their property must be returned to the churches, synagogues, mosques, and other responsible agencies of the particular faith. Establishment of new congregations, building of new churches, selection of clergy, and the free choice and direction of religious leadership must be granted.

3. *Freedom to propagate the faith.* Liberty to preach, teach, and to spread the faith must be restored. An honest search for spiritual truth and the duty to accept and teach it require this freedom. There must be full liberty for religious education in Sunday schools, parochial educational institutions, youth groups, confirmation classes, Bible and other sacred literature study groups, and all teaching ministries considered necessary by the religious body. Restrictions on printing, importation, distribution, and use of Bibles and other sacred writings, and upon hymnbooks and religious literature should be completely removed. Seminaries and other institutions for the training of theological leaders must

be permitted. Spying and censorship by government agents to trap and harass ministers and believers must cease.

4. *Freedom of mutual cooperation.* The right of churches and all religious bodies to form associations, within their national borders and beyond, for proper administration and fellowship, must be recognized. This must include the right to carry on cooperative benevolent, educational, welfare, and missionary endeavors, at home and in foreign lands. Free exchange of persons, ideas, and materials with other religious groups must be permitted.

Such are the basic essentials for true religious liberty.

Many details could be added to this outline. Many other liberties will naturally flow from the granting of these fundamental freedoms of conscience and worship. All may be summed up in the principle that religious liberty is total, and not divisible at the whim of atheist dictators and their bureaucrats. The principle was well stated by the Great Teacher:

"Render unto Caesar the things that are Caesar's, and unto God the things that are God's."

THE TRUE NATURE OF COMMUNISM

How can this program to regain and sustain religious liberty be accomplished? How can this vital step in religion's forthcoming victory over communism be taken?

If religion is to conquer communism, we whom the Marxist leaders honor by calling us *believers* must dedicate ourselves to three vital tasks:

First, we must understand and teach others to know the nature and history, the purposes and programs, the strengths and weaknesses of communism.

Second, we must use all the moral and spiritual power we possess, bringing it to bear upon the many weak spots in the Communist fortress.

Third, we must utilize every political and governmental weapon at our disposal, in favor of human freedom and against Marxist tyranny.

It is essential to understand our enemy, as thoroughly as it is humanly possible, in this historic struggle for the survival of religion with all its attendant blessings. Surely in this study we have explored, necessarily in brief, the origins and nature of the worldwide revolutionary movement. We have noted its beginnings and development as a monolithic, dictatorial regime in the Russian motherland, its expansion to other areas according to Marxist plan, and throughout all, its basic thesis of atheistic materialism. So let us summarize:

According to Communist leaders all the way from Karl Marx, there is no God, no Creator of the universe, no spiritual existence of any kind. There is only physical matter, its origin unknown and unexplained. Since in Communist theory there is no Supreme Spiritual Being, man did not become a living soul, but only a bit of organic matter, alive but no more so than all other organic matter about him. Logically then, since man has no spiritual nature, what he calls *religion* is nothing more than a collection of superstitious illusions.

Nikita Khrushchev expressed the matter for Marxists of all times and for all tongues when he said in a Moscow radio broadcast:

"I believe there is no God. I freed myself long ago from such a concept. I am a partisan of a scientific point of view, and science and faith in supernatural forces are irreconcilable opinions which exclude one another necessarily if one is consistent to the end in scientific knowledge." *

Now, say the Marxists, as social "classes" developed, the property owners, who were all exploiters of the working class, decided they could use religion as a tool for further exploitation. If the working-class man believed in a spiritual life hereafter, he might just be more satisfied with his wretched lot on this earth, and the cunning, greedy capitalist could make even more profit out of him. Therefore, religion is a "vestige" of hated capitalism, and since capitalism is the enemy of the people's revolution it must be completely abolished and religion eradicated with it.

Absurd, you say? Unbelievable in this day when 75 per cent of the working class, the skilled and unskilled laborers in the free nations, are capitalists in the sense of owning property and investments? Not at all! Let us remind ourselves that Marxist leaders are still in deadly earnest in their determination to dominate the world, although embarrassed that with popular education spreading around the globe their preposterous ideologies are being exposed for the monstrous lies they have always been.

The true nature of Communism was well described by J. Edgar Hoover, Director of the U.S. Federal Bureau of Investigation, in these meaningful words:

Khrushchev gives the answer to those who still repeat the shabby, deceitful phrases of Communist dogma, when he de-sanctifies Stalin one day and on the next day rehabilitates him as a good Communist. . . . The answer also comes from Mao Tse-tung, the Chinese Communist dictator, who without apparent shame admitted that 800,000 of his countrymen had been liquidated between 1949 and the beginning of 1954.

The answer comes from those Americans who were victimized by the Communist deception of claiming credit for reforms and advances which the Party did not deserve.

Most informed Americans now know that the Communists adopt a cause only to exploit it for their own ends. Communism does not mean better housing, improved social conditions, or a more strict observance of civil rights. The vast majority of Negro leaders have rebuffed the Communists' attempts to exploit them. By forcing Party members out of positions of authority and even from union membership, true trade unionists have shown their awareness that Communists seek to disrupt the legitimate mission of labor unions.

Communism, in brief, has bitterly indicted communism. Communist practice has indicted Communist theory; Communist actions have indicted the perverted use of such lofty words as "peace," "justice," and "liberty." But we cannot afford the luxury of waiting for communism to run its course like other oppressive dictatorships. . . . The call of the future must be rekindled American faith, based on our priceless heritage of freedom, justice, and the religious spirit.*

MARXIST PROMISES ARE HOLLOW

As we enter this enlistment for the duration of the struggle against atheist Marxism let us realize that we are fighting an enemy already defeated. We need but to press the advantage we now hold to complete the victory.

Communism has failed throughout the world.

In three major aspects communism is a colossal fizzle. It has failed *politically, economically, and spiritually.*

Karl Marx thought, or at least ardently hoped, that once the Red banner of the world Communist revolution was raised the "working people" of one nation after another would rally beneath it. This did not happen. As we have seen, the infant constitutional government of the Russian homeland was seized by the throat in 1917 by Lenin and choked to death. A fledgling monster of potential tyranny was given its birthright, and has now grown to be a huge, moronic giant, lashing about to destroy what it cannot understand and cannot control.

Not one country of those containing the more than 900 million people now under communism has freely voted for its adoption.

In every instance, communism has been thrust upon the people by the ruthless tactics of the Marxist warlords and rulers. It has gained control only by infiltration, subversion, and seizure of power, backed by military might and the dread secret police.

Even where communism is supported by a segment of the people, that support was gained by deceit and chicanery. Communism, masked as the friend of the workers, the champion of the oppressed, the creator of equality and opportunity, gains followers who do not suspect that once they are in its grasp communism will drop the mask, and the cruel face of dictatorship with its oppressions, degradation, and poverty will be revealed.

Herein lies the failure of communism politically: its control over the people and its denial of their liberties belies all its fine promises of a "people's government." The matter is well summarized in a publication issued by the Americanism Commission of the Veterans of Foreign Wars:

> The Communist ruling class has never risked giving the majority a free voice in government. The Communist party has always retained its control through a series of infrequent, fixed, single-party, noncompetitive "elections." They offer no choice of candidates or issues. Communism keeps the majority in line through arbitrary and harsh persuasion. Any citizen attempting to act independently is liquidated.*

Communism has failed politically because of its record of falsehoods and betrayals of the hopes of humanity for progress and peace. Its members in the United Nations use that organization only to advance the revolution. Its proposals for disarmament would only weaken the free world in its fight for survival. The repeated avowals of its leaders for "peace" are now recognized throughout the world as false as counterfeit banknotes.

"Peace" is a wonderful slogan. Everybody is for peace on earth. People everywhere would gladly abandon war, now and forever. But "peace" on the Communist pattern means only the lack of opposition to Marxist expansion that will result—they hope and expect—from the liquidation of all opposition. Nowhere on earth is there a better example of "peace" as desired by Communist rulers than in Hungary. It is the peace of subjection, the peace of a graveyard where lie buried the hopes of freedom.

Communism has failed *economically*. Marxism claims to be able to satisfy all the needs of the people by *materialistic means*. That is supposed to be its basic appeal. But that promise has proved to be hollow. Nowhere on earth has communism been able to supply material things in quantity to sustain standards of living comparable to those of the free peoples.

So communism flunks the one big course in which it is supposed—by its leaders and dupes—to excel. Since it denies the things of the spirit, there is not much left for it to boast about.

The reason why communism has not, and cannot ever, supply the needs of the people is clear. The answer is written in bold letters in the Soviet Union, in Red China, in Cuba, and in all the captive areas: economic progress can be made only under conditions that permit the enjoyment and exercise of human liberties, and especially the right of self-government, including the shaping and changing of policies as the times and needs of the people demand.

Communism totally ignores the basic facts of economic life: that abundant production, whether from the factory, the soil, the office, or the professional workshop cannot be forced by government planning and decrees; that deep in human nature is pride of ownership and its accompanying desire to create; that production depends in large measure on private initiative and rewards for work well done; that when initiative and rewards are eliminated, all the pressure of a monolithic dictatorship, all the threats and punishments that can be heaped upon a sullen, unresponsive citizenry cannot match what freedom does for those who possess it.

Apologists for communism and deluded fellow-travelers will point out that "the Russian people are so much better off than they were under the Tzars," and that "the Chinese people are steadily improving in production," and "give Castro time and he will overcome the shortages in Cuba."

In 1972 the Kremlin's leaders have been forced to import massive quantities of wheat and other food items from the Western World in order to assure adequate national food supplies for the U.S.S.R. Such agricultural crises in the years since the Communists came to power occur far too frequently for the 'vagaries of the weather' to be solely to blame for Soviet crop failures.

While most of the captive countries did somewhat better, all face the continuing lowering of industrial and agricultural production. Witness again the contrast between free Germany and Soviet Germany, between West and East Berlin divided by that Communist wall.

The fact is that no Red-driven slave can or will outproduce the free man. The Russian people may be better off than they were under the Tzars, but *without* the shackles of these nearly 50 years of Marxism, and *with* constitutional self-government, they would be far more advanced and prosperous today than they are.

So the Red leaders, swallowing their curses at the hated "capitalist'" nations, come hats in hand like beggars, pleading to be sold wheat and other foodstuffs to keep their people alive and working. They would not be asking for help from the governments and peoples they pretend to be excelling if their systems of "Socialism" had not fallen flat. The Marxist politicians, being practical fellows, understand full well that no boiler without some outlet for its steam can withstand the pressure when the fires are hot. They know that all the oppressive control they can muster, backed by all the threats and terror of secret police, will not be able to contain a population if its members get so fed up they would rather die than live any longer as slaves pulling the oars of Marxist galleys.

THE ULTIMATE FAILURE OF COMMUNISM

Communism has failed *spiritually*. Marxism is itself a religion: an ideology that admits no higher loyalty than to itself. Its spirituality consists in denying that which is spiritual. Since it offers the stones of atheism when believing children ask for the bread of life, since it offers serpents of persecution instead of the fish of reverence the people need for spiritual food, communism cannot hope to succeed in winning true loyalty.

Herein lies a great truth, the sword that can pierce the Marxist armor of cruelty and deceit:

Communism bears within itself the seeds of its own destruction, for it possesses not the strength that can come only from righteousness, but the fatal weakness of inherent evil.

It is precisely in its crusade to eradicate religion that Marxist tyrants best display the true nature of communism. They would eliminate from all life that which gives it meaning in the present and hope for the future. They would deny the sacred calling of priests, rabbis, ministers, and all religious workers, whose spiritual leadership gives order, cohesion, and dignity to worship.

They would snatch away forever from human hearts the firm belief that God is the Father of all mankind and that all mortals are His children. They would stamp out the calm assurance that comes from communion in prayer with the Creator, the joy of praise in song, the warmth of spiritual fellowship with brothers and sisters in the faith.

They would deny to believers the stewadship of possessions to sustain places of worship and to propagate the faith at home and abroad; to help the sick, the distressed and the weak; to inculcate principles of morality, decency, and righteousness among children and youths.

They would rob all future brides and grooms of religious ceremonies to bless their union as God intended, deny to the bereaved the consolation of spiritual faith and hope, and take away from every person the assurance that this which is mortal will someday put on immortality.

They would continue to uproot from every community in the

world the places of worship with the sacred and beloved facilities, casting away all the symbols which indicate mankind's belief that "righteousness exalteth a nation, but sin is a reproach to any people."

The Marxist leaders would have mankind abandon love of wives and husbands, children and relatives, friends and neighbors, as "bourgeois sentiment." They would have us discard kindness, mercy, meekness, self-sacrifice, charity, honesty, and brotherly love as capitalist nonsense and not needed in the atheist paradise on earth. They would have parents raise children not for the fulfillment of the Creator's intent, not to raise them in the fear and admonition of the Lord, and not for the joy of family life, but only to further the interests and greed of the all-powerful State.

Understanding the nature of communism and what its continued existence and extension throughout the world would mean for religion, can believers fail to answer the challenge to join battle? Let us assemble, even as Gideon of old assembled his meager band of warriors and led them to complete victory.

We have the weapons. Let the trumpets sound! *

* It is obviously impossible for lack of space to carry on a lengthy discussion of the nature, aims, and tactics of communism in this work. Fortunately, materials on the subject are available from many denominational publishers and suppliers of literature. Such publications, ranging all the way from pamphlets to volumes, have the approval of the reader's fellowship, whatever his faith or denomination may be.

Accordingly, we are happy to present in the appendix of this book a list of sources where studies of communism may be obtained, with identification by name and address of the religious fellowship that sponsors and offers the materials.

We append also a list of sources of materials published by the United States Government dealing with communism. We realize that there are numerous private sources of information available to those concerned with the subject. It is our hope that readers may take advantage of the materials which religious leaders and other recognized authorities feel are essential to an understanding of communism and how to deal intelligently with its menace. *The Authors*

CHAPTER NINETEEN

SPIRITUAL WEAPONS
ARE POWERFUL

The Rev. Walter M. Ciszek, a Jesuit priest, son of Polish parents who immigrated to Shenandoah, Pennsylvania, decided as a young seminarian to devote his life as a missionary to eastern Poland. He was influenced in this decision by reading an encyclical of Pope Pius XI. He studied in Rome, and as a priest of the Eastern Rite of the Catholic Church was assigned to Albyrtyn, Poland, in 1937.

When the Nazi and Soviet forces took over Poland according to agreement of the Hitler-Stalin pact, the Reds raided Ciszek's office, destroyed his books and papers. Father Ciszek volunteered to go as a worker in the Caucasus area, and for a year was a laborer there. Then the Reds arrested him as a "spy of the Vatican." For five years he was imprisoned in Moscow, much of the time under "interrogation" by Communist tormentors. At the close of the war he was sent to Siberia, and for ten years, while at forced labor in the salt mines, nothing was heard of him in the outside world.

Father Ciszek had been known as a robust, versatile athlete, a friendly, affable man. News that he was alive reached friends in Europe and the United States in 1955, and Father Ciszek was shifted to Abakan concentration camp near the border of Mongolia.

Appeals went out from prominent Catholics and churchmen of other faiths, in many countries, for his release. When the appeals became embarrassing to the Kremlin's "de-Stalinization" program and the "coexistence" policy, Khrushchev ordered Father Ciszek's freedom. He reached New York on Columbus Day, October 12, 1963, lean and gaunt, but with firm step and head held high. A few days later he celebrated a Solemn High Mass of Thanksgiving in the parish where he was born and reared. In a brief address to friends afterward, Father Ciszek declared:

"During all the twenty-three years in Communist prisons I never forgot that I was a priest."

"Did the Soviets break you?" he was asked.

"Break me? They didn't even bend me!" he replied.

From the experiences of Father Ciszek, including his release, we note two significant facts: There is nothing so strong as spiritual faith. And the pressure of church people upon the shaky structure of Red terror can win concessions from the Marxist tyrants.

We believers in religion, of all faiths, have before us the second urgent, immediate task: to use our moral and spiritual weapons in the battle to win freedom of religion and thus roll back the crusade for atheism in the Communist world.

These weapons are the strongest of any at the disposal of free peoples.

We do recognize that it is necessary for governments and citizens of the free nations to maintain military strength sufficient to repel aggression in a world beset with those who defy order, justice, and international peace. We cannot here discuss what military strength is needed to hold at bay the forces of lawlessness. We realize with sorrow that the government of the United States of America feels obliged to appropriate more than 50 billion dollars annually for this cause. We know that if this stupendous amount plus the total amounts spent annually by other free nations could be used by private citizens and families for the support of religious causes, and by both private and public agencies for health, education, welfare, and human betterment generally, it would be a happier world.

But the fact remains that we have moral and spiritual weapons to be used against Communist tyranny, aggression, and expansion, more powerful than those comprising our military defense. The first to be mentioned is not within our borders at all. It lives in the minds, hearts, and souls of the faithful believers in human liberties now living behind the monolithic iron curtains of Communist control.

WHAT THE TYRANTS FEAR MOST

The current Red rulers and their associates in the Kremlin do not fear our atomic and hydrogen bombs, our guided missiles and our huge defense establishments. In this complacency they are joined by Red Chinese Mao, by Cuba's Fidel Castro, and by all other top Marxist dictators and their fellows. The whole pack of them know that the free world, led by the United States of America, will never start a "preventive war," or any other kind of war. They realize that a "shooting war" could be thrust upon us only by their own miscalculations and actions.

While the Red Chinese and the Soviet bloc leaders currently differ over how far they should go in defiance of the peace-keeping efforts of the "war-mongering" nations, they do not fear wanton aggression on our part.

They fear most of all the burning desire for liberation and for the restoration of self-government of those they have enslaved.

That is the most awesome weapon in the hands of free peoples. The Communist leaders are practical politicians. They know that their oppression and tyranny have not endeared them to their victims. They know that their denial of the precious right of religious liberty has made them evil in the sight and thoughts of those they have persecuted. They have not forgotten how the East German workmen on June 17, 1953 with their bare hands assailed the Soviet tanks in the cities and towns of Ulbricht's captive colony, and they know that if that uprising had been supported by the free world all Germany would now be free. They shudder as they recall the revolution of the Hungarian fighters for freedom and how it might have started a wave of uprisings for liberation all over eastern Europe.

The last thing the Communist leaders want, at least those in the Soviet bloc, is war. They are aware that war would touch off the fires of rebellion in every captive area. They cannot trust the military forces of their captive peoples. And they know that all the efforts of their own Soviet military forces would not be sufficient to stem the tide of revolution.

The Marxist leaders' counterweapon to this desire for freedom is *time*. Time, filled with a period of false "coexistence." They know that if, despite their failures and difficulties, enough time goes by to permit their bringing up a few atheist generations, *all hope of liberation will be gone*. The new Communist generations will not remember the God of their fathers nor care for the ancient religious faiths. This is the only weapon in the Communist arsenal that can prevent religion from conquering communism: it is the loss of all hope of living again in freedom.

"How can I ever convince the people of this great country, of which I am now a naturalized citizen, that the people of Hungary are losing all hope of freedom?" asks our friend Dr. Alexander Haraszti, the man who bound up the wounds of so many of the victims of the Soviet tanks and guns in that bloody rioting of October 1956 in Budapest.

"The uprising was one of the great rebellions of history against tyranny. Now the survivors are losing hope. They do not believe the pious statements of politicians in the free countries, who seem to say that they are for human freedoms when they have no programs to attain them for the enslaved in Communist lands."

From time to time, the dictators of the Red Russian empire have signaled they would like to work out a deal for "peaceful coexistence" with the United States. Remembering how Stalin so completely duped the American statesmen into granting his every request, they would pledge hands-off in U.S. spheres of interest in exchange for a *"status quo"* understanding in Europe.

Such a "deal" would consign the 70 million captive peoples of eastern Europe to perpetual captivity. As though these men, women, and children were nothing more than cordwood or sacks of potatoes, they would be bargained away—for what? For hollow promises that the Marxists might keep hands off U.S. spheres of interest.

The United States has no spheres of interest except to help all peoples live in freedom, with justice and peace. It is unthinkable that leaders of the United States would consider such an evil, heartless, shameful exchange, whether "after the 1964 presidential election" or any future election. The deal would mean abandoning all moral principles, admitting that might makes right, and that a peace with justice is not worth working for. It would certify for all time that the fate of our neighbors who fell among thieves who beat them, stripped them of their raiment, and left them half dead is none of our concern and so we'll just pass by on the other side.

"WE WILL NEVER FORGET YOU!"

How use this moral and spiritual weapon, this worthy longing for liberty? Believers of all faiths and kinds in one voice may declare:

We will never forget you! First of all, we will never forget to keep you in our prayers. We will never become so smug in our own presumed security that we cast your plight from our minds. We shall never thank God for our own priceless freedom of conscience and worship without remembering to ask Him to strengthen our faith in your ultimate deliverance from evil.

Next, we of the free world will never cease our efforts to influence your leaders to grant to you the independence you desire and deserve. By all peaceful means we will work as well as pray for your liberation. We will arouse public opinion in your behalf, throughout the world. We will never forget you!

Finally, keep the faith yourselves! Resist, by every method you can devise, these intensified efforts to teach your children and youth the satanic principles of godless materialism. Tell your young people that atheism can never eradicate the blessings of religion. Tell them that by God's help they can enjoy the comforts, the consolations, the assurances of eternal life, the fellowships that spring from the fountain of religious faith. Keep the faith, and we will match your faith with ours.*

As we move into our campaign to regain religious liberty we may need to clear our minds of the grave error of equating *peoples* with their *Marxist governments*. We may be concerned about imputing guilt by association such as implying that the leaders of Red regimes are "the Russians," or "the Hungarians," or "the Chinese." Let us make a sharp distinction between Communist-ruled people and the Marxist regimes that rule them. Let us abandon such expressions as "enemies" and "opponents" when speaking of the men, women, and children that made up the populations of countries with which a free nation was in conflict during past wars, and also of Communist-dominated countries today.

The *peoples* of Japan, Germany, and Italy were NOT our enemies during World War II. It was the expansionist and aggressive policies of the Japanese war lords, of Hitler and Mussolini, rather than the wishes of the vast majority of the citizens of those nations, that drove them into the unspeakable tragedy of war. It was the cruel and aggressive policies of the Red China regime, backed by the USSR, that drove the Chinese people into war against their small neighbor, the Republic of Korea.

Let us abandon forever the loose thinking that calls a Marxist regime an "ally" of the free world, past, present, or future, when no dictatorship can in a true sense be a friend and supporter of our way of life and our aspirations for a true peace based upon liberty, justice, and security for all.

Freedom has no enemies among the peoples of the world. All who love liberty and are dedicated to its preservation are friends.

Let us also abandon such expressions as "East versus West" in speaking of the activities of Marxist regimes that violate the liberties and security of free peoples. Such a geographical division of humanity is inaccurate and unfair. It is true that the homeland of Marxist control is Soviet Russia in eastern Europe and Asia, and the great subcontinent of China, decidedly an "eastern" nation, is now under Red control. But communism did not take over in either place because the area was "East" but because the people had no effective way to prevent it.

Certainly Generalissimo Chiang Kai-shek, who fought the Red advance in China until his resources were exhausted, is not of the "West"; nor is Carlos Romulo, statesman of the Philippines; nor Charles Malik of Lebanon, formerly president of the United Nations Assembly; nor Kiyoshi Togasaki, member of the board of Japan International Christian University and vice president of Rotary International, nor millions more Easterners like them who are vigorous opponents of communism. Not by any means could Cuba of Fidel Castro, Communist leader of the "Western" Hemisphere, be called "East" yet its regime is as Marxist as that of the USSR.

To strengthen the sinews of our campaign in popular thinking, let us use the more meaningful expressions: "The free world versus the Communist governments," "The free peoples and the captive peoples." Let us never dignify the false implications in such Marxist designations as "The German Democratic Republic" (for the Soviet Zone dictatorship) or "The People's Republic of China" for the Red control, without adding some explanations in behalf of truth.

THE BATTLE MUST BE WAGED

As the campaign to demand religious liberty progresses, we shall doubtless be reminded that the Communist leaders are "moving in our direction" to grant greater personal liberties and civil rights, and that efforts on the part of religious believers and church groups might "rock the boat," "delay the process of softening," or some similar bit of wishful thinking.

Let us never lose sight of our goal nor be deterred from its pursuit. Either the "softening" is genuine or it is not. If it is genuine, then Khrushchev and the Kremlin leaders are ready for concessions to the free world.

The first and major concession to be made is to grant true freedom of conscience and worship.

On the other hand, the relaxing of tensions may be a mere tactic in the cold war, a strategic retreat by Marxist rulers in order to gain time to solve more pressing problems and to recoup losses in power and prestige. The best possible way to find this out is to press for religious freedom. If that freedom is denied, then the coexistence policy is a fraud; still worse, it is a trap to entice free peoples into believing that communism has really changed for the better.

If only *some* concessions toward religious freedom for people under communism are granted, even though reluctantly and grudgingly, to that extent progress toward our goal has been made. So on both counts the battle must be waged, the challenge of Marxist "coexistence" accepted and tested.

Already some church groups have assaulted the Red citadels and found that with persistent pounding the hard shell of Marxist resistance gives way. After four years of pressure from Catholic leaders in the United States, in 1959 the Soviet Union granted permission for a chaplain to serve Catholics in the foreign diplomatic community of Moscow. The position had been vacated in 1955 when the Rev. Georges Bisonnette was expelled without explanation. Father Dion, Assumptionist priest of Worcester, Massachusetts, is now spiritual adviser to about 150 persons of his faith in the Soviet capital.

Members in exile of the Latvian Evangelical Lutheran Church in November 1963 issued a forthright appeal for the restoration of religious freedom in Latvia and the other Baltic states. It contained these words:

> Our concern for the extension and preservation of human freedom involves the special concern for the freedom of worship. Although the Church may strive to accomplish its mission under the most adverse circumstances, it can fulfill its work best only in a free society that guarantees the freedom of worship. We reject the thesis that a dying Church is somehow better than a living one!

The Latvian Lutheran statement spelled out other items of religious freedom, summarized in these words: "Freedom of worship is the freedom of the Church to develop its own life without outside interferences." This appeal, given widespread undercover reading in Latvia and Estonia, aroused considerable concern among Red commissars in those captive nations.

In February 1964 the Council of National Unity, representing the 100,000 Polish Catholics living in exile in Great Britain and Ireland, at its annual Congress issued an appeal to the United Nations and other international organizations against the "blatantly inhuman" anti-Catholic activities of the Communist government in Warsaw. The appeal jolted heavily the Gomulka regime both for its boldness and for its accurate bill of particulars.

The specific oppressive measures mentioned as levied "under pressure from Moscow" include: Catholics dismissed from their jobs because of attendance at mass, persons punished for receiving holy communion, schools stripped of crosses and crucifixes, teachers arrested and fined for giving religious instruction out of school hours, nuns removed from hospitals and charitable institutions, priests and parishes penalized by exorbitant taxes. One of the newest Communist restrictions, the statement said, involved curtailment of religious publications "and a corresponding increase in ever-growing volume of atheistic literature." The appeal declared:

"People of Poland, whether living in their own country or abroad, have a right to defend the faith of their ancestors from Communist aggression. They have a right to hope that all people with a conscience will join in this solemn protest against religious persecution in Poland and condemn it."

On March 3, 1964 an interfaith committee was formed in Paris "to throw light on the situation of Christians in the Soviet Union." Jean Marie Dominic, a Catholic, pinpointed for the committee and for world opinion various types of religious persecution meted out by Red governments, and called for united action to oppose the antireligion campaign in the USSR.

In April 1964 a conference on the persecution of Jews in the Soviet Union, held in Washington, D.C., and sponsored by the Union of American Hebrew Congregations, issued a vigorous denunciation of the intensified oppressions of Jewish leaders and members under communism. An appeal was made "to all those in the USSR who genuinely desire the eradication of the evils of Stalinism and who, with us, thirst for truth, justice, and decency; we appeal to the Soviet authorities to act in this matter on the basis of their own ideological, constitutional, and legal commitments. We fervently hope that the following specific steps may be taken."

The appeal listed restoration of Jewish education, reopening of cultural institutions, permission to establish formal religious bonds with Jewish communities abroad, permission for Jews to leave the USSR, and "a vigorous campaign against anti-Semitism should be undertaken."

The wide publicity given this conference stung propaganda boss Ilyichev to deny that anti-Semitism existed in the Soviet Union, and anyhow, "corrective measures" would soon be taken.

FRIENDSHIP IS A POWERFUL WEAPON

Among the moral and spiritual weapons which believers in religion hold in their hands are the resources to be helpful to peoples in need. After an earthquake had virtually destroyed the city of Skopje, Yugoslavia, in July 1963, with the loss of about a thousand lives and with 3,000 injured, financial and material aid for the stricken survivors began pouring in from church groups all over the world. The World Council of Churches raised nearly half a million dollars to provide 100 prefabricated houses. The Lutheran World Federation, the Catholic Welfare Conference, Methodist churches in Germany and Switzerland, and the "Bread for the World Movement" were among the larger contributors.

Disasters such as the Skopje earthquake present an opportunity for members of religious bodies to remind the people in Marxist lands, in a substantial way, *that they are our friends, not enemies.* By every possible means, believers in free countries should emphasize that they understand the difference between the *people* and the *governments* that deny the people the blessings of true religious liberty.

The failure of Communist regimes to supply the physical needs of their subjects also opens doors for believers, in churches, congregations, and denominational groups, to be helpful. The free nations are lands of abundance. In the United States, surplus farm commodities are piled mountain high. Despite political complications and transportation costs ways and means should be found by all who believe that "I am my brother's keeper" in my concern for his well-being, to see that abundance is shared by those who are hungry and impoverished, particularly in the Communist areas.

Why should not an interfaith conference be called especially to consider this matter and come up with suggestions which denominational groups might agree upon?

In the land of greatest abundance, the United States, why should not peoples of all faiths *give* of their abundance to peoples behind the Marxist barriers? Millions of dollars' worth of food and feed grains, dairy and poultry products, and cotton are stored in warehouses under governmental control. This surplus had better be sold for token amounts than deteriorate into waste, if its use helps to pierce the shell of Communist enmity with a message of friendship and helpfulness from people to people.

Suppose that ships could be loaded with surplus agricultural products and should head for the coasts of Red China and Cuba, and that by sea and land transportation the products could be brought to calling distance of the Berlin Wall, the barbed wire and mine-fields of Hungary, Poland, and other imprisoned regions. Suppose that messages, day and night, spoke out in the language of the area:

"This is a gift from people who are your friends! All we ask is that you come and get it!"

What would the Red rulers do? If they permitted the acceptance of the gifts of food, feed, and materials, a tremendous propaganda victory would be won by those who believe in a spiritual brotherhood of man.

If the Red dictators refused their own people the needed proffered aid, still a victory would be won in the admission of Marxist leaders that they are more interested in keeping their people sealed off from "capitalist" friendship than they are in their welfare.

We have in our possession a collection of poems by a young Russian author, a lay churchman who served time in a Siberian concentration camp for his religious activities. The poems were smuggled out of the Soviet Union. While the verses lose much of their rhythm and beauty when the expressive Russian language is translated into English, still they breathe the spirit of the outlawed religious faith which believers in the free world must help to rescue. Here are some quotations:

I Know How to Live

At times when I am short of food,
Or suffer pangs of thirst,
I praise God for all things,
And continue to strive for Heaven.
In all my toils and exertions,
In my exhaustion without sleep,
In sorrow and in trouble,
When sadness is seen in my tears,

Under the burden of malignant gossip
And calumny of those who slander me,
In distant exile and in days of persecution,
In prison, under the weight of fetters,
May I remind you that at the end,
Paul said praises even when
He was badly beaten and imprisoned.
Yes, he knew how to live with God!

I Want to Walk

I want to walk so that in this land of sins
I may be witness of the only way,
The way of God's sentinels, the Holy Prophets,
May I walk with them, shoulder to shoulder,
May I not falter nor fall by the way,
May I not bend my cowardly back.
May I walk so that my tired brother
Can hear the moving rhythm of my steps,
And filled with inspirations, speed
His steps toward the sacred dream.

Sound the Victory!

Hail to you, flourishing tribe of Christ,
Born in a period of heavy storms.
You have met many threats in recent times
And have been challenged to the last decisive fight.
The battle regiments must stand united like a wall;
Godlessness is coming to fight a fierce battle.
Close your ranks more tightly!
Sound the victory! Let the sacred flame
Burn brighter over the ruins of evil!

CHAPTER TWENTY

BELIEVERS OF THE WORLD, UNITE!

"Workers of the world, unite! You have nothing to lose but your chains!"

With these stirring words Karl Marx and Friedrich Engels ended their *Communist Manifesto*. This revolutionary trumpet call has sounded many times since to rally the "workers" to overthrow the "capitalists" and establish communism throughout the world.

Believers of all religious faiths, let us unite! Let us join to overcome the godless force that would crush all religion and would build a completely atheist society. We have nothing to lose but the chains of persecutions, restrictions, and harassments that bind our fellow believers in all Marxist lands.

And what have we to gain?

We can gain a world rid of the most reactionary ideology of modern times. We can gain a world in which young people everywhere can plan their futures without enforced military service, and can enter freely into their chosen professions, their homemaking, and their community life. We can gain a world cleansed of the knock on the door at night by the dread secret police; a world without the arrests, imprisonments, and tortures of atheist Marxist rulers.

We can gain a world in which people everywhere and of all creeds may again rear their altars and light their fires of religious faith, unhindered and unafraid.

To accomplish this history-making task, we must add to our

program of moral and spiritual pressure the weapons of direct political action.

Let us hasten to agree that this *does not mean* taking the churches and the church organizations which we cherish into "politics" or governmental affairs. It *does mean* that as individual believers we can join hands across denominational lines in this matter of universal concern. We can unite as believers in God and in the unalienable rights of His children of all races and kinds to influence our public servants to help accomplish the most important mission confronting us in this modern age:

It is to regain religious liberty for all people and roll back the tide of Marxist atheism.

If ever there was a common program worthy of ecumenical cooperation, surely this is it. If ever the clear call sounded for religious unity to accomplish a specific task, that clear call is sounding now.

This crusade for religious freedom can and should supplement all other efforts at ecumenical cooperation, for peoples of *all* faiths and expressions of reverence suffer religious persecution somewhere in the atheistic Marxist empires.

In this common effort of Catholics and Protestants, of Christians and Jews, of Muslims and Bahai, of Buddhists and others whose religious faith prompts concern for fellow men, there need be no sacrifice of cherished beliefs. There need be no surrender of principles or creeds, no giving up of hallowed practices of church, denomination, or fellowship.

All believers, each in his own way or in collective effort within his fellowship and group, may join the ranks of those who now stand at Armageddon and battle for the Lord.

DIRECT ACTION IS NEEDED

Citizens of the free world, remembering that their public officials are servants of the people and not their masters as in Marxist nations, should carry the crusade for religious freedom directly to their governments at every point where action is desired.

We the people may start with our foreign offices (the State Department in the United States) to insist that the basic violation of human rights in all the areas of Soviet imperialist colonial rule be corrected. The basic violation stems from the broken promise by the USSR that after World War II there would be *free elections* to establish new and permanent governments in the countries of eastern Europe, from Poland to Bulgaria. If this pledge had been carried out, freedom of religion would certainly have been recognized and preserved in these countries.

"When are these people to have free elections?" the Red leaders should be asked by spokesmen of the free nations, day by day, month by month. In the embassies of all countries, in the United Nations, in international conferences, the question should be pressed until the consciences of statesmen everywhere are seared with it.

Meanwhile, religious leaders and groups should point to the wording of peace treaties and demand their observance. All treaties following World War II involving the eastern European countries included provisions that were intended to guarantee freedom of religion, along with other rights which free men consider unalienable.

An example of all such treaties was the one signed with the representatives of the Romanian government by the Allied powers in Paris in August 1947. It was duly deposited with the foreign offices of all signatory nations and with the United Nations Treaty Division, and includes this provision:

"Romania shall take all measures necessary to secure to all persons under Romanian jurisdiction, without distinction of race, sex, language or religion, the enjoyment of human rights and the fundamental freedoms, including freedom of expression, of the press and publication, of religious worship, of political opinions and of public meeting."

Not one single freedom "guaranteed" in this solemn treaty exists in Red Romania today. There is not a semblance of freedom of religion, nor of speech, press, assembly, or political opinions publicly expressed.

Similar treaties, broken and held in contempt, exist for other captive countries. Let believers urge their officials to ask, day by day, month by month, in the embassies and in the United Nations:

"When are you going to grant freedom of religion promised to your people?"

Peoples of the free world have direct access to their public officials, the legislators who express the popular will in the making of laws and the members of executive departments who administer them. Officials in free republics are men and women of religious faith, eager to cooperate in matters pertaining to the preservation of our spiritual heritage. Believers should appeal to them to use their powerful influence to arouse world opinion in behalf of human liberty.

Countless examples of such cooperation by public officials could be cited. U.S. Senator Jacob Javits has taken up the appeals of Jewish leaders and members of his faith in many countries of the world for relief from religious persecution in Soviet lands. In a speech on the floor of the Senate, Mr. Javits discussed this problem, and declared:

> The State Department suggests that religious groups themselves in the United States on their own initiative could give appropriate publicity to the violations of the rights of their coreligionists in the Soviet Union, and that private appeals to the USSR on humane grounds are in order.
>
> Enough evidence is piling up against the Soviet position so that government-to-government protest is in order. As far back as 1890 our government never hesitated to protest the persecution of Jews, at that time by the Tzarist government. I see no reason for its reluctance to do so now. I believe the facts are beginning to point up serious dangers and I urge our President to instruct the State Department to protest *now!*

Such appeals, piling as high as is the evidence of religious persecutions, would prove an irresistible force to move Red leaders to grant greater freedom of conscience and worship.

Lutheran Bishop Otto Dibelius of Berlin-Brandenburg has said, "The experiences of the recent past only confirm what for a Christian has always been a basic tenet of his faith: that no single man, nor group of human beings, nor any political power on earth, can prevent or even impair the presence of the Church." *

These sentiments express a great truth, but Bishop Dibelius

doubtless realizes that if people of religious faith and courage win the cooperation of their servants in government, the presence of the church in the struggle against its mortal enemy has gained a powerful ally.

No Greater Impact Could Be Made

The crusade for restoration of religious liberty behind the iron curtains of Communist rule should be carried with full force to the representatives of the free world in the United Nations, and through them to the representatives of the Marxist governments. It is true that the UN is made up of *nations* as members, but the charter begins thus:

"We, the People of the United Nations—"

Those words express the founders' hope that "we, the people" would have some say in the conduct of the organization.

Despite the weaknesses of the UN, despite its prostitution by Marxist nations for the profit of their Communist revolution, it can at any time be utilized by the people as a forum for the expression of grievances and appeals for redress from injustices and oppressions.

The very words of the UN charter open the doors for action in this matter. Continuing with the preamble we find that we the people are determined "to reaffirm faith in fundamental human rights, in the dignity and worth of the human person. . . . To establish conditions under which justice and respect for the obligations arising from treaties and other sources of international law can be maintained. . . . To practice tolerance and live together in peace with one another as good neighbors."

Article 55 of the charter declares that the United Nations shall promote "universal respect for, and observance of, human rights and fundamental freedoms for all without distinction as to race, sex, language, or religion."

There is no greater human right than to enjoy freedom of reverence, of conscience, of the practice of one's spiritual faith.

In the Universal Declaration of Human Rights, adopted on December 10, 1948, by the General Assembly of the United Nations at the Palais de Chaillot, Paris, are these significant words:

Everyone has the right to freedom of thought, conscience, and religion; this right includes freedom to change his religion or belief, and freedom, either alone or in community with others and in public or private, to manifest his belief in teaching, practice, worship, and observance. Everyone has the right to freedom of opinion and expression. . . . Everyone has the right to freedom of peaceful assembly and association.

On November 25, 1960, the draft of the Charter of the Rights of Man was approved officially by the UN. Religious freedom "in all its forms" is specifically assured in Article 18 of this charter. The draft was accepted by the USSR and all its Red colonial regimes.

Let us use these expressions and pledges in the Declaration of Human Rights and the Charter of the Rights of Man in our crusade to restore religious liberty. By giving them wide publicity we shall remind the whole world of the violations of these rights in the persecutions of religion under Marxist governments.

No greater impact could be made upon UN members than to press now, and keep pressing, for the restoration of true freedom of conscience and worship. Yet since the writing of the eastern European peace treaties no serious discussions have been carried on between officials of the United States government and those of the Red regimes over refusal of the latter to permit this liberty. A spokesman for the State Department explained the reason:

"The matter is such a sensitive one with the Communist governments that we fear its being raised would complicate other matters under discussion and escalate irritations."

Translated, this means: "The Reds know they are guilty of persecutions of religion and they'd just rather not talk about it or be bothered with it."

They will *not* talk about it unless and until they are confronted with this vast injustice by aroused and righteously indignant world opinion, formulated into specific programs of action. Let us then as individuals and groups urge our political leaders to agree that no concessions can be granted the Soviet Union or any of its "satellite" governments, in trade, in travel, in exchanges of farm, industrial, and educational personnel, until moves are made by the Kremlin and its subordinate regimes to grant religious liberty.

Let this concession be the primary essential to continued betterment of relations.

No mention was made of freedom of religion in the negotiations between the United States government and the USSR, Poland, Czechoslovakia, and other hungry Red areas concerning the 1963 purchases of wheat and foodstuffs. Such negotiations doubtless will continue far into the future. So will negotiations for nonstrategic machinery and industrial, farming, transportation, communications, and construction equipment of all kinds.

Official spokesmen for free republics should be made keenly aware by the united voice of religious leaders and organizations that all such negotiations with Red regimes should begin with the demand that they cease persecutions of religion and grant genuine liberty to believe, to practice, and to propagate one's faith.

"GRANT YOUR PEOPLE FREEDOM!"

All the areas under Marxist control are seeking the flow of money from foreign visitors. Tourism has become the source of Big Capital in the Socialist camp. Tourists from America and other free nations bring in good hard currency. In Czechoslovakia we found that American dollars, if spent by tourists such as we, were worth twice as much as ordinary dollars. Poland advertises for tourists. Hungary is reaping the rewards of tourist trade. Even Bulgaria, most backward of eastern European countries, is working out arrangements with many hated "capitalist" governments for a share of the profits from tourism.

According to statistics of the U.S. State Department, approximately 10 million persons obtained visas to visit abroad during the years 1959-1963, and the numbers are increasing every year. Many of these visitors go for business reasons, but most of them visit relatives and familiar scenes in the Old Country; get quick refresher courses in music, art, and drama; do amateur writing and photography; or simply enjoy a bit of vacation in a foreign land.

"You want us to visit your country?" believers in religion might ask. "We would like to do so. But it would be embarrassing for religious people from abroad to visit you and find insufficient places of worship on our day of reverence. If you want tourists in the future, grant your people freedom of religion!"

Citizens in the free nations who believe in religion should support and strengthen the propaganda efforts of their officials where such efforts are in keeping with spiritual truths and ideals. Two projects in the United States may be mentioned as examples:

During the first two years of the administration of President Eisenhower the Division of Religious Broadcasts of the Voice of America was given effective direction by Dr. D. Elton Trueblood. This noted educator, author, and churchman presented programs of vital interest to believers in every land, with special messages to sustain and encourage the spiritual faith of those behind the iron curtains. This important service has remained in capable hands during succeeding administrations.

Presidents Kennedy, Johnson, and Nixon have urged support for the Voice of America and for its specific programs that broadcast facts and discussions of interest to peoples of all religious faiths.

In June 1959 the U.S. Congress unanimously passed a Joint Resolution designating the week following the Fourth of July as "Captive Nations Week." The resolution was sponsored and supported by Democrats and Republicans with equal enthusiasm. It declared:

"Whereas the enslavement of a substantial part of the world's population by Communist imperialism makes a mockery of the idea of peaceful coexistence between nations and constitutes a detriment to the natural bonds of understanding between the peoples of the United States and other peoples . . ."

The Resolution named the areas whose national independence has been subjugated by the Soviet Union and continued:

Whereas these submerged nations look to the United States . . . for leadership in bringing about their liberation and independence and in restoring to them the enjoyment of their Christian, Jewish, Muslim, Buddhist, or other religious freedoms, and of their individual liberties . . . Resolved by the Senate and House of Representatives of the United States in Congress assembled that the President is authorized and requested to issue a proclamation on the Fourth of July 1959, declaring the week following such day as "Captive Nations Week" and inviting the people of the United States to observe such week with appropriate ceremonies and activities. The President is further authorized and requested to issue a similar proclamation on each succeeding Fourth of July until such time as freedom and independence shall have been achieved for all the captive nations of the world.

This Resolution struck an exposed nerve in the anatomy of Marxist oppression, and the cries of pain were loud indeed. Dictator Khrushchev exploded with denunciations of such an action, labeling it "an act of provocation risking atomic war." The great double value of the Resolution was, and is, the tremendous surge of hope and comfort it gave to the captive peoples, and the fact that it disclosed the intention of Marxist rulers to hold fast their colonial subjects and to make the Sovietizing of these once-free peoples a permanent thing.

For these reasons, if for none other, the Captive Nations Week Resolution should be offered and passed by the U.S. Congress and proclaimed by the President each year. Surely it will have the active support of all who in good conscience believe that "the enjoyment of . . . religious freedoms and . . . individual liberties" is the right of all men.

PROPER WEAPONS MUST BE USED

Let us not lose sight of the true weapons we as believers hold in our hands and chase off after those that are superficial and pointless. Let us for example insist that our officials abandon such bizarre stunts as sending a man or men, a woman or women, to the moon. Responsible scientists inform us that no gain in knowledge of space could possibly make up for the enormous cost of this project, estimated to exceed $50 billion.

Let us ask our statesmen, seriously: "What is to be gained by the proposed moonshot, calculated to drain off such huge resources from American taxpayers?" Backers of this fantastic project would have us believe: "It would be a triumph in space over the Russians." "It would raise our prestige among the neutrals and uncommitted nations."

"To beat the Russians" we do not have to descend to the level of their atheistic materialistic sputnik-makers. We can beat the Soviet rulers in world prestige by championing the cause of humanity on earth rather than competing with them in projects of outer space. It is certain that the Communist Imperialists do not care one whit how much the free world spends on such spectaculars. In fact, they would be delighted if the people of the United States and other free nations spent themselves into bankruptcy for boastful projects in outer space.

Just a small fraction of the vast expenditures for a moon shot, used to encourage the people now enslaved to keep up their resistance and to assure them that some day they can be independent, would place free peoples far ahead in prestige among the responsible leaders of the world.

Although the task may be difficult, champions of religion should employ determined efforts to steer their statesmen away from ideologies that can only weaken or render impotent the crusade to restore religious freedom in Communist lands. For example, there is the notion that *some* Marxism is better than others, and therefore the better Communists should be encouraged to break away from the mainstream of Marxism. Since Josip Tito of Yugoslavia is "independent" of Moscow, they assert, he should be given material aid from the United States. "Poland will pull farther away from the Soviet Union," it is said, if its Red rulers are also given some American aid, and so on.

Such ideas are born of a lack of understanding of the nature of Marxism, or of wishful thinking, or fear of meeting these issues squarely. Marshall Tito did not "pull away" from the Soviet bloc; he was expelled from the Cominform bloc at the behest of Stalin because Tito was a Communist leader in his own way. Always since his expulsion Tito and his clique have made it entirely clear that they are as dedicated Marxists as ever.

Surely it has also been made abundantly plain by Marxist leaders themselves that in their attitude toward spiritual matters *all* Communists wear robes cut from the same cloth of irreconcilable enmity. The use of any kind of aid to Red regimes is to fall into the trap of Communist thinking which holds that material well-being is all that counts, anyhow! And to presume that material aid for *some* Communists because they *may* pull away from the others is no more moral nor effective than for the government of Chicago, New York, or any other city to try to bribe one set of lawless gangsters to oppose another set, with the idea that thereby all gangsters would somehow be weakened as public enemies.

Some thinkers have even suggested that the free nations should come to the aid of the Red Russian regime in its rift with Red China, because it might help "to widen the rift." Former Congressman Walter H. Judd, once a distinguished medical missionary to China, has tersely answered that suggestion:

"Communists fight among themselves only when they are in trouble, as the USSR and Red China both are. When in trouble, Marxists not only fight among themselves; they also leave off their worst aggressions for a period of so-called 'co-existence.' Neither activity should fool any intelligent person in the free world."

Let us keep steadily, unwaveringly, to the course. Let us formulate and make known our demands in behalf of liberty. Let us say to the Marxists:

We stand for that which helps your people. But first help them yourselves—by restoring their right of worship.

We are glad to share our abundance, our trade, our artists and musicians. But give back to your own people the enjoyment of religion in its faith and practice.

We would be glad to share our architects and builders with you, but let them plan and build again the houses of worship.

We would be happy to improve relations with you, but prove your good intentions by releasing from your jails and concentration camps all prisoners condemned because of religious activities. Some have languished there for twenty years and more. Set these captives free.

A WHOLE FUTURE TO GAIN

Can religion conquer communism, or is the task too great, are the obstacles too formidable, is the victory not worth the battle?

Let any who question the power of religious faith remember that all human progress has flowed from the fountain of spiritual forces. Religious principles have conquered countless injustices through the centuries from the time of the great lawgiver, Moses, who expounded the Ten Commandments as a guide to just living.

Let us remember in humble gratitude that religion has been the guiding light for the transformation of lives, the establishment of family and community stability, the basis for progress, in all the ages of human history. Its gleaming rays have banished the dark shadows of ignorance and superstition. Its life-giving warmth has conquered the fear of death. Its truth has been and will ever be the fountain of all liberty. From spiritual ideals have grown the great systems of education and research that have freed the world of much of its disease and suffering.

"I am come that ye might have life, and that ye might have it more abundantly," said Jesus of Nazareth.

Let us remember with grateful hearts that religion has conquered much of the cruelty of ancient times and made possible human sympathy and helpfulness. Religion has all but conquered human slavery and its power can conquer the enslavement of Marxism.

Let any who question the power of religious faith remember that against great odds the chosen people of Jehovah kept alive the belief in the one true God. Infiltered right and left by those who worshiped false gods, assailed constantly by powerful enemies, tempted to abandon the faith of their fathers for the easier worship of material things, the Hebrew people were brought up sharply and reminded of their great spiritual heritage by prophets and leaders who refused to be discouraged.

"Behold, the Lord's hand is not shortened, that it cannot save; neither is his ear heavy, that it cannot hear," trumpeted that great spokesman for the Almighty, Isaiah. "Arise! Shine! For thy light is come, and the glory of the Lord is risen upon thee!"

Whatever the believer's faith, as he faces religion's greatest challenge for survival let him take heart by remembrance of a rugged follower of the Nazarene Teacher, the Apostle Paul. Persecuted, beaten, imprisoned, tormented by infirmities but never wavering in his belief in the ultimate triumph of a righteous cause, he wrote to his friends in the struggling fellowship in Rome:

If God be for us, who can be against us?

Believers of the world, let us unite in the crusade to roll back the ominous menace of atheistic communism. We have nothing to lose but the chains that bind our fellow believers, and a whole future to gain for humankind.

REFERENCES

Chapter II

Page 32. Hunter, Edward. *The Black Book on Red China*. The Book-mailer, Inc., New York.

Page 34. *The Jews in Eastern Europe*. Publications, 83 Charlotte St., London.

Chapter IV

Page 49. Lyons, Eugene. *Our Secret Allies: The Peoples of Russia*. Duell, Sloan and Pearce, New York; Little, Brown and Co., Boston.

Chapter V

Page 61. Galter, Albert [Giovannetti, Alberto]. *The Red Book of the Persecuted Church*. The Newman Press, Westminster, Md.

Page 66. Galter, Albert. *Ibid*.

Chapter VI

Page 70. Lyons, Eugene. *Op. cit.*

Page 73. Gsovski, Vladimir. *Library of Congress Study Report*. Washington, D.C.

Chapter VIII

Page 97. Galter, Albert. *Op. cit.*

Chapter IX

Page 105. Markham, R. H. *Library of Congress Study Report*. Washington, D.C.

Chapter X

Page 119. Fletcher, Jesse C. *Bill Wallace of China*. The Broadman Press, Nashville, Tenn.

Page 123. Fletcher, Jesse C. *Ibid*.

Chapter XI

Page 134. Hoover, J. Edgar. *Masters of Deceit.* Henry Holt and Co., New York

Chapter XII

Page 138. Lowry, Charles Wesley. *Soviet Total War.* In report of September 23, 1956, House of Representatives, Washington, D.C.

Page 143. Visser't Hooft, W. A. From report by Religious News Service, New York.

Page 148. Jones, Francis P. *Documents of the Three-Self Movement.* National Council of Churches of Christ, New York.

Chapter XIII

Page 153. Solyom-Fekete, William. *Library of Congress Study Report,* Washington, D.C.

Chapter XIV

Page 163. Schalk, Adolph. Quoted in *Library of Congress Study Report.* Washington, D.C.

Page 169. Abashiya, Audu Kwasau. Reported by Religious News Service, New York.

Chapter XVI

Page 195. Wells, Charles A. *The Wells Newsletter,* Princeton, N.J.

Page 196. Goodwin, Dean. *Crusader, American Baptist Newsmagazine,* Valley Forge, Pa.

Chapter XVII

Page 202. Udvarnoki, Bela. From article in *Christianity Today,* Washington, D.C.

Page 203. Schneiderman, S. L. Quoted in report by Religious News Service, New York.

Chapter XVIII

Page 214. Khrushchev, Nikita. Broadcast monitored by Voice of America, U.S. Information Service, Washington.

Page 215. Hoover, J. Edgar. *Op. cit.*

Page 216. From *"What the Citizen Should Know about Communism,"* Veterans of Foreign Wars, Kansas City, Mo.

Chapter XX

Page 236. Dibelius, Otto. Quoted by Religious News Service, New York.

SOURCES OF STUDY MATERIAL

The authors have been informed that material relating to the subject of this book may be obtained from the following church-related and other organizations. While the authors cannot vouch for the material thus available, we do feel that each group listed may be of some assistance to those concerned for the victory of religion over communism. If the reader's church or fellowship is not listed, we suggest that he contact his own denominational headquarters.

CHURCH-RELATED ORGANIZATIONS

Seventh-Day Adventists, General Conference, Office of Research, 6840 Eastern Ave., NW, Tacoma Park, Md.

Assemblies of God, Department of Publications, 1445 Boonville Ave., Springfield, Mo.

American Baptist Convention, Division of Christian Social Concern, Valley Forge, Pa.

National Baptist Convention, USA Inc., 3101 S. Parkway, Chicago, Ill.

Southern Baptist Convention, Christian Life Commission, Nashville, Tenn.

Catholic Church, National Catholic Welfare Conference, 1312 Massachusetts Ave., NW, Washington, D.C.

Christian Churches (Disciples of Christ), Division of Church Life and Work, 222 S. Downey Ave., Indianapolis, Ind.

Church of Christ, Scientist, Committee on Publications, 107 Falmouth St., Boston, Mass.

Church of God, Editor of Publications, 1080 Montgomery Ave., Cleveland, Tenn.

Church of the Nazarene, 6401 The Paseo, Kansas City, Mo.

Evangelical United Brethren, Board of Publication, 601 W. Riverview Ave., Dayton, Ohio.

American Jewish Congress, 15 E. 84th St., New York, N.Y.

Church of Jesus Christ of Latter Day Saints, 47 E. South Temple St., Salt Lake City, Utah

Reorganized Church of Jesus Christ of Latter Day Saints, The Auditorium, Independence, Mo.

Lutheran Church, Missouri Synod, Lutheran Building, 210 N. Broadway, St. Louis, Mo.

Mennonite Church, The General Conference, 722 Main St., Newton, Kan.

Methodist Church, Board of Christian Social Concerns, 100 Maryland Ave., NE, Washington, D.C. Commission on Public Relations and Methodist Information, 475 Riverside Drive, New York, N.Y.

African Methodist Episcopal Church, General Board, 1724 Villa St., Nashville, Tenn.

United Presbyterian Church in the USA, Office of the Stated Clerk, 410 Witherspoon Building, Philadelphia, Pa.

Presbyterian Church in the US, Office of the General Assembly, 341 Ponce de Leon Ave., Atlanta, Ga.

Protestant Episcopal Church, Office of the National Council, 815 Second Ave., New York, N.Y.

United Church of Christ, Council for Christian Social Action, 289 Park Ave., New York, N.Y.

NATIONAL RELIGIOUS, CIVIC, AND PATRIOTIC GROUPS

American-Jewish League Against Communism, Inc., 79 Madison Ave., New York, N.Y.

National Association of Evangelicals, Office of Public Affairs, 1405 G Street, NW, Washington, D.C.

National Council of the Churches of Christ in the U.S.A., Committee on Christian Literature, 475 Riverside Drive, New York, N.Y.

The Church League of America, Division of Information, Wheaton, Ill.

Foundation for Religious Action in the Social and Civil Order, 1346 Connecticut Ave., NW, Washington, D.C.

National Education Association, Lay Relations, 1201 Sixteenth St., NW, Washington, D.C.

The American Legion, National Americanism Commission, Box 1055, Indianapolis, Ind.

Veterans of Foreign Wars, Americanism Commission, Kansas City, Mo.

GOVERNMENTAL AGENCIES

U.S. State Department, Publications Division, Washington, D.C.

Federal Bureau of Investigation, Justice Department, Washington, D.C.

U.S. Senate Committee on the Judiciary, Washington, D.C.

House Un-American Activities Committee, Washington, D.C.

INDEX

251